The End of Peacekeeping

THE END OF PEACEKEEPING

Gender, Race, and the Martial Politics
of Intervention

Marsha Henry

PENN

UNIVERSITY OF PENNSYLVANIA PRESS

PHILADELPHIA

Copyright © 2024 University of Pennsylvania Press

All rights reserved. Except for brief quotations used for purposes of review or scholarly citation, none of this book may be reproduced in any form by any means without written permission from the publisher.

Published by
University of Pennsylvania Press
Philadelphia, Pennsylvania 19104-4112
www.upenn.edu/pennpress

Printed in the United States of America on acid-free paper

10 9 8 7 6 5 4 3 2 1

A catalogue record for this book is available from the Library of Congress.
Hardback ISBN 9781512825237
eBook ISBN 9781512825244

CONTENTS

1. Critical Interventions and Knowing Peacekeeping: An Epistemic Project — 1

2. From Civilizing Mission to Global Color Line: Coloniality in Humanitarian Work — 33

3. The Limits of the Singular: Intersectionality, Binaries, and the Coloniality of Gender — 67

4. Where's the Peace? The Martial Politics of Peacekeeping — 103

5. For the Peacekept: Decolonizing, Demilitarizing, and Degendering Peacekeeping — 130

6. Toward Archives and Ends — 159

Notes — 167

Bibliography — 171

Index — 185

Acknowledgments — 197

CHAPTER 1

Critical Interventions and Knowing Peacekeeping: An Epistemic Project

Introduction

In 2003 when I was in my first permanent academic post, I was approached by a colleague with a proposal to develop a joint research project on gender relations and peacekeeping. At the time, I had been devoted to my work on gender, representation, and development and knew very little about military settings or studies of peacekeeping. My then colleague proposed that we combine our respective knowledge of gender and militarization and gender and development to examine sexual exploitation and abuse (SEA) in postconflict/peacekeeping settings, in light of reports and documentation by various humanitarian organizations in the early 2000s (UNHCR and Save the Children, 2002; Rehn and Sirleaf, 2002; Human Rights Watch, 2002). Both of us immersed ourselves in a variety of literatures, learning that peacekeeping emerged after World War II and was developed by the United Nations (UN) Security Council (SC) to maintain peace in former conflict zones. Subsequently, numerous UN member states[1] volunteered to send troops, officers, and experts for this global civil service of "peace." In particular, the multinational forces were expected to collaborate in order to halt the outbreak of further armed violence and civil war by keeping former warring parties geographically and physically separated. From this initial research, and having reviewed multiple investigative and policy reports by nongovernmental organizations (NGOs), we eventually began a research-council-funded investigation of gender relations between international male peacekeepers (UN) and local women living in UN peace operations.[2] The aim of this research was to better understand everyday experiences of security and insecurity and to focus on relations between local beneficiaries of peace operations and those tasked with providing humanitarian assistance and aid for peacekeeping. The results were subsequently published as a book, *Insecure Spaces*, and revealed that peacekeepers' presence has conditional effects on experiences of security and insecurity (Higate and Henry, 2009). While conducting fieldwork in Cyprus, Liberia, Haiti, and Kosovo from 2004 to 2007 for the funded research, we realized that we had entered peacekeeping sites at the precise moment that it had become quite difficult to talk about sexual exploitation and abuse, let alone sexual relationships; the silence was likely because the UN had introduced informal policies to curb such incidents, aimed at disciplining peacekeepers rather than addressing underlying social inequalities and power imbalances (Kihara-Hunt, 2017). In any case, our research was led by our respondents' needs and issues, which were different than those identified in our originally formulated research. Our study morphed into an altogether different project as we responded to recurring themes that emerged from our conversations with our respondents, who included local beneficiaries and international UN peacekeepers. Our final conclusions were that *who* kept the peace, and *where* this peacekeeping happened, mattered a great deal in shaping people's experiences of security and insecurity, and indeed, of peacekeeping itself (Higate and Henry, 2009).

While the guiding question of that early research period was essentially *how* people (the peacekept[3] and the peacekeepers) experience security and insecurity, there was another question haunting this research. It is a question seldom asked in studies of militarized and male-dominated processes such as peacekeeping and humanitarian aid: how does peacekeeping come to be known? That is, how do scholars and practitioners come to understand peacekeeping when they read about it, work within a peacekeeping mission, or gender, for example, while reinforcing traditional military aims and objectives (Cruz et al., 2017). This is further reflected in scholarship which focuses on macro issues of operations, doctrine, effectiveness, responsibility, and neutrality (Williams, 2020; Bellamy et al., 2010). By providing a critical overview of what has been lost, I argue that it is vital for peacekeeping scholarship to return to some of its more critical and (perhaps for that reason) undercited scholars, who provide important conceptual framings and interventions and prompt a reimagining and repoliticization of peacekeeping. In doing so, I provide scholars with a more comprehensive and complex learning journey that may give rise to a more epistemically nuanced and politically urgent positioning within the scholarship.

Unacknowledged Histories: Feminist, Critical Race, and Antimilitarist Theories in Peacekeeping Studies

It is vitally important to scrutinize the boundaries of what constitutes peacekeeping scholarship, especially given how much academic work informs policy and practice but does not reflect theoretical innovations. If one looks deeply enough, however, it is possible to find feminist, antiracist, and antimilitarist theorizing and practice within the peacekeeping literature. In the following section, I provide an overview of literature that I believe is central to understanding the current state of peacekeeping studies. This early work provides the critical tools with which to understand peacekeeping as a knowledge project itself, and explains to some degree why these works have been sidelined in research. Rather than an exhaustive account of all of the relevant literature, I trace a critical history of the theoretical interventions within peacekeeping studies that lay the groundwork for my analytical frame. And of course, as I demonstrate throughout the book, coming to know peacekeeping is itself a project that is both partial and incomplete.

What I want to make visible is the way in which certain theoretically informed work has been *disappeared* from or pushed to the margins of peacekeeping studies. Why is it that some theories and conceptual framings have lost traction—especially those interested in gender, race, and militarization? For example, in 2002, Cockburn and Žarkov's edited collection *The Postwar Moment* provided a compelling account of the variation in militarized masculinities in peacekeeping and the effects of these on gender relations in postconflict settings (Cockburn and Žarkov, 2002). One of the first collections to examine peacekeeping from the perspective of feminist peace activism, the book provided an important contribution to peacekeeping studies more broadly—yet it is rarely cited in mainstream peacekeeping studies texts. Cockburn and Žarkov's book preceded key interventions in the field of critical peacekeeping studies (Pugh, 2004; Richmond, 2004; Ramsbotham and Woodhouse, 1996). For example, the earlier critical and foundational work takes issue with the "liberal peace agenda," Global North–led peacebuilding, and the economic inequalities found in the aid industry itself (Chandler, 1999; Ramsbotham and Woodhouse, 1996; Paris, 2001). Yet these texts, as critical as they are (or are not), make very little or no mention of thinking about axes of difference and systems of oppression based on gender, race, class, and sexuality. Even more curious is the absence of *The Postwar Moment* in later texts that take as their subject matter the impact of gender on peacekeeping (and vice versa) (Smith, 2018; Otto and Heathcote, 2014). A key chapter in *Postwar Moment* is committed to obtaining an understanding of the perspectives of women who sell sex to peacekeepers (Cockburn and Hubić, 2002). In this chapter, Cockburn and Hubić show that what women want is not the elimination of paid sex in peacekeeping contexts but rather, solutions that promise financial and physical security in these unequal encounters. While they speak from an agential perspective, the women in Cockburn and Hubić's study identify safety and security as key demands rather than as evidence of a need to be "rescued." This early feminist political economy perspective on sexual exploitation and abuse in peacekeeping adds to the literature on peacekeeping economies by showing the power of the market and how it functions socially, even under postwar conditions (Higate and

Henry, 2009; Jennings, 2014). While this chapter is empirically original, even groundbreaking in its arguments and access to those involved with peacekeepers, it also contributes to theorizing peacekeeping as an epistemically contested field. Here Cockburn and Žarkov situate the larger text as stemming from their own unique standpoint and position within feminist peace activism. This book is one of several by Cockburn that advances a feminist peace politics and is clearly influenced by feminist standpoint theory (Smith, 1987; Cockburn, 2008). I discuss the importance of this perspective later in the chapter and throughout the book.

A text parallel (and comparable) to Cockburn and Žarkov's is Whitworth's *Men, Militarism, and UN Peacekeeping*, which investigates the gendered issues raised by peacekeeping as an exclusively male enterprise premised on conventional military ideology and values (Whitworth, 2004). It documents some of the gendered and colonial legacies of such deployments in Cambodia and Somalia, revealing how violence was perpetrated by peacekeepers and then covered up through the rhetoric of national "niceness" and notions of benign peacekeeping. The work is one of the first to extend ideas about military masculinity to the context of peacekeeping, providing a crucial feminist intervention into the otherwise androcentric and Eurocentric scholarship. This elision is partly a result of representations of peacekeeping that continually emphasized a number of noble masculine-martial values—the "duty to serve," though here not in the narrow service of one's country but in a larger and more lofty, global sense as a cosmopolitan calling (Bergman Rosamond and Kronsell, 2018). If a reader visits the photo gallery on the United Nations Peacekeeping home page, a catalog of "honorable" images of peacekeepers is readily available that features peacekeepers carrying women, holding the hands of small children, and rescuing food and other essential supplies. As Duncanson argues, the epistemic investments in the narrative of "forces for good" have been a long time in the making and tend to be used to "offset" problematic acts— for example, the sexual abuse and torture of local women, girls and boys—by military men, or those that have apparently exhibited [negative] "military masculinities" (Duncanson, 2013). Whitworth's intervention can be read alongside parallel feminist work that reveals the androcentric bias of modern science for its double standards and mistreatment of women (Tuana, 1989). While much of the focus of Whitworth's book is on Canada's gendered and racial investments in varying versions of peacekeeping, the analysis is applicable to other Global North peacekeeping nations. And consequently, if peacekeeping is androcentric in its foundations, then it is not surprising that what we learn about peacekeeping reflects this bias.

Whitworth's analysis is followed by an important book edited by Mazurana, Raven-Roberts, and Parpart with the apt title *Gender, Conflict, and Peacekeeping* (Mazurana et al., 2005). For the longest time this was one of the few collections that provided a critical overview and early analysis of gender training for peacekeepers (among other important issues raised by feminist antimilitarists) (Mackay, 2003, 2005; Puechguirbal, 2003; Mazurana et al., 2005). The book was timely, being published in the early stages of the introduction of gender awareness training into in-mission training, in practice delivered by a number of recently appointed "gender advisors." These advisors were assigned to each peacekeeping mission and tasked to ensure that gender issues were adequately addressed in all aspects of operations (Bastick and Duncanson, 2018; Holvikivi, 2021). Feminist analysis of gender relations in peacekeeping missions has since grown as its own subfield of peacekeeping scholarship, yet the works highlighted above have rarely been incorporated into macro analyses; in particular, Mazurana et al.'s edited collection is not cited as frequently as work subsequent to that publication. These three key studies (Cockburn and Žarkov, 2002; Whitworth, 2004; Mazurana et al., 2005) made outstanding original and explicitly feminist contributions to the field, drawing on the work of women's organizations; theorizing from feminist international relations and peacekeeping studies as well as peace and conflict studies, development studies, and global studies; and engaging across multiple disciplines and sectors including humanitarian aid, disaster relief, and military studies. Yet their relegation to the margins of scholarship on peacekeeping (and even within gender and peacekeeping) highlights the increasing erasure of these important "politicizing" texts. I suggest that this is in keeping with a general trend of *depoliticization* in the field of peacekeeping practice and research. This depoliticization looks like many other normative global projects that minimise the role of inequalities and geopolitics when writing about peacekeeping. This trend may also be related to the rapid and recent availability of journal articles online, which means that digital searches bring up the more cited and downloadable journal articles rather than older chapters in edited collections. But it is not by accident that texts concerned with challenging the Global North, male domination and power; the pervasiveness and perniciousness of militarism and militarization within conflict and postconflict spaces, and the co-optation of watered-down notions of gender equality as a means to a military end have become marginalized in peacekeeping citational practice.

At the beginning of the millennium, a few key texts emerged that drew on postcolonial, critical race, and critical development studies theorizing. These works ranged widely in conceptual approach, but all engaged with peacekeeping as practice. Among these, Razack's *Dark Threats and White Knights* stands out (Razack, 2004). It was, for me, one of the most groundbreaking exposés of violence committed by the global "good guys"—Canadian military peacekeepers posted to Somalia in late 1992. While the book outlines the details of the legal investigation and misconduct case of a specific regiment, it draws on theories of race and nationalism and makes visible the legacy of colonial power in contemporary peacekeeping. In particular, Razack details not only the ways in which certain nations use peacekeeping to reinforce racism and mythologizing views of themselves as "civilized" (humanity entrusted with the responsibility of bringing those apparently in need into civility), but also unwraps how *who* is selected to keep the peace is reflected by the global division of labor and the inequalities produced by racial capitalism (Robinson, 1983; Du Bois, 1915, 1903). In this way, Razack's "global color line" is unveiled throughout the book and shows how racial tropes, ideas, and colonial practices enabled, excused, and even normalized racialized and militarized violence by Canadian troops in Somalia.

As a way of pointing to the influence of some key feminist and postcolonial scholars' work, I provide a brief overview of some other critical scholarship that has also faded from incorporation and acknowledgement in peacekeeping studies. Zisk Marten and Pouligny offered critical accounts of international interventions, exposing how the practice of peacekeeping is itself out of touch or incompatible with and resisted by local groups (Zisk Marten, 2004; Pouligny, 2006). These texts were aimed at both academic and practitioner audiences and contained specific examples of imbalanced power relations in peace operations. Zisk Marten focused on the parallels of peacekeeping with empire, while Pouligny canvased local populations and grassroots organizations to understand the experience of peacekeeping "from below." Unlike Razack's book, which explicitly engages with peacekeeping from the perspective of critical race and postcolonial theories, these works were clearly influenced by related ideas and concepts. They used close textual or interview methods to gain insights from those located "below," and made a series of critical recommendations for challenging those in positions of power in peacekeeping contexts, rather than seeking to restore power firmly with institutions such as the UN, the EU, and NATO. Although not explicitly postcolonial or evidently influenced by critical race theories, traces of these important interventions by Pouligny and Zisk Marten are evident in the subsequent and popular works of Autesserre, a scholar well regarded in the field who has continuously written the peacekept into accounts of postconflict contexts (Autesserre, 2010, 2014, 2021). While Pouligny, Zisk Marten, and Autesserre were influenced by critical perspectives, they do not engage directly with critical theories of gender, race, and coloniality in their work.

Some other contemporary texts, namely work by Duffield and Paris, also echoed the sentiments of much of this literature and unequivocally challenged the motivations, foundations, and effects of peacekeeping; but even their critiques reinforced ideas about peace, conflict, and development studies as essentially *a-gendered* fields of study (Duffield, 2001; Paris, 2001). Scholars drawing on postcolonial and similar critical paradigms saw peacekeeping itself as emerging from colonial, neoliberal, and disciplinary responses to conflicts and other systems of power and control, and not simply a benign response to conflict (Zanotti, 2011). Notably, these scholars did not always acknowledge the gendered foundations, possibly because gender as a concept ended up being relegated to the interpersonal rather than structural.[4] Instead, peacekeeping scholarship of the early 2000s was characterized by a division between those scholars arguing for critical (i.e., postmodern) approaches to peacekeeping and those invested in solving the apparent problems of peacekeeping practice, with the feminist and postcolonial scholarship remaining mostly on the margins of both. That the majority of those in the mainstream school are scholars based in Global North institutions, reflects the geopolitical and epistemic interests of such scholarship.

Work that did not feature in these debates provided important critical grounding, and I review these works to bolster my argument that peacekeeping studies could be more politically radical in its scope. Rubenstein's book *Peacekeeping Under Fire*, for example, although rarely cited or present on any peacekeeping syllabi, is based on an anthropological study and involved some "deep hanging out" with peacekeepers (Rubenstein, 2008). Rubenstein was interested in what experiences from the ground could tell scholars about the realities of peacekeeping, rather than in specifically addressing the experiences of the peacekept. His work shows how anthropological theories and methods could be employed to offer new and different insights. Rubenstein's account centers on the cultural modes by which peacekeepers engage others inside and outside their own militaries as well as construct their own identities in situ (Rubenstein, 2008). In a similar vein, Higate and I focus on the performative context within which civilians and military peacekeepers are embedded, and theorize the spaces of peacekeeping as evolving from a range of cartographic practices—all of which influence the experiences of security and insecurity of those living and working in peacekeeping missions (Higate and Henry, 2009). Influenced by military anthropologists and sociologists, Rubenstein and then Higate and I used theories of the symbolic, performative, and socio-spatial to argue that peacekeeping is a militarized power project that physically and psychologically reorders postconflict space (Higate and Henry, 2009; Rubenstein, 2008). This allowed an original extension of securitization theories to include the more affective and experiential elements of security analyses and thus provided an opportunity to question the foundations of peacekeeping, rather than attempt to fix peacekeeping without the knowledge of its own evolution. Similarly, Zanotti used a Foucauldian framework to make the case that peacekeeping is not only a "civilizing mission," as Paris suggests and Razack argues, but is based on containing and managing the peacekept (Zanotti, 2011). Any of the above works which center the peacekept is of primary importance to this book. This is because by a focus on problem-solving alone, the peacekept are sidelined, minimized, and even patronized by peacekeeping's governing gaze, and consequently the subject of peacekeeping becomes depoliticized. Thus, in the first decade of the twenty-first century, scholarly work on peacekeeping contributed to a particularly critical archive of knowledge about different aspects of peacekeeping ranging from its ideologies and foundational thinking to its practices of recruitment and reach, and finally to its impressions and influences on local and indigenous populations. Although not exclusively based on critical theories or suggesting more critically informed interventions, this particular trajectory of scholarship informs my own framing of the limits and possibilities of peacekeeping and peacekeeping studies.

From 2011 onward a number of comprehensive books on peacekeeping or related areas were published. I summarize their contributions here to acknowledge that there have been some continuities of commitment to feminist and antiracist perspectives, but that these do not always recognize the critical interventions of earlier scholarship. These include feminist texts where issues of gender, international law, militarism, and representation have been foregrounded (Harrington, 2010; Kronsell and Svedberg, 2011; Duncanson, 2013; Otto and Heathcote, 2014; Pruitt, 2016; Karim and Beardsley, 2017). I provide a snapshot of some of these texts to impress upon readers the types of works that have entered the scholarship and, in some cases, have helped to constitute mainstream knowledge of peacekeeping. For example, while Harrington's work is cited infrequently, it is a foundational (but not unproblematic) account of the history of sexual exploitation and abuse and sex trafficking within peacekeeping contexts (Harrington, 2010). Kronsell and Svedberg's edited collection is an excellent complement to that of almost a decade earlier from Cockburn and Žarkov, although there is less geopolitical commentary and focus than in the previous decade of scholarship (Kronsell and Svedberg, 2011; Cockburn and Žarkov, 2002). This means that the space for analyses of processes of racialization are marginalized at the expense of thinking about violence from a predominantly Global North perspective. As previously mentioned, Duncanson's account of military narratives of "progress" goes some way toward repoliticizing discussions around military masculinities, begun by Whitworth a decade earlier (Duncanson, 2013; Whitworth, 2004). However, only one chapter is devoted to thinking through the role of empire in molding liberal narratives of progress, and the book prioritizes gender as the primary axis by which to understand peacekeeping as an enterprise. Otto and Heathcote's edited collection draws on a much wider range of geopolitical contexts and provides socio-legal insights into issues including violence by peacekeepers and increasing the number of women peacekeepers in missions—a task not too dissimilar to that taken on by Mazurana, Raven-Roberts, and Parpart in 2004 (Otto and Heathcote, 2014; Mazurana et al., 2005). The book is explicitly feminist but is invested in how legal, policy, and practice frameworks can enable different forms of intervention. Thus, the collection situates itself in direct dialogue with the women, peace, and security agenda rather than the field of peacekeeping studies itself. Pruitt's study is the first book-length analysis of women peacekeepers and, though it is less cited than other books of a more quantitative nature, provides some much-needed analysis of the lived experiences of women working in peacekeeping (Pruitt, 2016). It fails, however, to address issues of the "global color line" put forward by Razack in 2004, and which I discussed in one of the first articles on women peacekeepers from the Global South (Razack, 2004; Henry, 2012). I would extend this criticism to an important and compelling research account culminating in the publication of *Equal Opportunity Peacekeeping* by Karim and Beardsley (Karim and Beardsley, 2017). This book is an ambitious analysis of empirical data which maps some of the impact of the presence of women peacekeepers on gender relations, operational effectiveness, and security more broadly. The book is comprehensive in scope and rigorous in terms of the qualitative and quantitative methods employed. It thoughtfully imagines how peacekeeping could be better balanced along gender lines. However, the study only partly draws on feminist approaches, and even less on postcolonial, and antimilitarist theories and the more evidently political analyses outlined above. In fact, *Equal Opportunity Peacekeeping* positions itself in the problem-solving peacekeeping studies school (rather than feminist International Relations). As the title suggests, women peacekeepers are denied equal opportunities and thus face a number of challenges in recruitment, deployment, and in-mission training. But there is little critique of the incorporation of women into the colonial and military projects that make up peacekeeping. Peacekeeping is taken at face value (as benign) and assumed to be inherently good or neutral. I argue that the book "makes war safe for women" rather than pursues the peace ends that Shepherd argues should be essential to critical feminist accounts (Shepherd, 2016).

Some works have concentrated on particular aspects of peacekeeping from a critical perspective. Sloan looks at how military peacekeepers have been mismatched with peacekeeping practices and how the increasing use of force works against the founding principles of the UN (Sloan, 2011); Cunliffe examines the unequal burden of peacekeeping as distributed among Global South contingents and how these maintain legacies of colonialism (Cunliffe, 2013); and Autesserre examines peacekeeping at the level of the everyday, conducting in-depth research with a number of actors present in the peacekeeping landscape from ordinary citizens to activists and peacekeepers (Autesserre, 2010, 2014). Autesserre's interventions are compelling accounts of some of the fault lines of peacekeeping. Although I would not classify Autesserre's work as falling neatly into any peacekeeping "school," her study omits much of the critical work cited and discussed above. Finally, de Coning, Aoi, and Karlsrud center their analyses on the dissonance between peacekeeping doctrine and the new era of peacekeeping challenges and obstacles (De Coning et al., 2017). This edited collection reflects almost nothing of the contributions of earlier feminist and critical race scholars, nor does it mirror the detailed insights and findings of much of the work from 2007 to 2017. Problematically, in contrast to its predecessor (Thakur et al., 2007), the collection does not include a single chapter on gender, despite the increased number of quantitative and qualitative studies of women peacekeepers and reporting and exposure of incidents of sexual exploitation and abuse incidents in peacekeeping missions (Higate and Henry, 2004; Nordäs and Rustad, 2013). I provide a brief overview of these more recent texts because I argue that they reflect the contemporary state of peacekeeping studies—often a field that does not know its own diverse conceptual and empirical history and that commonly refuses to take up antiracist, antisexist, and antimilitarist political positions.

Finally, there are interventions in the scholarly literature that warrant recognition. Two texts that do not engage gender substantially but provide an important framing for thinking about the "necessity" of peacekeeping as a global governance practice include *Peacekeeping in the Midst of War* and *Power in Peacekeeping* (Hultman et al., 2019; Howard, 2019). Both of these books focus on assessing and measuring "effectiveness" through analysis of different sources of data. Both are critical in the sense of examining where peacekeeping fails and where it has been effective in reducing fatalities, or where it contributes to the positive transformation of the host country. Hultman et al. tend to rely on some problematic language about conflict, as in the section "Saving Humanity from Hell," which reinforces ideas like those about the Democratic Republic of Congo first depicted in Conrad's *Heart of Darkness*, which Razack deftly unpacks (Hultman et al., 2019; Razack, 2004). In fact, Razack's opening page quotes Conrad as a way of grounding her analysis in postcolonial critique from the outset. Howard avoids such polemical connotations but is concerned to engage the mainstream scholarship and invested policy makers. When Howard speaks about "power" in peacekeeping, she does not draw on the critical Foucauldian understanding of power that other scholars might rely on; rather, she writes about the power of peacekeeping to effect positive change in the lives of the peacekept (Zanotti, 2011). Similarly, Westendorf's book *Violating Peace* is an excellent intervention in peacekeeping studies which is concerned to engage the topic of sexual exploitation and abuse from a theoretical and empirical perspective (Westendorf, 2020). As the first in-depth exploration of sexual exploitation and abuse, the connection between SEA and conflict-related sexual violence, and the impact of these types of activities on long-lasting peace, the book provides a much-needed analysis of how peacekeeper practices can disrupt the entire peacekeeping project. The book includes critiques of androcentric peacekeeping, colonial logics, and the problems of reliance on militarized interventions. Having said this, *Violating Peace* strays from the bolder critical stances that earlier scholars take up: Zanotti's compelling Foucauldian account of peacekeeping as surveillance (Zanotti, 2011); Harrington's historical tracing of sexual imperialism (Harrington, 2010); Cockburn and Žarkov's curation of chapters on variations in militarized masculinities (Cockburn and Žarkov, 2002); and work that questioned peacekeeping's right to existence in the first place (Chandler, 1999; Pugh, 2004; Mac Ginty, 2016; Richmond, 2004). Yet the book does not feature significantly in mainstream peacekeeping studies, perhaps because it is so overtly politically feminist (a good thing in my opinion!). But as peacekeeping practitioners have said to me before, "if a book is not useful to us in the field, what is the point of writing it?"

Methodological Approaches and Situating the Researcher

The scholarship and research material that is the catalyst for and substance of this book, respectively, emerges from almost twenty years of observing and discussing in depth with a range of peacekeepers inside and outside the peacekeeping field. It also is based on many years of fieldwork directly in conversation with individuals living and working in peacekeeping spaces—those who I refer to as the peacekept but who are not the sum of this conceptual label. Men and women struggling to survive war, violence, insecurity, and trauma inside peacekeeping environments are often those overlooked in studies of peacekeeping as a set of social relations. This book attempts to recenter the focus of peacekeeping studies through qualitative methodologies. I say qualitative methodologies so that the techniques I used are generally recognizable, but so much of what makes up this book is also derived from moments of silence, in the gaps in conversation where individuals could not speak for fear of weeping and opening up the grief they had buried deep within their psyches. In approaching peacekeeping through these methods, my aim is to disrupt the seamless narrative of peacekeeping as innocent or inherently good in character. My aim is to use critical theories to intervene in the epistemic project.

I am influenced by multisited ethnographic approaches and have conducted interviews, focus groups, and group interviews and participated in various formal and informal activities alongside UN peacekeepers and local NGO workers and other humanitarian aid staff. One fieldwork journey stood out for me and indicates some of the ways in which I draw on my observations, field notes, transcripts, and archival documents to sustain my arguments about the need to come to peacekeeping knowledge from different angles and perspectives. The first involves "shadowing" a small grassroots organization in Kosovo that allowed me to join them in some of the work they were doing on behalf of the UN. I spent several days observing Relia and Mihas as they provided services to Romani communities living in Mitrovica or beyond.[5] Relia was a young woman and had ambitions to work with the UN or an international nongovernmental organization. As part of the day's activities, we met with a journalist who was reporting on the Romani community and their experiences of postwar life; we met on a cool winter day outside a new housing development. I was struck by how generous my hosts were in sharing the day with a relative stranger, easing my comfort wherever possible. I was welcomed into Relia's parents' home in the evening, where we shared a few words of Hindi/Hindustani when we could no longer find English words to help us communicate. What this fieldwork prompted was a desire to include these more subtle and moving moments into my overall book project in order to be able to witness and give space to those living in peacekeeping missions who fall under the radar, so to speak.

Throughout the book, I speak to conversations and dialogue that I was fortunate enough to benefit from. I was lucky in that my status as a tenured academic at the London School of Economics and Political Sciences (LSE) afforded me the socioeconomic privilege of protection and security, although because of my own racialized appearance, I was not always granted the authority that a white researcher might have been allowed. On one occasion in Liberia, as I sought permission to interview women peacekeepers, I was told by the then chief of staff of the mission that even though I "appeared like a perfectly nice young lady," he didn't know where I was from and what LSE stood for. Throughout my fieldwork days, I was disciplined and my access was limited by a range of senior peacekeeping officials and gatekeepers, almost all of whom were white civilian staff. During one of my field trips, I was confronted by a member of the security staff while exiting the canteen in the UN Headquarters. The security officer grabbed my pass, which was on a lanyard around my neck, and angrily said, "I've already cancelled your pass!" When he saw my name on the pass, not the name of another researcher with whom I had met and conversed and who had recently left the mission site, he quickly recognized his mistake. That researcher was another woman of color. Thus, the ways in which peacekeeping functions day to day also provided epistemic and practical challenges to my own work and research.

While fieldwork trips spanned an almost fifteen-year period, it was two moments that reminded me of my contradictory position within peacekeeping spaces and scholarship. On 12 January 2010, I was about to begin a new term of teaching at my university. As I was working and listening to the news, I learned that a massive earthquake had struck Haiti.[6] I quickly penned emails to some of my former respondents with whom I had kept in touch since 2006, when I first began fieldwork. Over the next days and weeks, I learned the consequences of environmental disasters and corresponded with both peacekeepers and the peacekept as the devastation and death unfolded. As the book reveals, peacekeeping spaces are filled with a range of losses for individuals and communities, and this has been a theme that almost every peacekeeping scholar has been concerned with. In this regard there is some humanity in our research cultures and common scholarship. However, there is also the knowledge that as a researcher you are bound to make connections with a range of people, develop friendships, and perhaps even come to be attached to neighborhoods and familiar leisure spots. The earthquake in Haiti put into focus that these attachments are themselves legacies of colonial and Eurocentric histories. That, as a researcher, I can allow myself emotional bonds in spaces to which I do not belong is important to acknowledge. Part of what I do in this book is to provide that feminist killjoy intervention—to tell the story that no one wants to hear about peacekeeping spaces and to channel the witnessing of devastation in a meaningful way (Ahmed, 2016). I do this in order not to step away from my responsibility as someone committed to an abolitionist position vis-à-vis formal peacekeeping.

In 2014, shortly after my last trip to Liberia, it was announced that a deadly virus and public health epidemic had begun in West Africa.[7] News again traveled among myself and other peacekeepers that I had known from their postings in Haiti and Liberia. As in 2010, many peacekeepers and UN national staff left the mission as the pandemic took hold. Some found work elsewhere, while others managed and watched as the entire peace project was put in lockdown mode. While I was not conducting fieldwork at this time, I was developing a grant proposal that would have entailed doing work in the cities of Buchanan and Monrovia. Again, I was reminded that to do research on peacekeeping is to put oneself in the midst of postconflict recovery. Postconflict recovery lasts a lifetime in most cases, and to abandon such sites would involve some sort of moral mind tricks to assuage feelings of guilt. However, what I want to emphasize is that there is no "god trick" perspective (as Haraway refers to it) that can will away Global North power, even if I situate myself as part of the critical community I write about in this book (Haraway, 1988).

I have previously accounted for the contradictory position that Global North researchers face when conducting peacekeeping fieldwork (Henry et al., 2009). While most of researchers are in positions of privilege and can exercise power over respondents, there also needs to be recognition of the ways in which those marginalized along lines of race, class, and nationality can complicate these relations of power. My own positionality as a woman of color within Anglo-American gender studies, peace and conflict studies, and international relations as well as humanitarian aid, diplomatic, and military cultures also placed me on the margins in several ways. But as I repoliticize peacekeeping in this book, then it is only fair that I do so by giving an account of myself and my contingent, contradictory, and sometimes complicit role in the field.

The Need for Critical Theories

My review of the critical thought on peacekeeping has inspired me to draw on a range of theories and ideas from feminist, antimilitarist, and critical race scholarship in order to extend and deepen my analysis of peacekeeping as an epistemic project. As I have shown, peacekeeping studies is a varied field, and it has undergone some quite important political shifts. These are both specific and nonspecific to peacekeeping studies. Like many other left-leaning and critical theory subfields, peacekeeping studies has always had proponents intent on reforming peacekeeping as a practice. However, my observation is that peacekeeping studies, in particular, should be a site in which scholars take a more politically honest foothold—where they engage in using critical theory to take up a moral and political position about how global governance practices should or should not continue into the future. What theories might enable scholars to move in a more politically accountable direction? But before I pursue this more ontological question, let me outline what I mean when I argue that peacekeeping is an epistemic project.

To argue that peacekeeping is epistemic is to recognize that the practice of peacekeeping—everything from the Security Council's decision to establish a peace operation and deploy civilian and military personnel until the "draw down" and the moment the last UN worker leaves a particular office—constitutes a body of knowledge. This knowledge is not a raw and natural resource that emerges organically but is instead the product of discourses, structures, and power relations in motion. Revealing this takes away any mysticism about peacekeeping as a purely altruistic and innately humane and reactive practice. Calling peacekeeping an epistemic project illustrates the consciousness and conscientiousness by which decisions are made about who will be the keepers and who will be the kept. This line of argument is inspired by the work of geographers and by the book *Insecure Spaces* (Higate and Henry, 2009). In this previous work, we conceptualized peacekeeping as a socio-spatial power project and argued that when peacekeeping missions are established, they fundamentally alter social and physical landscapes, contributing to new experiences of security and insecurity. This unpacking of peacekeeping as far from being a benign and neutral process in postconflict settings has led me to a new analysis around epistemology.

Because peacekeeping sites engender complex social relations, it is easy to witness the ways in which both peacekeepers and the peacekept resist and challenge the various power relations within which they find themselves embedded, and the ways in which these sites reflect wider structural and global inequalities. They are spaces that produce knowledge about the locale, but also about peacekeeping itself. I will outline a relevant fieldwork experience from Liberia to illustrate my argument about epistemics. At the end of a day of interviews, my colleague and I were heading back to our hotel when our driver, Luke, asked us if we were ready to close the day. We said yes, and he told us he knew a short cut which would help us to reach our destination quickly and efficiently. As he wove his way around the outskirts of Monrovia, the vehicle suddenly came to an abrupt stop as we entered an old hotel car park, which now had a Swedish peacekeeper "manning" the gate. Luke and the peacekeeper entered into a heated debate, battling it out as to who exactly was in a position to control that entrance and access to roads. Luke protested by saying that he "*always* used to take this shortcut" (his emphasis). He eventually capitulated and complained the whole journey back that he frequently took that route and was aggrieved that he could no longer travel freely in "his own country." We never forgot that incident and the humiliation that we could read on his face as he sat in silence on the rest of the journey. This confirmed to me then, and now, that peacekeeping not only transforms space and place but actively rearranges knowledge of those spaces such that some individuals feel displaced and confused while others feel authorized and empowered. One could almost say that Luke was gaslit in that moment—that he was epistemically marginalized and made to believe that he did not "know" his own city. And it was this encounter that reminded me that peacekeeping can never exist outside of knowledge production and the power relations that form the backdrop of humanitarian encounters.

The work of Massey is instructive here in thinking through space and its transformation into knowledge. Massey maintains that globalization and its effect on our society can be understood through an understanding of both space and time. That is, in the contemporary era we can see that the world is indeed "speeding up" as well as "spreading out," and the compression of the two is evident as global interconnectedness and interdependency becomes more prevalent (Massey, 1994). In this way, Massey suggests that cultures and communities are merged owing to rapid growth and change, as "layers upon layers" of histories fuse together to shift our ideas of what the identity of a "place" should be. Massey "repoliticizes" space and moves away from space as empty matter or as stasis, and toward an understanding of space as intersecting with temporality. Furthermore, Massey demonstrates how individuals are positioned in spaces and differentiated by race and gender; for example; she argues that those who move freely have more power. She writes:

> Now I want to make one simple point here, and that is about what one might call the power geometry of it all; the power geometry of time-space compression. For different social groups, and different individuals, are placed in very distinct ways in relation to these flows and interconnections. This point concerns not merely the issue of who moves and who doesn't, although that is an important element of it; it is also about power in relation to the flows and the movement. Different social groups have distinct relationships to this anyway differentiated mobility: some people are more in charge of it than others; some initiate flows and movement, others don't; some are more on the receiving-end of it than others; some are effectively imprisoned by it. (Massey 1994, p. 156)

Massey used these ideas of flows and movements to think about relations of power and inequality on a global scale, as well as in regard to the local or domestic when she identifies the gendered division of labor as such a site where power geometries can be illustrated. In relation to peacekeeping as an epistemic project, I might then ask what it means, for example, to have peacekeepers (or "foreign" military men) living and working in a particular location—Bosnia, Kosovo, Haiti—for so many years. What power geometries are at work? How has their own mobility and rootedness in these spaces helped to constitute peacekeeping? How has this shaped what peacekeeping scholars know?

If research on sexual exploitation and abuse tells us that the presence of all-male military peacekeepers results in "peace babies" (Vahedi et al., 2021), then this confirms further that peacekeeping has consequences (unintended or intended) and cannot simply be conceived of as a neutral and peaceful presence in a previously conflicted place (Thakur et al., 2007). Why then does the UN continue to populate peacekeeping missions with all-male military squads, in spite of this well-established knowledge of the root causes of sexual exploitation and abuse of the peacekept? What are the collective investments that various states have in the discourse that peacekeeping "saves lives," and that these "unintended" consequences are a rather minor matter in comparison? It may be that male peacekeepers, as the most likely trained soldiers of a nation, provide the possibility of security in a now fragile context. Yet we know from research that this is not logically what transpires (Higate and Henry, 2009). In our research in Haiti, we were struck by local women's accounts of increased insecurity, something the women believed stemmed from the presence of particular groups of men: armed peacekeepers and corresponding armed bandits (Henry and Higate, 2016). Women recounted how certain contingents used aggressive combat tactics, which in their view fueled violence, insecurity, and injury rather than engendered peace. Research conducted by a multinational team of scholars show the multitude of effects of peacekeeping in Haiti, among them victims of sexual exploitation and the fate of children fathered by peacekeepers (Vahedi et al., 2021; Lee and Bartels, 2020; Kolbe and Hutson, 2006). The fact that most UN peacekeepers are men and are mobile—the very skewed power geometry of it all—meant that peacekeeping could indeed foster insecurity, perpetuate colonial-style relations, and impoverish women and girls already economically and socially marginalized. Thus, my emphasis here is that there is an invaluable contribution that critical theories such as Massey's can make toward repoliticizing peacekeeping scholarship.

What Massey and feminist geography inspire further is the importance of a politics of location, both in terms of geopolitics and in relation to epistemic situatedness. As I show throughout this book, those feminist and postcolonial scholars engaged in critiques of peacekeeping often drew on explicitly epistemic theories and concepts—such as feminist standpoint theory (Collins, 1986; Smith, 1987). Standpoint theory, especially that developed by Black feminists, is interlinked with a range of other concepts and theories but is especially associated with the development of intersectionality (see discussion below) (Crenshaw, 1989). Importantly, returning to feminist standpoint theory allows me to do two things in this book. The first is to better understand the epistemic nature of peacekeeping. Here, peacekeeping is not only what the UN "does" but is a form of constructed knowledge about conflict and postconflict spaces and societies. But who constructs this knowledge? Peacekeeping officials, military and civilian peacekeepers, humanitarian agencies, global governance directors and elected officials, the peacekept, peacekeeping scholars, and students all contribute to what can be known about peacekeeping.[8] What feminist standpoint theory does is to remind us that peacekeeping knowledge, like all knowledge, is always partial and depends on where individuals are standing, in multiple senses of the word. For example, I ask, where are those producing or contributing this knowledge located in the world? Are they sitting in the UN Headquarters in New York, far away from the visceral effects and aftermath of war? Are they writing from the academic "ivory" tower? Are they corresponding from home or from their barracks in Haiti? Or is it from the internally displaced people's (IDP) camp in which they have been living since the conflict ended many years ago? To argue that peacekeeping is an epistemic project is to acknowledge that accounts of peacekeeping are not only partial and situated but depend on the relative power of standing (Cockburn, 2008). An example of this is evident from my fieldwork observations. The differences in life quality and outcomes between peacekeepers and the peacekept is very obvious when moving around the mission. If there is ever any doubt that there are multiple worlds and forms of knowledge, it is confirmed in that moment when the mission's special representative of the secretary general (SRSG) comes in and out of the city—they are ushered to and from the airport by a convoy of expensive luxury vehicles with a police and military escort. Sometimes traffic is jammed up for hours as a result of this journey. An entire city can be disrupted in this performance of security and high status. To point this out as contributing to peacekeeping knowledge is to repoliticize the field.

Further examples will confirm this argument. If I include the persistent number of cases of sexual violence and abuse of local girls and boys in peacekeeping missions such as those documented in Haiti, Liberia, and the Democratic Republic of Congo, I can see another way in which the concept of the color line might be epistemically useful. I might ask, as Razack invoking Du Bois prompts us to ask, which bodies of color matter? Which bodies are available to the peacekeeping gaze and project? And which peacekeepers should do the hard and soft labor of militarized peacekeeping (Henry, 2015, 2019)? Which women should come to fill the ranks in order to decrease incidents of sexual exploitation and abuse committed by male soldiers (Henry, 2012)?

In following Twitter activity from the official UN Peacekeeping account, the UN consistently and repeatedly "thanks" peacekeepers for their "service." Peacekeepers who have been killed on duty are honored for their "sacrifice." Tweets show pictures of male peacekeepers hard at work helping to construct buildings and distributing water or other supplies. This type of representation is cliché, despite all the changes in the composition of peacekeeping labor that might challenge such a stereotype. The UN is heavily invested in maintaining traditional ideas of duty and sacrifice, even as it changes the "face" of peacekeeping by promoting initiatives to increase the number of women peacekeepers. But the reality is that male peacekeepers have relied on peacekeeping deployments to send remittances home—for many breadwinners it has been a lifetime career (Henry, 2015). But the color line is not simply a gendered or economic one. The color line functions in contemporary peacekeeping by putting some of the most vulnerable individuals into fragile situations (Cold-Ravnkilde et al., 2017; Cold-Ravnkilde and Albrecht, 2020). Thus, in Chapter 2, I take Razack's appropriation of the Du Boisian concept of the global color line and use it to better understand global divisions of labor among peacekeepers, and point to how these divisions create the conditions for unequal peacekeeping. This chapter uses critical race and postcolonial theories to analyze current and upcoming peacekeeping practices which involve the soldiering of those deployed by a global system of racialized and unequal labor. In Razack's study of peacekeeping violence by Canadian peacekeepers in Somalia, she argues that Canadians come to *know* themselves in intimate ways through the color line (Razack 2004, p. 9). The color line, according to Du Bois, is the "problem of the twentieth century... the relation of the darker to the lighter of races of men [*sic*] in Asia and Africa, in America and the islands of the sea" (Du Bois, 1903, p.15). Drawing on this work, Razack unpacks modern peacekeeping as a color line "with civilised white nations standing on one side, and uncivilized Third World Nations standing on the other" (Razack 2004, p. 10). This, she suggests, is what structures the relationship between peacekeepers and the peacekept. Importantly, she points out that it does not matter where the peacekeepers originate from; either way they are bound up in the imperial project. Thus peacekeeping, yet again, seen through this analytical framework, is not an innocent and impartial rescue mission; it is not simply about saving and securing lives but rather is part of "race pleasure" and in what Agathangelou and Ling would refer to as a "desire industry" (Agathangelou and Ling, 2003; Razack, 2004). In this way, revisiting the critical concept of the color line allows another reveal of the epistemic foundations of peacekeeping. Whose lives matter in peacekeeping?

A related concept informs my arguments about epistemic power and peacekeeping. Intersectionality has made its way as a buzz word into a range of disciplines and fields of practice that perhaps the scholar most associated with the term, Crenshaw, could not have predicted (Davis, 2008; Crenshaw, 1989). In introducing this concept, I am not suggesting that we return to intersectionality in peacekeeping studies, because as far as I know it never had a place (Kappler and Lemay-Hebert 2021)! However, I have been loosely tracking the introduction of the concept into international relations, critical military studies, and peace and conflict studies more recently. Intersectionality is a theory that emphasizes intersecting systems and structures of oppression. It is the idea that women experience oppression through various configurations and levels of intensity. Patterns of oppression are interrelated and work together to influence intersectional systems of power. This includes race, gender, class, ability, and ethnicity, for example (Crenshaw, 1990, 1989; Combahee

River Collective, 1983). Crenshaw developed the theory from her own and others' experiences and unique perspectives. It is a term developed out of the experiences of economically vulnerable Black women and the multiple discriminations experienced by this group, particularly in the US. Recently, I have witnessed the adoption and appropriation of the concept of intersectionality in analyzing military masculinities and have written extensively about this, drawing on my work with women peacekeepers from the Global South (Henry, 2017, 2021). In this work I caution against using the concept to simply represent multiple differences. For example, the use of intersectionality to understand ethnic minority men's experiences within the military has been insightful but draws away from acknowledging the privilege and power some men continue to hold (Henry, 2017). Using intersectionality this way does an injustice to the emancipatory and revolutionary roots of the theory in the first place. However, I do see a place for intersectionality in the context of peacekeepers from the Global South and for increasing attention to the peacekept. First, thinking with intersectionality enables scholars of peacekeeping to pay attention to prevailing global inequalities. As scholars show, intersectionality can help challenge the idea of discrete and singular positions of disadvantage towards an understanding of inequality as intersecting, interlocking or even forming a matrix (Crenshaw, 1989; Razack, 1998; Hill Collins, 2002). Such an approach has allowed me to understand the experience of women peacekeepers as precarious and marginal, while also paying attention to how they may simultaneously occupy positions of relative privilege vis-à-vis the peacekept. The Indian women peacekeepers I spent time with and spoke to in my research consistently positioned themselves as agents "superior" to those local women they were tasked to protect. This "move" reflects the performative and therefore productive side to peacekeeping as an epistemic project, one that enables peacekeepers to reaffirm their national and gendered identities. Global sisterhood then, especially in peacekeeping policies, is a myth that intersectionality helps to reveal and challenge (Henry, 2012). In this way, drawing on intersectionality to understand the experiences of peacekeepers also bolsters my argument that what we know about peacekeeping is contingent on where we stand and who we listen to when learning about practice.

Intersectionality also offers another avenue of resuscitation. It can draw our critical eyes toward those who are subject to and governed by peacekeeping and the various ways in which individuals are situated both as victims of, and agents within, peacekeeping missions. Of late it appears that peacekeeping studies is becoming less and less about those who are the beneficiaries of such practices. Intersectionality helps to ask, In what ways is the color line enforced? In what ways are social inequalities compounded and experienced by the "peacekept"? Thus, in Chapter 3, through the use of the concept of intersectionality, I demonstrate how different axes of power, privilege, and identity shape the ways in which peacekeepers occupy the peacekeeping space. Continuing to focus on how peacekeepers are not "equal," I move away from thinking solely about gender when it comes to women peacekeepers. What other axes of power feature in the lives of Global South peacekeeping women? Drawing on empirical work conducted in Liberia and Haiti, I show how women peacekeepers are positioned in paradoxical ways. Pressured to conform to a range of gendered and militarized norms, women peacekeepers are expected to both maintain and disavow embodiment along a feminine-masculine continuum. The chapter goes on to analyze how essentialized and binaristic views of women and men reinforce patriarchal expectations within martial institutions, trapping soldiers into stereotypical roles and producing women soldiers who are never "fit for purpose." In addition to the issue of women peacekeepers, the chapter explores how an exclusive focus by the media and the UN on sexual exploitation and abuse as gendered simultaneously reinforces colonial ideas about peacekept women as inherent victims. Here, I explore how viewing peacekept women as consenting agents challenges the dominant feminist thinking embedded in the UN system of gender training and initiatives to prevent sexual exploitation and abuse. By using the work of critical scholars, I approach these seemingly positive developments in peacekeeping (the inclusion of women into the ranks) with skepticism.

What assumptions are there in the knowledge that women will somehow make peacekeeping "better"?

Chapter 4 returns to feminist peace and antimilitarist scholarship. Evident in the work of Whitworth (2004), Cockburn and Žarkov (2002), and Mazurana, Raven-Roberts and Parpart (2005) is that the foundations of peacekeeping are not in peace thinking or conflict resolution but in martial power. Importantly, this is the one area of scholarship that has been consistently undercited and underacknowledged as the peacekeeping literature has developed since the early 2000s. This is also where I further reveal the *politics* of peacekeeping and what is entailed in contestations over what constitutes "appropriate" analyses of peacekeeping as practice. The chapter explores how concepts such as militarization and martial politics provide the necessary framing for reviving a more critical, political, and moral account of contemporary peacekeeping. This means understanding peacekeeping as a militarized epistemic project. Here I turn to a number of scholars interested in theorizing militarization (Enloe, 2000) and martial politics (Howell, 2018). If recent scholarship demonstrates that peacekeeping can be made more effective by tinkering with mandates, logistics, and operational procedures (Hultman et al., 2019; Howard, 2019), then what room is there for feminist peace perspectives on the need to reduce, if not eliminate, attachments to military values, culture, and ends (Chisholm, 2022)? To expose the epistemic roots of peacekeeping is to reveal its attachments to martial power. Finally, the chapter examines how the continued male domination of peacekeeping and the Global South burden of "boots on the ground" mean that peacekeeper fatalities and risks form the justification for an increase, rather than reduction, in military might. Troop-contributing countries such as Brazil have been advocating for targeted and elite military actions to counteract peace "spoilers" and to protect UN peacekeepers and property (Williams, 2020). Thus, the martial foundations of peacekeeping have become increasingly sedimented, and the problem-solving scholarship does not critique this long-standing investment in and dependence on the military.

The book explores how the global color line, geopolitics, and racialization determines who keeps the peace and what the cost of this labor might be; how gender, among other axes of power, impacts the ways in which the presence of women peacekeepers reinforces patriarchal norms and how the introduction of specific feminist framings reproduces and maintains colonial ideas and binaristic thinking; and how returning to critical feminist scholarship on the military and its ideological and practical foundations might lead to advocating for defunding the military in peacekeeping. Subsequently, Chapter 5 turns to more recent work on the need to engage in decolonization. If peacekeeping is the epistemic project I propose it to be, it requires critical framing and in-depth understanding if it is to be challenged, dismantled, and/or reassembled. What is observable is that along with a number of works sidelined in contemporary peacekeeping studies, there is also an increasing pattern of marginalizing the peacekept. Thus, even in work exploring women peacekeepers (Karim and Beardsley, 2017) and the necessity of peacekeeping (Hultman et al., 2019), the peacekept are constructed as just one among many variables, or objectified simply as the ground on which mandates and other policies are written. Decolonizing peacekeeping means challenging what we know about peacekeeping and thinking seriously about those who are acted on by peacekeepers and the peacekeeping industry. Thus, returning to the important work of critical scholars is of essential importance to thinking about who the referent of peacekeeping as epistemology might be (Pouligny, 2006; Zisk Marten, 2004; Autesserre, 2010, 2014). Shifting the gaze away from peacekeeping as a technology or as practical transformation and toward those who feel and experience peacekeeping requires serious investigation into how contemporary peacekeeping practices maintain colonial relations of power. This must be reflected in the peacekeeping scholarship itself. Decentering the Global North and global governance institutions provides an opportunity to challenge the pervasive racism, sexism, and militarism that endures. This applies to the actual practices and the scholarship and allows for a politicization of peacekeeping knowledge.

I conclude by extending the epistemic analysis of peacekeeping as a repository of knowledge about gender, race, and militarization. Viewing peacekeeping as epistemic allows a recognition of the endurance of patriarchy and global systems of racism and colonialism, and the ways in which martial power continues to persist, even in contexts where peace is supposed to prevail. Importantly, peacekeeping as epistemic provides an opportunity for thinking about the agency and resistance by those who have endured peacekeeping. If the foundations of peacekeeping are not attended to, is peacekeeping just a continuation of the heteropatriarchal, colonial, military-industrial complex? In what ways can a different journey through peacekeeping scholarship provide the basis for a repoliticization of peacekeeping studies toward a more decolonized, degendered, and demilitarized future?

CHAPTER 2

From Civilizing Mission to Global Color Line: Coloniality in Humanitarian Work

> My contention is that Canadian atrocities in Somalia disappeared into the national mythology of "clean snows" and innocent peacekeepers-noble intermediaries between the superpowers. This process relied on the construction of Somalia as the opposite of Canada, as nothing but heat and dust. Somalis (both those in Somalia and those who come to Canada as refugees) have become the embodiment of disorder and dirt. A spatial technology of domination is at work here beyond the level of metaphor. The very concrete practices of violence against Somalis enabled individual soldiers to imagine themselves as men from the land of clean snow, men whose duties in bringing order to Somalia required violence. I argue that Canadian troops saw themselves as colonizers, civilizing the natives and imposing order on the "chaos of tribal warfare." When their violence was interrogated in a public inquiry, it disappeared into this old colonial story, now reframed as a story of peacekeeping.
>
> (Razack, 2000, p. 128)

Introduction

I regularly revisit Razack's important and undercited text *Dark Threats and White Knights* (Razack, 2004). I do so to immerse myself in the only comprehensive account of peacekeeping as a colonial practice, a paradigm supported by critical theories and empirical evidence, including documented legal cases of violence committed by peacekeepers. Despite the groundbreaking revelations of Razack's work and the startling scale of acts of violence perpetrated against the peacekept in a variety of missions since its publication, peacekeeping studies appears to have little to no interest in providing a commentary on violence committed by peacekeepers. While it is the case that the field of peacekeeping studies has included broader concerns around sexualized and gender-based violence in conflict and engaged in research in this area, arguably this has attracted greater attention than acts of violence or other crimes perpetrated by peacekeepers (Westendorf, 2020). Instead, work from 2017 to 2020 focuses disproportionately on violence or potential violence *against* peacekeepers (De Coning et al., 2017; Cruz et al., 2017; Hultman et al., 2019; Williams, 2020; Howard, 2019). This focus goes some way in suggesting that the majority of insecurity in peacekeeping missions is experienced by peacekeepers rather than the peacekept. At the same time, I argue, it helps to construct, support, and reproduce a narrative that serves to justify the activities of peacekeeping and peacekeepers.[1] This is not atypical in military thinking and practice more broadly (Chisholm, 2014). What Razack's persuasive argument about peacekeeping as violence contributes to the scholarship is that it exposes the national-specific foundations of peacekeeping. Razack shows how incidents of peacekeeper violence are discursively managed away—they become erased from broader narratives about peacekeepers and peacekeeping and are often folded back into ongoing national mythologies. Stories of peacekeeping provide particular understandings of peace, conflict, nation, and "development," and it is this knowledge that I seek to engage throughout this book. In particular, Razack's work complements the argument that I make in Chapter 1: that peacekeeping is an epistemic project shaped by the gendered, racialized, and militarized politics of global governance.

When Razack argues that peacekeeping is a colonial project, it means that peacekeeping cannot be understood without, or separated from, the histories of colonialism and imperialism that precede the development and design of modern peacekeeping practices under the auspices of the UN. While Razack primarily focuses on an example of Canadian peacekeepers committing crimes, her broader argument about peacekeeping as colonial (violence) is applicable when peacekeeping is understood as constituted by more than the sum of individual peacekeepers' actions. Thus, the power of peacekeeping emanates from the discursive knowledge that is produced by the UN and in and through the practices that constitute it. In this way, peacekeeping both reflects and produces colonial relations (among others). Modern peacekeeping is implicated in colonial relations of governance by virtue of constructing postconflict societies in certain forms and by the effects of practice in terms of ideas about geography and nation that are perpetuated in the multiple "performances" (Henry, 2015; Higate and Henry, 2009). To state that peacekeeping is implicated in a colonial matrix is to acknowledge that geopolitical inequalities are not suspended or eliminated in times of peacekeeping. In some cases, these inequalities might be extended or exacerbated during the postconflict phase (Henry and Higate, 2016). Historically, peacekeeping has borrowed from international development and humanitarian aid in terms of framing the beneficiaries and the geopolitical context. Kothari demonstrates this in a similar context when she shows how contemporary development and aid workers have inherited their occupational and professional cultures and protocols from colonial rule and administration (Kothari, 2005a, 2006a; Kothari and Wilkinson, 2010). For example, time served in the British Colonial Office prepared contemporary development workers through an immersion in Orientalist thinking (Said, 1978) as a result of their own racialized and privileged positioning and Eurocentric beliefs in a moral and civilizing duty to shape the lives of those considered racially inferior but equally in need of "rescue" (Razack, 2004; Kothari, 2005b, 2006b). As mentioned in

Chapter 1, Paris' early work on peacekeeping upheld wider postcolonial critiques of peacekeeping, but in time Paris became convinced that, on balance, peacekeeping was better than nonintervention alternatives (Paris, 2001, 2002). Paris' argument, shared by many scholars, is a turn away from a more critical account of the enduring legacies of colonialism in peacekeeping, in a similar vein to most of the problem-solving scholarship. Other scholars have pointed out that Global North domination of peacebuilding and intervention efforts reflects both epistemic and political investments in colonial-style relations (Abrahamsen, 2000; Autesserre, 2014; Duffield, 2001; Tudor, 2023), yet colonialism is rarely mentioned in relation to the actions of peacekeepers vis-à-vis the peacekept.

This chapter considers in greater depth the insights offered by Razack (and others) about the ideology and discourse of peacekeeping as an epistemic and colonial project, through empirical examples. First, I outline the ways in which colonial ideologies persist in shaping relationships within peacekeeping spaces, with the UN as an organization/institution, and among peacekeepers and between them and the peacekept, although I explore this in more detail in the penultimate chapter. Borrowing again from Razack, I argue that the peacekeeping space is one in which colonial or "racial scripts" are enacted. This happens regardless of which peacekeepers are present—it is an argument that Razack makes about the nature and legacy of coloniality in postcolonial peacekeeping contexts, and I extend it more broadly. The metaphor of the "frontier," for example, enables an epistemic interpretative frame that views peacekeeping as *for* something. I explore how peacekeeping's dominant orientation (ideology), as reflected through accounts from peacekeepers and my own observations in missions, reinforces various forms of inequality and perpetuates structural and other forms of violence (Farmer, 1996). I then turn to critical race theories (such as that of the global color line) to explore how Global South peacekeepers bear the burden of peacekeeping labor, and I demonstrate how this is rooted in global racial relations. I suggest that when close attention is paid to the geopolitics of peacekeeping labor, it becomes clear that peacekeeping is not exempt from global processes which similarly reflect racial and other social and structural hierarchies. Finally, I demonstrate that those who are sent to do peacekeeping work are placed in a contradictory position; they carry out the "dirty" work on behalf of a proxy state (the UN) and yet are constructed in informal discourses as simultaneously "developmental," unreliable, and/or as docile, innocent, and expendable. Essentially these workers are fit for purpose while simultaneously being cast as typical Orientals, Africans, and so forth. For example, colonial stereotypes about Global South militaries as "effeminate" or "brutish" (Higate and Henry, 2009) do not reflect the firsthand perceptions of peacekeepers (or the peacekept) but should be understood in the context of colonial histories, discourses, and politics; viewing them in this light makes possible an analysis in which peacekeeping practices mimic and perpetuate power differences. Colonial ideas about the human qualities and propensities, capacities, and limits of Global South populations are maintained within mission contexts by global governance discourses as well as by troop contributing countries (TCCs) and individual peacekeepers themselves, all of whom have different investments in the power of such discourses.

The Endurance of Colonial/Missionary Thinking and Practice

On a recent reading of Razack's *Dark Threats and White Knights*, I came across a piece of paper marking a particular page. Jotted down on that scrap were the contact details of a civilian peacekeeper that my colleague and I had approached and asked to interview in 2006. I distinctly remember that we had befriended this peacekeeper through his then girlfriend, who also happened to also be a peacekeeper. We spent an evening having dinner and drinks with them and another couple, who were both employed as civilian peacekeepers. Many civilian peacekeepers helped us in our research, and hosting that evening's meal was a means for us as researchers to show our gratitude for their time and willingness. Simple, quotidian acts of dining out in hotels, restaurants, and cafes owned and/or staffed by foreign merchants are themselves indebted to the legacy of colonialism; no less so are our fieldwork methods implicated in this culture and context, as we have previously acknowledged (Henry et al., 2009), and which I will expand on in subsequent sections of this chapter.

As we were sitting in a restaurant in Monrovia (owned by a couple who had established a similar hospitality venture in the peacekeeping mission in East Timor),[2] John brought up the issue of the book that I had been carrying around earlier in the day, which he had spotted sticking out of my bag when we were in the UN Headquarters building. The book's cover is a photograph sourced from the National Archives of Canada and shows five adolescent Somali boys bound and blindfolded in an unsheltered, sunny street, with a Canadian peacekeeper standing behind them, gazing off into the distance. This particular image had ignited some concern among the civilian peacekeepers, and a discussion ensued. They asked me for a summary of the book's main arguments. When I told them of the book's description of peacekeeping as a colonial project, they immediately objected to this particular framing. They were all well-educated; each of them had earned master's degrees, mostly in human rights or development studies, and some had followed a fairly "cosmopolitan" path of education and work. They were familiar with academic arguments about colonialism, development, and aid. Yet, despite their familiarity with such theories, they did not agree with the book's premise. John objected to peacekeeping being referred to in either colonial or imperial terms because, as he claimed, colonial practices were not initiated with what he referred to as "good intentions." He argued that peacekeeping attempts to improve people's lives in the aftermath of extreme violence and war conditions and has nothing to do with "extracting" from the land or community in order to profit. Maria, who worked as a civilian peacekeeper at the headquarters, had a different approach and acknowledged the differences between those tasked to keep the peace and those "forced" to accept the UN's peacekeeping presence. Maria's family was from the Global South, though in the US she had experienced economic and class mobility, which afforded her an elite education in the UK, Italy, and the US. François backed up John's account, telling his own story of how peacekeepers had helped him to escape violence and destitution when he was just a young man living in East Africa. Having since succeeded on his "own merits," though with the help of some aid workers and peacekeepers, he managed to secure for himself a role as a human rights officer in a peacekeeping mission. François regarded the peacekept population not as colonial subjects but rather as reluctant and sometimes ungrateful beneficiaries of humanitarian aid. And finally, Susanne had a slightly different perspective. Coming from a working-class family in Germany, Susanne felt that in many ways she shared much in common with the local peacekept populations' struggles to create better lives. She shared with the group how working as a human rights officer enabled her to earn a sufficiently good salary so that she would be able to buy a car for her mother back home. From her perspective, inequalities exist all over the world, and the only way for individuals to overcome these obstacles was through hard work. Despite having had a northern European experience of higher education very similar to that of her colleagues, Susanne was much less sympathetic to the framing of peacekeeping as a colonial project. Her conclusion was that if relations were unequal, it was not to do with peacekeeping, but the outcome of already existing inequalities that locals themselves perpetuated. This was common rhetoric among many civilian, police, and military peacekeepers—inequalities might exist, but peacekeeping does not "bring" inequality; these inequalities predate the peacekeeping mission.

The somewhat tense discussion stayed with me well beyond the field. How is it that those UN civilian peacekeepers who had both studied some critical theories and who had worked in missions were reluctant to take up such an analytical framework? Perhaps it is not surprising that so much of peacekeeping studies is similarly wary of employing such theories, because they do not necessarily fit with the firsthand perceptions of being a peacekeeper. On numerous occasions in the course of our fieldwork, I and my colleagues had discussed the colonial attitudes we perceived to be present among an array of civilian workers, but especially those working for the UN

(Henry et al., 2009). We concluded that the relatively privileged backgrounds of UN civilian peacekeepers, in particular, was a major factor in drawing the conclusion that peacekeepers reflect the coloniality of peacekeeping. However, as I documented in my article on the contradictory positioning of peacekeepers (Henry, 2015), from 2012 onward there were fewer civilian peacekeepers working as human rights officers and, conversely, far more formed police units and civilian police present in the older missions. These militarized peacekeepers did not exhibit the same forms of privilege, nor did they share John's altruism in wanting to improve lives and "make things better." Many police and military peacekeepers had left precarious and depressed economies back at "home," and for them, peacekeeping provided a unique opportunity to become economically and socially mobile. Strikingly, this group of peacekeepers regularly shared their contempt for the peacekept, as I show throughout this chapter. The privileged positions that peacekeepers occupy is always in a state of flux, for their individual personal circumstances are closely tied to the unstable socioeconomic contexts from which they have been deployed. This in no way undermines Razack's argument that peacekeeping provides a colonial stage. Instead, it shows how peacekeeper narratives attempt to contest colonial relations, either by framing vulnerability as belonging equally to (some) peacekeepers and to the peacekept, or by reinforcing colonial relations by claiming a Global South native "authority" and embracing neoliberal progress narratives (Minh-ha, 1989).

I begin this section by narrating a commonsense or lay reading of what privilege and power might look like to an observer interested in the "micropolitics of detail" in peacekeeping (Lutz, 2006). In early fieldwork, we saw civilian peacekeepers with expensive clothing, jewelry, and gadgets, dining in exclusive restaurants aimed at expats or foreign businessmen and living in gated communities of newly built apartments and houses (Smirl, 2015; Henry et al., 2009). As a researcher with significant economic privilege in these contexts, I frequented many of these sites, both as part of my official research and when I took time off. However, as peacekeeping missions extended further in time, the need for certain personnel decreased and the presence of "cheaper" collectivized, militarized units became the norm. These spaces of privilege and luxury dining continued to exist, but the numbers of peacekeepers among their patrons noticeably declined, and thus the conspicuous visibility of peacekeeper privilege diminished. One important conclusion that I continually reiterate in my work is that the types of peacekeepers who are deployed matters—not in contradiction of what Razack argues about colonial scripts, but to demonstrate the geopolitics that informs peacekeeping deployments. The composition of peacekeeping is important when trying to understand the qualitative impact of a mission on the peacekept. To give some empirical examples, I start by reflecting on the nature of some peacekeeping spaces.

Mamba Point Hotel, Monrovia. Hotel Montana, Port-au-Prince. Dazzlingly white, starched cloths on tables arranged in intimate groupings on sun- and rain-sheltered verandas, with views of the city unfolding in the distance. Through the lush green trees below, glimpses of shimmering water of swimming pools that inspired novels like Gil Courtemanche's *A Sunday at the Pool in Kigali* (Courtemanche, 2004). The hotels attracted a varied though mostly foreign or international clientele. The restaurants and cafes associated with the hotels were frequent meeting places for UN peacekeepers (mostly civilian or military officers). These hotels were testimonies to so much of the colonial past; in some cases they used terminology reminiscent of colonial times ("Time for Tiffin" on menus) or featured colonial practices as attractions. For example, at Mamba Point Hotel, built along colonial architectural design and style, "high tea" was served in the afternoon. At Hotel Montana, "chicken creole [*sic*]" was lavishly served, cooked in a "blander" style to accommodate more "refined" European tastes, priced at three times the cost paid by the poorer patrons of smaller local cafes and kiosks. Menus at these sites often reflected the international clientele, from complex sushi menus to extensive meze meals; these global plated food experiences were nevertheless created with the expat customer's palate in mind.

Many of our fieldwork meetings with peacekeepers took place inside these venues. By contrast, none of the meetings we had with civil society organizations or the peacekept transpired in any of these hotel restaurants. These sites of privilege provide evidence of some of the ways in which peacekeeping spaces reproduce global inequalities and racial hierarchies; they speak too of how researchers contribute to the perpetuation of inequalities in many of the same ways as peacekeepers.

The peacekept and peacekeepers occupied these sites in very different ways. Security guards and other hotel and cafe workers were always on the margins of the space, often milling about in the corridors and the "behind" spaces of hotels and restaurants. During breaks, they took their meals or rested in their designated areas, away from the eyes of the clientele who were sipping cocktails in the plush lounges and dining rooms unquestionably reserved for expats and foreign personnel (Chopra, 2006). Many restaurant staff would charge their phones while on duty, and would discreetly steal into the dining rooms to retrieve them, after which they swiftly retreated back to their permitted spaces. Within these white spaces of privilege, diplomats, expats, and wealthy businessowners could be seen with their escorts; it was readily known and acknowledged by peacekeepers that ambassadors and consular staff were not "ashamed" to present local young women as their dates (Jennings, 2014). Even the overflowing UN-branded, SUV-filled car parks evidenced what Lemay-Hébert calls the "white car syndrome"—that these cars reflect the status hierarchies and divisions that characterize peacekeeping missions (Lemay-Hébert, 2011). Use of these leisure spaces were divided along peacekeeping (external/foreign)/peacekept (internal/local) lines. While both the peacekeepers and the peacekept can be understood as laborers, there were clear and distinct axes of power that fell along lines of class, race, and gender.

But it was not just inside these relatively exclusive spaces that the privileges of peacekeepers and other humanitarian workers were revealed as helping to sustain colonial relations. On one occasion we were invited by the gender advisor in the mission to observe discussions in an oversight meeting and press conference on security sector reform at the UN Headquarters. Civil-military and police peacekeepers were present to attend and hear from experts in the mission. As the coffee break began, I stood outside the entrance to the building where the conference was taking place and ended up speaking to a peacekeeper who was taking a cigarette break. As he unwrapped his fresh packet of cigarettes, he discarded the plastic sleeve, along with his old empty packet, into the nearby garden area. When my eyes followed the wrapper and then returned to his eyes, he must have felt himself judged, for he exclaimed, "Well this place is a shithole anyhow. No one takes care of anything so that (pointing to the wrapper) is not going to make any difference." On several occasions while we were traveling in UN vehicles with peacekeepers to various sites, officers would open windows and throw out their used cups, soft drink cans, food wrappers, or cigarette butts. They made no effort to hide their littering and regularly pointed to piles of putrefying garbage to justify their actions. These small acts reflected their disregard for the habitats of others and the integrity of local people's rootedness to, and belonging within, these spaces. They were also reminders of the power inequality between peacekeeping as an institution, peacekeepers as agents of the UN, and the peacekept as local owners and occupiers of these spaces. In reflecting on Razack's argument at the beginning of this chapter about peacekeeping's complicity in the business of constructing knowledge about the peacekept and the mission space as a site of "dirt and disorder," it is clear that peacekeepers continually help reproduce this colonial image of spaces of aid as chaotic and uncivilized—in need of taming (Kothari, 2006a; Zanotti, 2011; Lemay-Hébert, 2017; Razack, 2004).

Much larger instances beyond measuring the UN's footprint on mission sites (Maertens, 2019) correspond with reports of a range of forms of violence, including chemical contamination in Kosovo (Latino, 2019) and the infamous case of cholera in Haiti, which became the subject of years-long investigations and lawsuits while the UN strenuously and consistently denied responsibility (Lemay-Hébert, 2014). While conducting fieldwork in Kosovo, I visited the site of a new housing development built to provide homes for Roma populations in areas that had formerly been declared uninhabitable by health authorities. The Roma community had moved away from an area which they believed to be contaminated and had managed, through EU funding, to find a new space to live. The journalist who was showing me and the NGO team that had facilitated various fieldwork visits around the new community recounted how French soldiers had been propositioning young Roma girls whenever they came on patrols in the area. She was particularly angry that having escaped one form of "pollution," her community was still left unprotected from other forms of harm.

Returning to the 2010 cholera outbreak in Haiti, which killed ten thousand Haitians, the UN steadfastly refused to accept responsibility, and instead attributed blame to the Nepalese peacekeepers, who were identified as the source of the outbreak.[3] It is interesting to note how little acknowledgment was made by the UN of the relatively weaker power of the Nepalese government in comparison, for example, to the Dutch government, which was recently held accountable for failing to protect civilians in Srebrenica over two decades earlier. Both of these cases, which revealed the deadly implications of the UN's dereliction in its peacekeeping responsibilities to the people it was meant to protect, spawned huge legal debates and discussion, yet few made the links between these incidents in the context of the global inequalities that form the backdrop of peacekeeping relations. The case against the UN was eventually proven via the Netherlands government, which was found culpable as under the mandate of UN troops and in failing to protect citizens against violence and genocide. Yet still for many years, the UN retained its reputation as a benign, neutral force for good in the aftermath of conflict (Hasanbasic, 2014). These judicial verdicts called into question the narrative of the UN as an objective institution. The cases mentioned above show how the UN perpetuates hierarchies and unequal relations among states; acts slowly to hold major world powers accountable for actions that potentially disrupt world peace; and causes harm to the peacekept populations—yet moves quickly to attach blame and responsibility for peacekeeper wrongdoings on nations that are less powerful on the global stage. Recall that Razack's study showed how violence committed by Canadian peacekeepers was subsumed under national mythologies and explained away through recourse to colonial ideas of the "third world" as a place of disorder. These discourses play a role in the perception of *where* the operational fault lies (as in the spread of cholera in Haiti), *which* peacekeepers pose a risk (and which are the carriers of disease, etc.), *who* should be protected by peacekeepers, and *what* should be the responsibility of governments who contribute peacekeeping contingents when operations go wrong.

It is not only at the macro level that the working out of colonial power is visible. Peacekeepers often shared their frustrations with individual projects they undertook with intentions to "improve" the lives of the peacekept. One white-identified[4] peacekeeper outlined how he decided to introduce a skills program to help the local community. Bruno had advanced martial arts skills and extensive knowledge of fitness and exercise regimes, and decided to offer self-defense training for local men and women in a city about two hours away from Monrovia. At his own expense, he produced flyers advertising free weekly sessions, which would cover basic fitness and security self-awareness, and in a spirit of generosity, provided cookies and soft drinks purchased from local suppliers. Seven or eight local men and women attended the first session. Bruno was pleased with the turnout and explained to them how the sessions would be organized going forward. After the second week, he realized that some people were entering the hall that he had booked for the self-defense sessions and heading straight for the free biscuits and drinks, and then sometimes leaving the session halfway through. He persevered until about the fifth week, when only two individuals attended. He was angry and expressed to me that, on the basis of his own experiences of having lived through a war, he had come to the conclusion that Liberians were incredibly "lazy" and would "get nowhere with their poor attitude." While Bruno declared himself sympathetic to the widespread poverty and hunger present in many Liberian communities—and was not initially judgmental of individuals coming to his classes to eat and drink the free food—his feelings of frustration grew and his anger toward the peacekept began to emerge. He also became demotivated and disillusioned about both his purpose as a peacekeeper more broadly and those around him who were supposed to "better the lives" of the host population. Many of Bruno's fellow contingent staff shared similar derogatory or disappointed views about the peacekept (Henry, 2015). Militarized peacekeepers from among his Balkan contingent used the shared experience of war and conflict as the basis for developmental arguments, drawing on Eurocentric and colonial ideas about national social "progress" and economic "development." The peacekeeper accounts oscillated between reproducing colonial rhetoric about "backward" Africa and self-negating discourses about their own struggles for survival in depressed economies back home in Eastern Europe.

Govran shared a similar, yet complex set of opinions on relations between peacekeepers and the peacekept. As partially recounted in my article on martial habitus and discursive strategizing by peacekeepers, I argue that many peacekeepers either already view the peacekept in ways that reflect colonial ideas of unhygienic people who are unperturbed about the "dirt and disorder" surrounding them, or come to view them as so by virtue of their indoctrination in the mission (Henry, 2015; Razack 2004; Zanotti, 2011). On one occasion, while I was meeting with a small group of peacekeepers for breakfast, I witnessed some of the ways in which colonial scripts are both enabled and contested by peacekeepers. Govran was frustrated by regular power outages, but more so by a blocked kitchen sink in his flat. He was trying to prepare his morning coffee when the sink started to back up. He was angry and frustrated with the recurring problem, and associated these daily irritants with the space of the peacekeeping mission itself (Henry, 2015). Govran recounted how the "filth of the country" was literally making its way back up the drains, leaving him with the responsibility of cleaning up the mess. When informed of the problem, the landlord of the apartment complex came to address the situation and proceeded to "lecture" Govran about how to "properly" dispose of coffee grounds. According to Govran, he and his flatmates "calmly" listened to the advice from the landlord and thanked him for attending to the issue. After the landlord left, they all abused the landlord for financially benefiting from the "chaos" of the country (and by extension, cheating them). The Lebanese landlord was quickly cast as a quintessentially "cunning Oriental" (Said, 1978) and the peacekept as embodying the space of "darkness" (McClintock, 1995). Govran's housemates laughed at his dramatic outburst (which was typical and expected of him) but generally backed up his beliefs as the conversation then turned to the "outrageous" costs of living in the mission. Thus, while these particular peacekeepers were not from metropolitan or colonial "centers," they were highly influenced by colonial rhetoric and drew on and adapted this rhetoric to speak with disrespect and disparagement about the peacekept; as they did so, it was clear that they were at the same time configuring their identities as distinct from, and superior to, those around them.

To reiterate Razack's important intervention that where the peacekeepers come from is only part of the picture of the colonial scripts enacted through peacekeeping, I suggest that the relationship between peacekeepers, and the manner in which peacekeeping space is acted on and populated, mimics colonial relations. Drawing on colonialist language and reproducing stereotypes of colonial subjects was quite common, as reflected in peacekeeper accounts in Haiti, Liberia, and Kosovo. In Kosovo, European peacekeepers regularly referred to the "overly" patriarchal nature of local men and national staff employed within UN offices. Local women (Kosovars) were thought to be overly "sexualized" judging from the way they dressed and conducted themselves in spaces of leisure such as bars and nightclubs. Iris, a senior police peacekeeper from northern Europe told me how she thought that local women working in the UN Headquarters (UNMIK) often dressed "inappropriately." She set about trying to "teach" local women how to dress "professionally," which included prohibition of clothes that she believed were intended for "nighttime." Iris offered her own explanation of why it was that young women generally did not have access to jobs in the hospitality and service sector: all cafes and restaurants were staffed by men, and this was so because of "Islamic prohibitions" on women working in public spaces. There was no reflection on wider patriarchal or colonial relations of power. Ironically, there was little reference to the presence of military and police personnel in as small a city as Pristina, Kosovo, where the demographics of gender were entirely skewed resulting in an overwhelming male presence, or to the concentration of white Global North militaries and mostly European police forces. Due to the design and organization of peacekeeping in Kosovo (UNMIK/KFOR), there was a concentration of peacekeepers from the USA, Germany, Austria, Sweden, Italy, and the UK, and contingents of police peacekeepers from the French gendarmerie and the Italian carabinieri. In this way, Kosovo as a peacekeeping space comprised a different array of peacekeepers than, say, the Democratic Republic of Congo ever has.

Finally, ideas about European or North American peacekeepers as being "less savage"—that is, less likely to be the perpetrators of gender-based sexual violence—were reiterated by civilian peacekeepers. When I asked about cases of sexual exploitation and abuse that came to light in 2006, I was quickly reassured that there had not been any cases of such, because Kosovo "wasn't like Africa, where women are very poor." The gender representative at UNMIK said that she was very aware of a number of long-term romantic relationships and even marriages based on "love and equality" between local women and male peacekeepers. Many peacekeepers from Finland, Germany, and the US had been deployed for a number of years longer than most contemporary peacekeeping missions allow—resulting in establishment of long-term transnational ties. When I probed further the gender advisor's understanding of what "equality" encompassed, her answer revealed that there was a discourse circulating about individuals becoming involved in relationships primarily driven by economic motivations. Such relationships were thought to take place "out there" (read: Africa), and had no place in European romance narratives (Baker, 2018; Westendorf and Searle, 2017; Alexandra, 2011). Forged as a result of pecuniary motives rather than based on romantic love, these "other" relationships were perceived to be more likely to be unequal, unlike the "free" relationships untainted by the aura of money presumed to be the hallmark of Western relationships. Even in such an intimate area it is possible to discern how certain Global North peacekeepers hold disdainful images of Global South people as mercenary.

One peacekeeper recounted an experience he had while posted to the mission in Haiti. One evening he had been at a party with a number of other peacekeepers, during which he and his girlfriend (another peacekeeper) had an argument. He had left the keys to his own apartment at his girlfriend's house and decided that he would try to get into his flat by procuring the help of nearby locals, rather than have to negotiate the return of the keys with her. In the event, he was unsuccessful in gaining access to his flat, and as it got later and later, he felt "forced" to accept an offer from a local domestic cleaner, who sometimes stayed in the flats of peacekeepers when they were away. She had offered to allow him to sleep in a vacant apartment, assuring him that she would sleep on the floor next to him. He eventually took up the offer, and later, was adamant that "nothing [had] happened" that night. In the early morning he returned to his girlfriend's flat to collect his keys and to try to make amends; he had received texts from her throughout the night asking of his whereabouts. She, however, had already been informed by peacekeepers that they had seen him entering the flat with the Haitian woman and was upset and angry at what she had perceived as an obvious sexual betrayal. He spent days convincing her that he was "not interested in black women" and that he would never have put his own or her health at risk by sleeping with a local woman.

The rhetoric of Black women's bodies as dangerous and contagious—as conduits of disease—was regularly repeated by men and women peacekeepers alike. A senior woman peacekeeper posted in Liberia told me during several meetings that she had observed young women "roaming the streets alone at night" and offered this as "proof" of the extended insecurity in the region. Her observation was not rooted in a feminist-inspired concern for the inequalities or sexual exploitation of peacekept women but by colonial ideas about African women's apparently loose sexual morality and their propensity for promiscuity (Mohanty, 1984; McClintock, 1995; Higate and Henry, 2004).

Narratives by peacekeepers about themselves, the regions they were working in, the peacekept and peacekeeping as an institution reflected a variety of racialized and colonial tropes and ideas. These structured how peacekeepers viewed their position within the peacekeeping space and beyond. They did not need to have a "brute" form of colonial power as part of their own national inheritance (as in the case of the Canadian peacekeepers whom Razack writes about) because power was produced through micropolitical details (Lutz, 2006). Rather, as Razack suggests with her reference to the colonial and racialized stage, the epistemic power to construct knowledge about the peacekept was itself a basis for how they viewed themselves and others. This epistemically skewed positioning was enabled by the larger structures and discourses of peacekeeping. And as Mohanty argues in her important text "Under Western Eyes," the image of the other is often about consolidating the construction of the self (Mohanty, 1984). This is why I argue that peacekeeping reflects these colonial histories in thought and practice.

The Global Color Line: Peacekeeping Labor and the Burdens of Care

The global color line, as previously defined, refers to the social division of the world into supposed discrete and distinct races of people; these differences are made visible by their external appearance, notably skin color. The idea of race as biologically stable and a "real" set of categories arranged in a neat and incontestable hierarchical order has persisted over hundreds of years of racial theorizing by Europeans, who assigned themselves as indubitably superior to all others. As superior beings their right to freedom was unquestioned and they could therefore claim rights in property over the bodies of presumably inherently inferior Black people, the historical inhabitants of what we loosely term the Global South (Du Bois, 1915; Robinson, 1983; Wai, 2012).

I have previously argued that Global South militaries perform the bulk of militarized labor in peacekeeping missions; it is by no means a coincidence but is instead the consequence of geopolitical inequalities grounded in ideas of race, which took hold during the eighteenth century and justified centuries of colonial slavery and imperialism, reducing Black and Brown people to the status of units of labor (Schaffer, 2013; Streets, 2017). Histories of colonialism have resulted in many countries in the Global South "revamping" their militaries in an effort to create jobs and boost their economy (Henry, 2015). Conflicts around the world have not limited who can participate in peacekeeping, and former Eastern Bloc countries such as Bosnia, Serbia, Croatia, Poland, Russia, Czech Republic, and Ukraine, among others, regularly send security personnel to peacekeeping sites for many of the same economic and political reasons as do Global South troop-contributing nations. Countries in the southern cone of South America have refashioned themselves as peace-promoting "forces for good" after periods of dictatorship and have made up the bulk of peacekeeping troops in contexts such as Haiti (Henry, 2012; Sotomayor, 2014). TCCs often have their own histories of racism that doubly influence their take up of racist and colonial rhetoric, as I have outlined in the previous section. Various economic crises have resulted in countries investing in military labor power, which has also seen the inclusion of women into the ranks. But these contemporary realities also mirror a wider and unequal global division of labor in which those inside and outside militaries in the Global South appear to serve once again as cheap sources of labor. While the UN pays equal amounts to TCCs, these funds are not always disbursed in ways that benefit individual peacekeepers in the same ways across the globe. As an example, a peacekeeper might receive a regular salary of approximately $2,000 per month alongside a much larger "hazard pay" and monthly stipend of upwards of $5,000 while on duty; it is quite a different situation where a peacekeeper is earning $6,000 per month on regular salary in addition to this pay[5]. Peacekeepers coming from states with national social protection schemes will also have access to free or state subsidized health care, education, and unemployment support and so have additional benefits afforded them. I was surprised by peacekeepers' comments when they described themselves as "economically trapped" by their peacekeeping role, despite having had to jostle to be chosen for peacekeeping deployment or specifically selected for an indefinite future of such work. They received extremely good monetary rewards but felt "trapped" because they could not easily leave a job where they were able to send generous remittances home to enable their children, for example, to have significantly better educational opportunities, in contexts of economic inequality and fragility in their home countries. As outlined in my article, many peacekeepers were able to use their enhanced income to make some fairly significant financial decisions, from paying off familial debts to sending their children to private or specialist education and sports training (Henry, 2015). White peacekeepers from the Global North, namely those from Canada, Sweden, Austria, and Germany, did not recount their experiences with such financial framings. In fact, for Canadian peacekeepers in Haiti it was financially viable to fly home during leave periods, in contrast to peacekeepers from much farther away, such as those francophone peacekeepers who had been deployed from West Africa or those dispatched from Eastern Europe. These peacekeepers often chose to forego travel back home during leave periods in order to save money, opting instead to send larger remittances home. This put a significant and unequal toll on some peacekeepers' mental health and familial relations. In the early 2000s, the UN-generated Brahimi Report issued recommendations and guidance as to what TCCs should be doing to discourage the consequences of traditional male-majority deployments; one such recommendation was for missions to facilitate better communication channels, for example, by providing computers and Wi-Fi access to enable peacekeepers and their families to connect (United Nations, 2000).

As I have previously written about, many peacekeepers were anxious about how their national militaries were perceived within the context of a cosmopolitan peacekeeping environment (Adebajo, 2002; Cunliffe, 2013; Duffey, 2000; Henry 2015; Barkawi, 2017; Bergman Rosamond and Kronsell, 2018). Several scholars have written on the problems of UN foundational thinking in the context of Africa, and this has drawn on postcolonial critiques more broadly (Wai, 2012; De Heredia, 2019). These anxieties around the imposition of peacekeeping morality on Africa as a result of racial science were also reflected at the level of the individual peacekeeper. In Chapter 3 I outline how a Nigerian lieutenant colonel felt that her mixed-race American section commander had undermined her in racialized and gendered ways. Senior male commanders often shared how they feared reputational damage by talking with researchers interested in documenting sexual exploitation and abuse. Many were keen to demonstrate that they themselves had no tolerance for poor discipline amongst their soldiers, or spent time demonstrating their extreme commitments to humanitarian aid.

Time spent with the Pakistani military was insightful as to the contributions of different military contingents, as well as their investments in upholding ideas of nation. On one of my field trips to the UN Mission in Liberia (UNMIL), I was told that Pakistani soldiers regularly played cricket on a large field in the hinterland close to an area called the Blue Lagoon. I was curious to find out more about the sporting activities of peacekeepers because on many occasions I had come across peacekeepers who used sport or fitness as both a relief from stress and boredom and a basis for achieving pious forms of masculinity (Higate and Henry, 2004; Henry, 2015, 2012). A Pakistani officer that I had met during one of the medal ceremonies had told me about the cricket playing. I was never able to track down where the "stunning" cricket pitch was located or indeed, any more information about cricket games played locally. However, I was able to gain agreement that I could visit the PakBatt (Pakistan Battalion) base through the senior commander (Civ-Mil Relations or SIMIC) in Monrovia. When I arrived at the PakBatt base with my SIMIC woman peacekeeper escort and guide, we were immediately taken to two locations where Pakistani peacekeepers were doing outreach work with local communities. In one context, the contingent was responsible for repairing school playing-field equipment and the school itself, as well as preparing meals for the village children. This was an impressive weekly program of aid in the form of improvements to school infrastructure and provision of food supplies. In another neighboring village, a mobile medical team provided education on malaria prevention and advised on common treatable medical conditions for rural populations. In particular, the PakBatt medical team went around different villages giving basic public health lessons in combating gastrointestinal diseases and malaria infections. These took place in small community gathering spaces and involved using diagrams and physical demonstrations, such that the PakBatt officers could instruct without the need to "translate" their own dialect of English to local Liberians.

After observing the extensive work of the battalion, I was invited to attend the PakBatt base for a meal followed by tea and a short tour of the facilities of the base. In contrast to my experiences with other contingents such as the Indian and the Ghanaian, Nepalese, and Filipino peacekeepers, I was *not* entertained with narratives about Pakistani peacekeepers as "better" than or "superior" to the peacekept. For the most part the Pakistani peacekeepers held any views that they might have had about the local populace close to their chests, and at no time did I hear any conversation among them that suggested they were condemnatory of local people. They did not reproduce colonial and racialized rhetoric (at least not in the short time I was in their presence) about the peacekept. Mostly they were intent on their duties, wanting to execute their mandates as efficiently as possible. However, their *performance* of humility in the service of upholding a national myth of Pakistani peacekeepers as hardworking and morally committed was foregrounded (Rashid 2020). Without romanticizing their own positioning of themselves inside global rhetoric of progressive nations, their accounts of peacekeeping work suggested that they were doing the hard labor of peacekeeping by focusing on tasks and operations. In doing so, they effectively erased their own positioning as the formally colonized within colonial histories (though I think their representations or positions are more fluid than among other TCCs). Relying on a form of martial efficiency, the PakBatt peacekeepers both challenged the coloniality of peacekeeping and at the same time subscribed to and reinforced problematic "myths" about UN "neutrality" and narratives of their own national superior morality and discipline.

Nevertheless, it seemed a long way away from my conversations with a range of civilian peacekeepers who reaped the benefits of their own privilege yet denied the possibility of peacekeeping as colonial or racial in foundation, function, or form. A final example of how racial and colonial relations of power are evident in peacekeeping spaces involves Razack's reference to "the stage" as an example of how colonial relations can be visualized and understood. Razack uses the stage to show how the exercise of colonial power is hidden via recourse to national mythologies. In the case of Canadian peacekeepers, Razack shows the investments Canadian peacekeepers had in the idea of Canada and Canadians as quintessentially good. Furthermore, she argues that what is evident in peacekeeping spaces is that colonial desires can be acted out, whether or not the actors themselves are familiar with or have previously inhabited colonial positions of power. Ironically, this next example involves a literal stage. While I was doing fieldwork in Liberia in 2012, I was invited to attend UN Idol, an event created by a civilian peacekeeper to "showcase" the array of talent of those working for the UN, including national staff. The event was held in a local convention hall across from the UN Headquarters building in Monrovia. As I sat enjoying the performances of many peacekeepers who would go on to garner reputations as near celebrities, I became acutely aware of the legacies of colonialism and racism that filtered into the auditorium. When several contestants from India appeared on stage, the Bangladeshi and Pakistani peacekeepers in the audience remained seated and appeared disinterested. When the Bangladeshi peacekeepers performed their musical numbers, the Indian police presence (which took up a large portion of the five-hundred-seat venue), were texting on their phones and refused to give the performers a standing ovation as did the rest of the spectators. The legacies of imperially engineered conflict in South Asia seemed to emerge in the spectacular moments of national representations. In the final voting period an inspiring group of young Filipino women performed a hard rock song that ended in a dramatic drum solo—there were huge cries of support from the Spanish-speaking peacekeepers (Peru and Argentina). Perhaps to the rest of the audience nothing was particularly amiss in the performances, either in regard to the studied downplaying of tensions between the Asian contingents or the eventual winners. For me, what was instructive was that the geopolitical divides that had been fostered by colonial administrations traveled with peacekeepers and affected their interactions with other TCCs as well as with the local population.

The stage became a space to prove one's national credentials and authenticity as talented, good-natured, cultured, and expressive people. Although it was ostensibly an opportunity for showcasing talent, I interpreted the event as another space in which peacekeepers could justify their roles as peacekeepers. In addition, they could display more "human" faces, dispositions, or their "natural" aptitude for humanitarian work—as demonstrated through showing themeslves as a multitalented and highly "developed" people. Not only did peacekeepers carry the weight of colonial baggage from their own countries, but they also drew on ideas of racial hierarchies and notions of superiority to position themselves mostly in opposition to other contingents scripted as racially inferior.

In the previous sections, I have taken the idea of peacekeeping as neutral and objective and challenged it further by demonstrating how both colonial scripts can determine the relations of power in peacekeeping spaces; I have also shown how the differential and unequal positioning of peacekeepers can result in a range of narrative strategies employed to show peacekeepers as good citizens, obedient soldiers, and generous and selfless humanitarians. In this way, I reveal the double-sided aspects of a racial and colonial reading of peacekeeping inspired by Razack and other critical theorists.

The Political Economy of Caring: Global South Women Peacekeepers

> Relatedly, research conducted through the lens of "militarization" has tended to foreground gender analysis, for example, through the concept of "militarized masculinities," or emulation of Enloe's focus on women's lives. Even if we are attentive to how this may play out differently for racialized or poor women, the analytical foregrounding of "women's lives" positions systems of gender as primary in understanding "militarization." Gathering considerations of race, disability, poverty and Indigeneity under gender by pursuing a methodology

focused in the first instance on the lives of women (or on masculinities) risks subsuming varied systems of power, leaving us unable to capture how they might work differently than gender. (Howell 2018, p. 120)

As I argued in two previous publications, not all peacekeepers are equal, and this is especially the case for peacekeeping women, who predominantly come from Global South militaries and are positioned by peacekeeping institutions in complex and sometimes problematic ways (Henry, 2019, 2012). In particular, Global South peacekeepers provide the majority of labor, and women from countries such as Nepal, Philippines, India, and Bangladesh have been deployed to a range of peacekeeping contexts to help address the UN's failure to promote gender equality in its mission sites (Karim and Beardsley, 2017). These national responses to UN calls have also enabled TCCs to vie for Security Council seats and to improve their reputations within global governance communities (Pruitt, 2016). But as Wilén argues, the "added burden" on women peacekeepers is not adequately acknowledged by militaries or peacekeeping authorities (Wilén, 2020). Scholars such as Wilén and Heinecken rightly point out that patriarchal trends in military service continue to dominate national and global institutions (Heinecken, 2015; Wilén, 2020); the imperative to address gender needs both inside and outside the forces is not placed on serving men but instead the burden is placed on the shoulders of women peacekeepers. Much of the burden appears as informal labor rather than written into formal rosters or contracts. Women peacekeepers participate in a variety of unspecified forms of labor beyond what their military training might include, from providing specialist and gender-specific care for victims of sexual assault; mentoring and training of women in the security sector; deterrence against sexual exploitation and abuse; transforming martial organizational culture from "boys will be boys" toward gender equality and inclusivity; and acting as inspirational role models for local women and girls who might not be familiar with seeing women (especially women who look like or closely resemble them) in authority or in professional roles (Wilén,

2020; Holmes, 2019; Pruitt, 2016; Henry, 2019, 2012; Karim and Beardsley, 2017). A number of problems arise for these Global South women, which are carefully documented in the studies cited above. The additional and unstated demands on women peacekeepers puts them in a distinctly disadvantageous position. First, along with their male counterparts, they generally do not hold any specialist gender knowledge or skills. Nor do they have advanced conflict resolution capacities or experience in community policing. Most of the women recruited from Global South militaries and police forces may not have the broader policing and advanced security sector skills that women peacekeepers from Global North forces have access to and have had experience incorporating into their work. This is in part owing to the staggered entry of women into forces and global inequalities in security institutions.

Of the women deployed to peacekeeping missions, the majority are contingent staff (lower-ranking military) from Global South countries; in contrast, the minority of women officers and senior-ranking military and police tend to come from Global North forces (Karim and Beardsley, 2017). This means that Global South women peacekeepers enter the mission with the least amount of status and power, reflected in assumptions about them as docile and compliant workers by peacekeeping powers. Although perhaps an unintended consequence, peacekeeping initiatives to achieve greater gender balance and equality have reinforced global gendered-racial hierarchies and color lines. The hierarchy of women peacekeepers reflects those of colonial structures of social organizing, albeit one that positions women according to their racial grouping, so that white Global North men are positioned at the apex of a triangular hierarchical structure, with women of color and those whose claims to whiteness are "suspect" occupying a broader middle mass, followed by Brown and Black women occupying the broad majority base. The existence of this hierarchy of women vastly undermines the idea that the more women that work in peacekeeping, the closer peacekeeping comes to equality.

What this discussion serves to illustrate is how, by considering gender as the primary axis of women's oppression, the unequal division of peacekeeping labor is masked. If Global South women peacekeepers are seen as laborers in the same way they are in other sectors (migrant domestic and caring work as nannies, nurses, and domestics), then they are not simply entering the peacekeeping stage as gendered actors. Global South women enter peacekeeping missions with the baggage of centuries-long histories of representations of them as "natural" laborers; often cast as sweatshop or domestic workers, or as field workers where their "nimble fingers" make them ideal for picking delicate leaves of tea and rice destined for Western consumption (Elson and Pearson, 1981).

Some of these ideas of their "natural" docility have seeped into Indian women peacekeepers' self-images, as evident when they referred to themselves as "better [than the male] candidates for the job at hand": highly disciplined, teetotalers, home oriented, and therefore more suitable than their male counterparts (Henry, 2012). On some days the women peacekeepers were retaking French classes to improve their prospects of future peacekeeping deployments to francophone mission sites such as Haiti and Democratic Republic of Congo, as they realized that despite their higher value as workers, they would need to maintain a competitive advantage. During the medal parade ceremony[6] that I recounted in the article "Parades, Parties and Pests" (Henry, 2015), it was clear that women peacekeepers were expected to "do it all": to demonstrate their physical prowess by performing various martial "tricks" while at the same time displaying themselves as the consummately "feminine" hosts during the entertainment part of the parade and celebration day. For example, peacekeepers were expected to dress in uniform during the morning ceremony and later to exchange their uniforms for formal (civilian) dress in the evening. While they claimed to be "the same" as the men, it was evident that in the evening part of the parade, strict feminine norms were imposed. The woman commander at the time of fieldwork was quite anxious in the days leading up to the parade ceremony as she was responsible for a number of activities with the local community, such as ensuring the efficient running of a mother and child clinic and reviewing her officers' presentation routines, while still carrying out close protection and shadow policing activities with mission staff and national police. In sum, they were proud of their moves toward self and professional improvement and their positive impact on local communities. For example, the squad hosted Bollywood dancing classes for local women as a bridge to connect with local people. None of these activities emerged from their specific martial skills (which were based in crowd control tactics, advanced weapons training, etc.) but were approved by senior commanders as a meaningful way to spend some of their time. But these acts of care and charity for the community were a form of labor that was appropriated by UN authorities as a way of showing virtuousness as well as usefulness. The relative expectations and achievements were starkly different both between men and women and between different national contingents. While there was praise for these women and their "achievements," there was little acknowledgement of the achievements of peacekeeping men. In some cases men were expected to "behave" and not engage in sexually exploitative relations, and this threshold was seen as extraordinary.

I was surprised by how much work women peacekeepers were doing across the days and nights. Just as the global division of labor is unsustainable, I observed these women's schedules as excessive. Ghanaian women peacekeepers carried out caring outreach work on the weekends, which meant that time to correspond with their families was sometimes cut short. Eleanor, a senior policewoman shared many of her struggles to be taken seriously among a multinational group of police under her command; despite having "climbed the ranks" she said she often faced "mutiny." When she did community work as part of developing national police capacities, she was perceived as doing "soft" work. Male police peacekeepers who were in special branch units, some of whom had "sharpshooting" expertise and experience, thought that community policing work was best left to (Brown and Black) women, though they did not think that their participation in community policing would have much impact; it would "never stop the gangs" or any other criminal activities. In a sense, women peacekeepers were often under the critical gaze of men and found wanting, or were seen as "deficient" men. When women peacekeepers from the Indian contingent would walk into headquarters, male peacekeepers could be seen openly giggling about their uniforms and their soldiering styles. In my interviews with peacekeeping men, they suggested that women were mostly "out of place." During some of the other medal parade ceremonies, such as that for Nepalese soldiers, women peacekeepers were specifically chosen to present gifts to the SRSG on the platform where VIP guests were seated. That women were expected to perform this more feminine "gifting" role was noticeable because there were only a small handful of women in the fairly large battalion. They were also tasked to welcome guests in the meal service after the parade and to serve food alongside their male colleagues. But in the dramatic performance that was scheduled for the late afternoon activities, no women were present. Instead, the story depicted in the short play involved peacekeeper men, posing as mythical embodied male *and* female figures (Henry, 2015).

Despite all this work, women peacekeepers were also simultaneously contained and managed by both their national commanders and the UN system. They had little mobility in the mission and were often viewed by Global North peacekeepers as docile and obedient—the "good girls." Gendered expectations of women's cooperative behavior in upholding the national reputation or their rank and role effectively restricted their movement in the everyday sense. They made less of an impression on the peacekept and their peacekeeping colleagues than is reflected in the UN rhetoric about gender parity. The UN capitalizes on the unequal global politics of peacekeeping labor to enhance its image as a "diversity champion." It does not challenge the "global color line" or the gendered burdens of providing security that exist for Global South women. This is because, as I argue in Chapters 3 and 4, gender is a foil for the acts and impacts of military expansion and empire building.

The Political Economy of Violence: Peacekeeper Deaths

In May 2021, a Malawian peacekeeper was killed by right-wing militants in the Democratic Republic of Congo. This was the first recorded death of a woman peacekeeper.[7] Peacekeeping scholars have been taking the issue of peacekeeping fatalities seriously for some time and indeed argue that peacekeeping has become more dangerous and challenging for those keeping the peace. Yet little of this work accounts for the racial, gendered, and militarized foundations of peacekeeping practice and thus continues to produce knowledge that marginalizes the perspectives of those most negatively affected, such as Global South peacekeepers and the peacekept (Williams, 2020; Thakur et al., 2007). Most of this work puts global-north-dominated perspectives at the center of what constitutes the truth or reality of peacekeeping. While there are very real material risks to Global South peacekeepers in particular, peacekeeping scholarship does not foreground how these larger global inequalities—or the global color line—are part of the design and organization of peacekeeping itself. Saying that peacekeeping has become a dangerous job is to deny peacekeeping's complicity in colonial relations, racialized hierarchies, male domination, and martial desires. That a Malawian woman peacekeeper was killed seems to have had little effect on the trajectory of scholarship, which speaks much more to Cruz et al.'s line of argument: that peacekeeping needs to be militarily fortified and intensified (Cruz et al., 2017). The death of a Global South peacekeeper could be a catalyst for a discussion about inequalities in peacekeeping labor. However, I argue that her death stands in for the supposed threats that peacekeepers and peacekeeping are subject to as evidenced in the dominant global governance discourses. The idea that peacekeeping is essentially an insecure practice, one that involves considerable danger and risk (both to property and persons), is the current and dominant epistemic position in much of the literature (Hultman et al., 2019; Williams, 2020; Howard, 2019; Dayal, 2021). Even though there is an extensive literature outlining the ways in which Global South peacekeepers are differently positioned in the peacekeeping industry, and the disproportionate risk and death that overshadows these Global South deployments, there is still little analysis of the roots of such inequalities in governance institutions themselves (Cunliffe, 2013). This is a problem because, as I argue in Chapter 5, the accounts allow the peacekept to become continually eclipsed, to use Razack's words, when their "pain is stolen" (Razack, 2007) and when peacekeepers are portrayed as the primary victims of violence (Razack, 2003). Furthermore, this denies the ways in which these deaths are embedded within the larger context of gendered, racialized, and militarized politics.

In early January 2006, a few months before traveling to Haiti to conduct fieldwork, I heard the news that the then force commander, General Urano Teixeira Da Matta Bacellar of the Brazilian military, had been found dead in his hotel room.[8] General Bacellar had been residing at Hotel Montana. Early reports indicated he had been shot, but it was not immediately clear if the injuries were self-inflicted. A few weeks after his death, a colleague and I arrived to begin our research, which explored the everyday experiences of security and insecurity in peacekeeping missions (Henry et al., 2009; Higate and Henry, 2009). For many of the military peacekeepers we spoke to, the death of their commander was still fresh, and the accounts about the everyday experiences of living in a peacekeeping mission were very much framed with his death in the background. Juan, a senior military commander in the UN Mission in Haiti (MINUSTAH), was deeply affected by the death of his boss and shared some of his thoughts more generally about peacekeeping problems. He was convinced that the general had felt enormous guilt about violence enacted against the civilian population by *Lavalas*[9] supporters, which the commander felt he had been unable to stop. Juan also brought up a number of prior experiences that he felt conveyed the difficulties peacekeepers face when they are posted to postconflict sites. Juan had been working in UN mission in the Democratic Republic of Congo (MINUSCO). He explained the many challenges he, in particular, faced while working in the context of multinational forces. It was difficult to get along with other officers and troops when communicating in English and with widely divergent military codes and cultures. What was commonly heard among senior military figures was that different command cultures and ideas were often a source of conflict for military officers in particular (Duffey, 2000). Used to having overall authority, many of the officers found themselves in positions of deference to commanders from other TCCs. The tensions of trying to work with different styles and levels of experience meant that peacekeepers often felt isolated, and in some cases even bullied, without an appropriate place to go to air their concerns. In the Democratic Republic of Congo, Juan had been under the command of an officer whose behavior he felt was erratic and unprofessional. There had been a number of incidents of violence against the peacekept, and Juan felt that his commander was only interested in protecting himself from reputational damage. Over the course of several interviews, Juan and I discussed different peacekeeping mission spaces, and he shared with me the belief that coming from Latin America, he was often assumed to be a "banana republic" soldier without any of the cultural "finesse" that those from France might have.

Juan, too, looked at the cover of a book I had carried around and noticed that there were peacekeepers from his country pictured in the background (*Peace Operations Seen from Below*; Pouligny, 2006). He was keen to reveal how much at risk he and his colleagues were, and how Global North forces had arrived in the mission and imposed what he felt was a colonial-like set of relations among the peacekeepers. According to Juan, while the Global South forces were "fighting among themselves" and facing "fire" from local populations, the UN had maintained a mandate that did not allow them to use force to "defend" themselves. As he had previously worked in an observer mission (see Chapter 4), he was used to traditional forms of peacekeeping where maintaining a cease-fire was the main overall objective. However, when peacekeepers from his country were killed and the UN decided to send in French special forces, he felt things were moving in unfair directions. As French forces were deployed, the mandate also rapidly changed, allowing the forces to now take over operations in the "hot spots" and to use deadly force if required (much of which has been documented in studies of interventions in francophone Africa; Berdal and Ucko, 2015). Juan and many of his colleagues shared their feelings of being underused and underappreciated—that somehow their lives were considered dispensable. Alberto, Juan's compatriot, had similar views. He suggested that there was a hierarchy of militaries and that some peacekeepers were seen as professional and "valuable" while others were seen as "incompetent." Ironically, many of these ideas about the "inherent" value of certain military peacekeepers were reflected in the opinions of the peacekept; for example in Haiti, some of the local population showed greater appreciation for the Brazilian forces' connection with local communities (Brazilian tanks carried two flags, one Haitian and the other Brazilian). However, women in many communities called into question the impartiality of Brazilian troops, whom they saw "hanging out" with known gang members (Henry and Higate, 2016). In earlier fieldwork, I noted that Irish and Swedish peacekeepers had garnered an image as both ideal humanitarians and troops with technological expertise and mastery, whereas Nigerian and Bangladeshi forces were seen as either "heavy-handed" or "effeminate nice-guys" (Higate and Henry, 2009, 2010). As I argue in Chapter 4, when peacekeeping is constructed as a risky business, the main concern of the UN is not necessarily the loss of peacekeeper lives, although much of the public discourse might suggest otherwise. Rather it is an ideological justification for martial means in peacekeeping contexts.

Conclusion

I began the chapter by reflecting on Razack's critical interventions in studies of peacekeeping, where she argues that incidents of peacekeeping violence can be understood to reflect colonial and racial relations of power. In particular, her account highlights how peacekeepers enable colonial scripts to play out by reinforcing Orientalist and racist discourses. Drawing on Razack's invocation of the Black Marxist and Du Boisian concept of the global color line, I suggest that looking at the impact of peacekeepers on the peacekept is one way to understand how colonial and racial power is manifested. Similarly, using the concepts of both the global color line and intersectionality as tools to think through the ways in which coloniality is retained and reproduced, it is impossible to dismiss or underestimate the multiple axes of oppression and privilege that affect Global South peacekeepers' experiences and interactions with the peacekept, as well as their own position in the larger peacekeeping picture. Nor can the fact be dismissed that Global South peacekeepers face a number of obstacles when they are assumed to be "stand-ins" either for gender equality or mainstreaming or for justifying the increased militarization of peacekeeping.

Which lives matter in peacekeeping? Turning to postcolonial and critical race analyses allows scholars to see peacekeeping as a colonial, racial, and epistemic project. I use the critical theories of the global color line and intersectionality to draw attention to the multiple ways in which structural axes of power are reinforced by peacekeeping, despite its carefully crafted and almost universal image as a "force for good." While individual peacekeepers may not intend to act in colonial ways or to perpetuate colonialist relations of power—an approach that John vehemently denied over dinner that evening—peacekeeping maintains global inequalities by relying on Global South labor, benefiting from the abundance of invisible and caring labor that Global South women peacekeepers provide, and by exploiting the rhetoric of duty, pride of service, and honor as a distraction from the inequalities that make it most likely that it will be peacekeeping women and men of the Global South who will die in the line of duty.

CHAPTER 3

The Limits of the Singular: Intersectionality, Binaries, and the Coloniality of Gender

In 2006, I was conducting research in Haiti and was granted permission to visit a Uruguayan battalion posted in Cap-Haïtien in order to meet and interview women peacekeepers. The battalion included about fifteen women: mostly soldiers within a contingent and two officers (a dentist and doctor). Upon arriving at the base, I was greeted warmly by the commander and introduced to the officer who was also acting as the main translator within the region. When introducing us, the commander apologized for his "poor" English and asked the officer, Rosa, to take over the conversation. I quickly apologized for my poor French and hoped that Rosa's English would be better than my Spanish (nonexistent!). Sadly, that was not the case, and I muddled along with my rudimentary French throughout the next days. Rosa and I quickly connected on many levels and spent the next few days together talking about all things to do with gender, peacekeeping, family, and life in general.

In 2012, I was conducting research in Liberia and was granted permission by the UN Gender Advisor's Office to visit the Indian Police Battalion in Monrovia. Upon meeting the police commander, who happened to be from the Indian contingent, I was warmly welcomed to India House, the headquarters of all Indian peacekeepers deployed in Liberia. He was a senior officer in the Indian Police Services, had extensive peacekeeping experience, and understood the nature of my research and the challenges I faced as a researcher. He invited me to attend India House whenever I could to enjoy meals and some social time with the all-women police squad of 100-plus women, as he knew that I was only permitted two "formal" visits by the UNMIL Public Relations Office. The contingent commander, Sita, helped to subvert this major restriction by inviting me, on this research trip and a subsequent one, to various events as a private guest. These events included daily puja/worship; watching Indian programs in the mess hall; meals both at India House and out at restaurants, and attending the medal parade as a VIP. While visiting we discussed family life among police officers, political developments in India, peacekeeping in West Africa, and not surprisingly, our mutual appreciation and love of food!

Introduction

I begin this chapter with memories of fieldwork among Global South peacekeepers, in particular with women police and military peacekeepers from Uruguay and India.[1] I do so to situate the forthcoming discussions within my own ethnographically inspired fieldwork conducted in peacekeeping missions across the past twenty years. Whenever I spent time with peacekeepers, I became aware of the ways in which peacekeeping spaces become complex and contradictory sites for the enactment of various identities (Henry, 2015). Identities are continually made and remade in these spaces, and these spaces engender certain types of lived experiences that in turn shape how peacekeepers view and conduct themselves, especially in relation to the peacekept. I entered peacekeeping spaces with lists of questions provoked by my reading and engagement with feminist and postcolonial scholarship, which I planned to explore with women in particular—both peacekeepers and the peacekept. Throughout the fieldwork, I learned that differences between peacekeepers and the peacekept are in a state of constant flux; they are at times exaggerated and in other moments, minimized. As I spent more time with peacekeepers, the stark differences—nay, inequalities—became evident to me between those tasked to provide peace and those required to receive it. The qualitative difference of what it meant to be a peacekeeper or peacekept from the Global North or South, to be of color, and to be Muslim or Christian was made distinct through individuals' own detailed and personal accounts of living and/or working in a post-conflict setting. While I shared much in common with many peacekeepers in terms of experiences of being a marginal subject working in a mainstream institution, through my own privilege as a researcher I was able to observe their struggles to fit into a gendered, racialized, and militarized organizational setting. Among the women interviewees I found a great deal of common ground, from the shared feelings of guilt to the frustrations of working in a male-dominated environment. Having left my own small children behind at home to conduct research, I found it easy to connect and empathize with the parents among them, as we shared stories and worries about our families. With the women, I built up a rapport and repartee quickly, and I looked forward to spending more time with many of them whom I interviewed and observed during my fieldwork visits. I was struck by how our perceived shared experience of womanhood (and sometimes motherhood) enabled me to gain the trust of many of these peacekeepers. Thus, although my analysis concludes that peacekeeping relies on colonialist savior narratives such as those invoked by Spivak's famous phrase "white men saving brown women from brown men" (Spivak, 1994), it also achieves this through reinforcing binaries—for example, by making and reinforcing a distinction between gender (social) and sex (biological). What I mean by this is that UN discourses (in policies, programming, and deployment patterns) and the ways in which peacekeepers themselves talk about their multiple identities and complex positioning in a variety of social, economic, and cultural hierarchies sediments, rather than challenges, the distinction. Of course, it bears underlining, as feminists have shown, that these popular understandings of sex as biology versus gender as social are in themselves problematic distinctions, for both—and here I want to stress the so-called biological sex—are social constructions (Tuana, 1989). I argue, however, that maintaining these distinctions is a necessary, rather than incidental, investment by the UN. In particular, its cautious definitions of sex and limited understandings of gender allow the UN to avert too-close scrutiny of its complicity in reproducing historical and contemporary inequitable relationships between the former colonizer and colonized and between the Global North and Global South. These histories continue to inform the militarist present of interventions in postconflict (and postcolonial) spaces.

As I read more extensively, at times across multiple disciplinary terrains, I found the use of critical theories such as those derived from feminist and postcolonial scholarship, for example, to be invaluable in developing a more nuanced understanding of the shifting power relations present in peacekeeping sites, and the ways in which peacekeepers try to position themselves toward, or against, multiple social, economic and cultural expectations (Henry, 2015, 2019). What I mean here is that peacekeepers are neither innocent vessels of the peacekeeping machinery nor uniformly powerful agents exercising and/or abusing power over the peacekept at every opportunity. Peacekeepers both produce and contribute to existing discourses on sex and gender (among other categories) by virtue of the ways in which they carry themselves as multiplex/intersectional subjects, and the way they position themselves with and against the peacekept—as I develop in the subsequent sections of this chapter. These and other empirical insights gathered over the years convinced me to revisit and draw on the perspectives, concepts, and theories of earlier peacekeeping studies, as well as feminist, antiracist, postcolonial, antimilitarist, and pacifist scholars. My return to this earlier scholarship seems more fruitful. I have found that recent scholarship on peacekeeping is marked by deficiencies in conceptual groundings that would push me toward the more critical, reflecting on some of the complexities of the lived experiences of peacekeepers to which I have been privy; moreover, the conceptual shortcomings made it difficult for me to go beyond thinking about and understanding peacekeepers as individuals or groups, and hence (initially at least) hindered my better understanding of peacekeeping as an epistemic project.

As I previously argued, current peacekeeping scholarship has omitted to address the critical concerns raised in earlier work—despite that this early work laid the foundations for thinking along multiple axes, and thus away from thinking of gender as the only or primary axis by which to critically appraise peacekeeping spaces and their social, economic, and spatial impacts (Cockburn and Žarkov, 2002; Enloe, 2000; Razack, 2004; Whitworth, 2004; Mazurana, et al., 2005; Väyrynen, 2004). While other disciplines from the arts to the sciences have all to some degree expanded their understanding of difference beyond gender, and understand identity as multifaceted and contingent, peacekeeping studies stubbornly continues to privilege a very selective version of what constitutes gender. One has to question why peacekeeping is so invested in neglecting explorations of the imbrication of gender with other modalities of difference such as race and ethnicity, which are particularly sidelined in peacekeeping scholarship. For example, peacekeeping scholarship has seldom reflected on and incorporated the substantive literatures that provide incisive critiques of global inequalities and geopolitics; racism and race relations in humanitarian contexts; and decolonizing initiatives in regard to sexuality, sexual relations, and transnational contexts. Nevertheless, although gender continues to have a place in the peacekeeping scholarship, feminist and gendered analyses of peace contexts are not always readily incorporated into "mainstream" peacekeeping texts. This is not wholly surprising, as feminist contributions from international law and international relations continue to be marginalized within these androcentric and white fields. Nevertheless, as I have charted, some significant critical work was embarked on in the early 2000s, and much of this has inspired further research trajectories around peacekeeping. Reflecting the legacies of earlier gendered critiques is Shepherd's *Gender, UN Peacebuilding, and the Politics of Space* (Shepherd, 2017). In this unique book, Shepherd draws on empirical work and applies a discourse analysis to peacebuilding more specifically. In doing so,

Shepherd unpacks the constructedness of knowledge about peacebuilding activities in postconflict contexts, and sheds much needed light on how this shapes the ways in which gender is both understood and integrated into programming. While Shepherd cogently demonstrates how gender can be weaponized to marginalize and disadvantage Indigenous populations, they invariably privilege gender as the starting and ending axis of analysis. While demonstrating the constructedness of gender and its inherent limitations, gender as identity, praxis, and so forth is reproduced as the principal category of identity, difference, or otherness that is consistently made visible in global governance contexts.

Consequently, in this chapter I reveal the limits of a solitary focus on gender in regard to three particular areas: (1) the lived experiences of women peacekeepers and their "situatedness" in global relations; (2) the discourse of "operational effectiveness" and women peacekeepers as a binary "foil" of empire; and (3) representations of sexual exploitation and abuse by peacekeepers and the implications for thinking with coloniality. Thus I examine how understandings of gender and women's sexed bodies permits both a crystallizing of sex and gender and distracts from the colonial relations of power that are implicated in the epistemology of peacekeeping and the subsequent associated practices. I employ the concept of gender both loosely and skeptically and demonstrate what the concept can do in a more critical vein; like Holvikivi, I put gender in its place so that it can be seen alongside the many other axes of inequality (Holvikivi, 2023; Zalewski, 2010). The chapter is broadly informed by a number of ideas and concepts drawn from and inspired by the work of critical scholars in the early 2000s. For example, I demonstrate how a martial obsession with "operational effectiveness" frames gender as a radical concept while contributing to instrumentalist and essentialist ways of thinking about women peacekeepers—not in keeping with much of the direction of feminist and gender theories more broadly. Ideas such as operational effectiveness further enable the very idea of gender, and women peacekeepers as militarized subjects, to serve as what Belkin refers to as "foils" (Belkin, 2012). I then show how thinking with intersectionality enables an examination of who peacekeepers are, what they do, and how they are situated in the epistemic project of peacekeeping. I do this through a Black feminist–inspired lens in order to analyze their experiences as products of structures or systems of power. Thus, I use intersectionality as a sensitizing concept to force attention to the different axes of power at play within peacekeeping spaces, and argue that this critical tool allows a much more nuanced account of Global South labor and of the contradictory influence that women peacekeepers may have on the peacekept environment. While few peacekeeping scholars have explicitly used intersectionality within their work, I argue that some of the critical foundations of earlier work point to theories like intersectionality as a way to analyze global forms of racism, heterosexism, and militarism. Following this, I reflect on the ways in which Global North perspectives on embodied soldiering provides opportunities for Global South women peacekeepers to challenge gender relations and enter a male military space—but simultaneously, women continue to be excluded and further subjugated to a range of power regimes. Drawing on the critical scholarship of the early 2000s enables me to focus on how Global North military norms become the invisible foundations of ill-formed judgments about women's capabilities in peacekeeping. Doing so not only reinforces ideas about gender but fixes categories further. However, my research shows the constructed nature of embodiment in peacekeeping spaces—its constant working and reworking along geopolitical lines and patriarchal expectations and norms. Finally, I turn to the issue of SEA in peacekeeping missions, where I suggest that postcolonial feminist perspectives can productively challenge some of the representations of peacekept women (and men) and perhaps point to a different way of understanding sexual relations in peacekeeping spaces. Here I suggest that what Lugones refers to as "the coloniality of gender" is reflected in the ways in which SEA is mandated against, and the ways in which it is understood to be primarily about the inherent power inequalities in gender relations (Lugones, 2008). This resonates with the work of Cockburn and Hubic, who early on in the peacekeeping scholarship highlighted the need to think carefully about which women are included and given agential status in postconflict settings (Cockburn and Hubic, 2002).

Intersectionality

Before turning to my critique of binaries, I want to provide a short introduction to the concept of intersectionality. I believe that the concept, not traditionally drawn on in peacekeeping studies, can offer a way of thinking that enables a return to more critical perspectives and can predispose peacekeeping scholars to think more analytically about the limits of peacekeeping practice itself. I take inspiration from previous works already mentioned because this scholarship continually reveals that issues affecting those on the margins must be understood from different standpoints (Collins, 1986) and that these standpoints are never simply about one axis of identity or system of oppression (Combahee River Collective, 1983).

Intersectionality has certainly found its way into a number of disciplinary and interdisciplinary conversations. However, intersectionality's radical roots deserve to be better integrated into feminist studies of the military, especially. I am skeptical of adoptions of the concept of intersectionality that ignore wider power relations at play; for example, I have previously demonstrated how using intersectionality can enable intersecting "differences" to be made visible, but that these differences can end up floating free from the main structures of oppression (Henry, 2017). I use the case of multiple axes of difference among Israeli soldiers as an example that demonstrates some of the ways in which hierarchies of gender (masculinity in particular), race/ethnicity, and class place militarized subjects in unequal ways and can potentially diffuse and depoliticize the concept's racialized components (see my discussion of Kachtan, 2017, and Sasson-Levy, 2011, 2016 in Henry, 2017). These examples of intersectionality at work in military institutions do the work of decontextualizing systems of oppression in a wider political context. In this way, those militarized subjects who are not a formal part of the military institution do not benefit from the intersectional analysis at work. For example, Palestinian men and women, equally bound by narratives of the martial, are not in the intersectional purview, and in this respect, intersectionality's application fails to elicit a comprehensive challenge to power outside the Israeli military institution. What I do is demonstrate how intersections of identity and difference can also be sites of both marginalization and privilege. I use examples from research conducted with peacekeepers from Global South[2] militarized forces (police, military, and private security) during fieldwork trips in 2006, 2011, 2012, and 2013. In this section, I extend some of that analysis by pointing again to intersectionality's potency and potentiality as a sensitizing concept that forces attention to structural forms of power and systems of oppression. The macro analysis that earlier peacekeeping scholars engaged in provides similar critical foundations.

What is intersectionality, and what does it have to do with peacekeepers, the peacekept, and peacekeeping knowledge? Intersectionality is a concept (among other things) that was initiated by the Combahee River Collective (1983, 1995) and then extended more fully by Crenshaw in two key articles (Crenshaw, 1989, 1990). Inspired by a number of influential scholars, the Combahee River Collective and Crenshaw drew on structural analyses of power, marginalization, and exploitation by the work of Black Marxists such as James, Du Bois, Davis, Hall, and Robinson, and the Black feminist theorists Lorde, Carby, hooks, and Hill Collins (James, 1938; Du Bois, 1915, 1903; Davis, 1981; Robinson, 1983; Hall, 1996; Carby, 1985; Collins, 2002; Lorde, 1984; hooks, 1981).[3] A parallel and intersecting body of feminist scholarship engaging with race and the coloniality of gender included Chicana feminist perspectives from Sandoval, Anzaldúa, Lugones, and Moraga (Sandoval, 2000; Anzaldúa, 1987; Lugones, 2008, 1990; Moraga and Anzaldúa, 1981). This is by no means an exhaustive list, but it does serve to ground much of the roots of intersectional theories within US and UK academic and activist communities. Crenshaw drew on this extensive body of scholarship and cultural critique to demonstrate why intersectionality as a metaphor provides a more inclusive analysis of how multiple systems of oppression operate simultaneously. Broadly defined, intersectional forms of oppression refer to contexts where there is no "single axis" that determines how an individual or group is marginalized or discriminated against. Individuals are never just simply women or men but are raced, sexualized, or disabled, for example, and their multifaceted identities are always contingent. Crenshaw concludes, for example, that discrimination against Black men is more often evidently rooted in their racialization, while when gender appears to be the determining factor it is white women who are seen as the primary victims (Crenshaw, 1990). This binarism is aptly summed up in *All the Women Are White, All the Blacks Are Men, but Some of Us Are Brave*, an anthology by the Combahee River Collective that drew attention to white feminism's exclusion of Black women from their analyses of gender oppression (Hull et al., 1982). Crenshaw, a lawyer, raised the question: where do Black women fit into legal judgements around oppression and systematic discrimination? Is it not possible that multiple systems of oppression may be at work simultaneously? What if those racialized as Black are marginalized because they are Black *and* women? Social or economic class adds another layer of systemic oppression—poor, Black women do not experience only one form of discrimination! Thus, early articulations of intersectionality sought to expand on ideas about standpoint and the politics of location to encourage an analysis of power that recognized the multiplicity and the contingency of different forms of oppression (Rich, 2003). Intersectionality has been taken up within a number of disciplines, but mostly in the space between (or among) those interested in analyzing the multiple burdens that Black women and women of color face, especially in the workplace. This is why I turn to intersectionality, in particular, when thinking about women peacekeepers from the Global South (and North to some extent); I want to explore the complex ways in which gender, race, and militarization underpin peacekeepers' experiences of privilege, power, and marginalization. But I also use intersectionality's roots in a range of radical theorizing to think about what it means to pay attention to the location of different individuals. Thus, I ask, where do peacekeepers stand? That is, how are they positioned and how do they experience peacekeeping from that place? And how can the perspectives of the peacekept be understood along similar lines?

As argued in the introductory chapter, peacekeeping is not a benign process that arises as an organic response to "inevitable" conflict situations. Rather it is a project based on very specific epistemologies and geopolitics, one that reproduces forms of power and oppression that bear striking resemblance to colonial systems of dominance. Importantly, peacekeeping is also a highly gendered and martial project, especially because it has historically comprised almost exclusively male military personnel, the consequence of widespread global patriarchal ideology about the proper and respective roles and spaces for women and men. This chapter is inspired by the ways in which intersectionality (and related ideas) can draw attention to a range of identities, categories, differences, and systems of inequality and oppression, and how this can lead to a questioning of peacekeeping scholarship and practice.

It's a Man's World: On the Limits of Gender Alone

Women peacekeepers from the Global South shoulder much of the burden of ameliorating the gender-imbalanced peacekeeping labor force. These women do not conform to the dominant Global North feminist expectations of them as likely "sisters" and role models for local peacekept women (Henry, 2012). What was important about this intervention is the challenge that my research poses to feminist ideas about "women" united in solidarity and possessed with the magical ability to bring about an end to patriarchy! Of course, I am not alone in disrupting the notion of sisterhood, global or otherwise, nor have I been the first to do so. However, my research conclusions abruptly depart from the majority of work on women peacekeepers, which has displayed a tendency to focus on issues of their operational effectiveness, and in this way has contributed to the reproduction of essentialist ideas about womanhood, femaleness, and the category of sex altogether (Karim and Beardsley, 2017; Wilén, 2020). By paying attention to intersectional differences among and between women, it becomes evident that the presence of women in militarized settings is not a panacea for gender inequality. Rather, their position in the domestic labor force places them in a contradictory position. On the one hand, they earn better as a result of higher UN payment standards, and, as other studies have demonstrated, garner respect from family and citizens for their contributions to national service (Holmes, 2019; Pruitt, 2016). Some peacekeeping mothers (and others with other caring responsibilities) are also able to negotiate childcare arrangements with their family at home—this is where the caring labor of extended family members played a significant role in enabling their "respectable" deployments in the first place (Henry, 2012, 2017). This means they can travel abroad for work and gain some important international experience to aid their progression in the male-dominated ranks of the police or military (Mäki-Rahkola and Myrttinen 2014).

Despite the opportunities provided by this "patriarchal bargain" (Kandiyoti, 1988), women peacekeepers from the Indian police faced a number of restrictions based on patriarchal expectations, such as limited freedom of movement in the evenings while off duty; being assigned duty tasks performed in exclusively same-sex configurations (close protection work), and through "no fraternization" policies that vetoed relationships between the peacekeeper and the peacekept, and by extension, severely narrowed women peacekeeper's exposure to the wider working environment of the mission. In addition, these restrictions also meant little to no interaction with women peacekeepers from other contingents, which prevented women from forming solidarities and alliances with the few women and women of color from Global North forces and those representing the Global South. Thus, while there was plenty to commend in the Indian army's deployment of a large group of skilled soldiers, the organization of their contingent relied heavily on gendered ideas of women's sexed bodies as being natural obstacles or hindrances to the effective performance of normal (i.e., male) soldiering, and as likely disruptions to the peacekeeping space

(Väyrynen, 2018; Pruitt, 2016). Their contradictory position—as women-soldiers—means that their very presence as peacekeepers challenges the gender order in some regards, while the women are also subject to the gender order in other ways. The Indian contingent commander of the all-women squad repeatedly assured me (but clearly also herself) of the women's "security" because they were married and had children, and were therefore less likely to stray from their official duties or, as her additional veiled comments suggested, were less likely to be the targets of male romantic attention. The implication here is twofold. The UN, and the TCCs, rely on expectations of women laborers as docile and compliant (Henry, 2012), and the second suggests that women's embeddedness in heterosexual family units means that they are less likely to compromise the reputational "integrity" of the community by engaging in misconduct. The politics of respectability (as married women with children) emerged strongly in the narratives of women peacekeepers. Importantly, I was never informed of the marital status of any of the peacekeeping men in the Indian forces.

If the gendered dimension is taken further and considered alongside the geopolitics of peacekeeping labor, intersecting factors at play become transparent. Global South peacekeepers repeatedly expressed their concern about being perceived as "developmental" forces (Henry, 2015). In trying to prove their worthiness, women officers were anxious to demonstrate various forms of respectability and often relied on martial capital and habitus (Henry, 2015; Holmes, 2019). This means that they strategically emphasized their martial skills and expertise and embodied an exaggerated version of a disciplined warrior to distract attention away from their (presumably weak) gender or their lower-class status (which was often reflected through their rank). For example, women peacekeepers from the Philippines were expected to remain on base or to travel beyond base only to get supplies, during the daytime and in the company of male soldiers tasked to drive and chaperone them. Women officers were almost never given the opportunity to drive vehicles, despite having advanced weapons training, forensic investigation skills, and aeronautic expertise—thus possessing proven proficiency in technological skills. In addition, all peacekeepers were expected to pass standardized driving tests, and the qualifications would mostly have been previously held. Yet for the most part Global South women peacekeepers were held to conform to "cultural" expectations that prohibited them from performing tasks that were seen to fall within the domain of male labor and, in some instances, reserved particularly for lower-class men.

At times, Global North ideas about gender came into direct conflict with Global South interpretations of appropriate gender performances. For example, a Nigerian lieutenant colonel was deployed to a division tasked with managing civil-military relations across the mission. While serving as deputy of this division, her senior officer—from the US military—had very different expectations of staff, especially around issues of communication and input. Thus, while the Nigerian lieutenant colonel respected and followed rank hierarchies and the military culture of deference, her Global North superior expected her to be (more) "communicative," "independent," and to "speak back" when asked for her opinion in training exercises. Frustrated by what he read as her reticence rather than her "by the book" behavior, the US senior officer said to me "women have been in the US military for some time now"—implying a linear arc of development in national armed forces—and complained that she "needed to step up" or "step aside." Despite their partial shared African heritage, this Nigerian deputy felt that her commander had behaved toward her in a manner that she considered racist. She told me that she felt she was being constantly attacked and criticized, and that this was a form of "American" snobbery and an instance of sexism. The commander felt that the deputy was weak and displayed poor leadership, and he openly cast aspersions on her credentials in front of her junior colleagues. In conversation with her outside the headquarters offices, she revealed her deep sense of frustration at the lack of respect she felt she was given. She outlined how hard she had worked to achieve her rank and the prestige afforded her by virtue of being selected—all negated, in her words, by the insensitive US commander above her.

Here, an intersectional sensitivity allows a view into the complexities of gender, race, class, and geopolitics within peacekeeping spaces. The Nigerian officer's presence as a woman peacekeeper played only a partial role in her experiences; other structural issues—her nationality, her blackness, culture, and her religion and class—possibly peeled back further layers of the "onion" of intersectionality. This episode demonstrated for me the importance of critical analyses that begin from listening to what women peacekeepers have to say about their experiences.

How can women peacekeepers' experiences be understood in ways that underline the intersectionality of multiple modalities other than or in addition to gender, and which together play a substantive role in shaping power relations in such a militarized environment? Taking on Cynthia Enloe's famous question "Where are the women?," I suggest that we ask further which women we are speaking of when we invoke this question (Enloe, 1993). Inspired by the structural critiques of earlier scholars, I argue that paying attention to more than gender can broaden our understanding of the realities of women who are at the margins of peacekeeping practice and knowledge.

Enforcing Binaries, Enhancing Empire: The Problem with Effectiveness

Working with intersectionality and other associated concepts and theories from critical race theory provides an opportunity for a revaluation of the peacekeeping scholarship by focusing on some of the attachments to gender that are reproduced through a single-lens approach. As I stated previously, much of the debate on women peacekeepers has centered around issues and concerns to do with their contributions to "operational effectiveness," although there has been a great deal of pushback from feminist scholars (Skjelsbæk and Tryggestad, 2010; DeGroot, 2001; Stiehm, 2001; Jenne and Ulloa Bisshopp, 2021; Karim, 2017; Carreiras, 2010). "Operational effectiveness" is a term commonly used to refer to the quality of the practical realization of the varied goals of a military, although the term "effectiveness" is not necessarily always used consistently in either peacekeeping practice or scholarship (Diehl, 1988). Sometimes "effectiveness" is used as a shorthand for well-functioning, harmonious, or even diverse military organization and capabilities. For example, recent developments of Norwegian gender equality measures in relation to compulsory military service suggest that it is not only Norway's cultural and legal commitment to gender equality that motivates the inclusion of women, but the broader goals of enhancing capabilities and diversity of personnel which leads to effectiveness—although some scholars have suggested that this discourse masks a process of "sidelining" women in militaries (Newby and Sebag, 2021). Whatever the interpretation, this has been and continues to be, I suggest, a problematic focus because it invariably and unproblematically centers and valorizes military values and norms while leaving unchallenged essentialist ideas about the primacy of gender and embodiment; it limits the terms of discussion and stifles possibilities for structural transformation. This tendency to re-center gender as the primary, if not the single marker (and thus part of a unitary and primary system) represents a departure from earlier scholarship which prioritized structural analyses. Within this body of earlier work, it is possible to discern an uncompromising willingness to name peacekeeping spaces and experiences as significant elements of global power relations (Cockburn and Žarkov, 2002; Enloe, 2000; Mazurana, et al., 2005; Razack, 2004; Whitworth, 2004). Thus, intersectionality provides yet another opportunity to question the logics of a feminist approach that does not recognize the interconnectedness of systems of oppression and markers of identity. Again, asking which women are sent to keep the peace and what "qualities" they possess—however, to what extent success can be achieved in regard to gender balance, mainstreaming, and sensitization in peacekeeping departments is always questionable.

Scholarship about women's contributions to peacekeeping has emphasized women's capacity to "meaningfully" contribute to peacekeeping operations alongside their male counterparts

(Bridges and Horsfall, 2009; Skjelsbæk and Tryggestad, 2010; Olsson and Tryggestad, 2001; Wilén, 2020; Karim and Beardsley, 2017; Karim, 2017). Early work examined women's potential and capabilities as peacekeepers and showed what women's experience of integration into militarized peacekeeping looked like (DeGroot, 2001; Mazurana, 2003; Sion, 2009; Valenius, 2007; Stiehm, 2001). Much of this early literature attempted to challenge essentialist ideas about women's natural or unnatural abilities in regard to performing military labor. A parallel body of literature challenged discourses about women's supposed disruptive presence, and this research provided conclusive evidence that the presence of women soldiers would in no way detract from effective military outcomes; these scholars argue in favor of women's deployment but criticize what Wilén refers to as their "added burden" (Olsson and Tryggestad, 2001; Heinecken, 2015; Wilén, 2020). "Added burdens" are the invisible labor and unstated expectations that fall on women soldiers specifically—these range from making the institution a friendlier place to actively combating predatory behavior and illicit activities. The weight of responsibility that disproportionately falls on women peacekeepers to address issues of gender imbalance and gender sensitivity more broadly is of course not applied to male soldiers. Yet another body of scholarship proposes that women are prevented from participating equally in peacekeeping, and that evidence demonstrates that they are as capable and effective as men (Karim and Beardsley, 2017; Karim, 2017). While much of the work I have outlined above and in the previous chapters has been mentioned and therefore cited, so much of the politics of feminist antimilitarism, postcolonial, and critical race interventions and accounts that examine heteropatriarchal relations as causal of war and violence is absent from these works. For example, while Karim and Beardsley's comprehensive study of women peacekeepers provides recognition of this large body of work, it fundamentally fails to link militarism with inequalities and violence more generally. Unlike earlier texts that emphasized the negative impacts of war and militarism on marginalized subjects, their book takes up gender equality aims without a sufficient framing of martial power and its investment in maintaining inequalities on a global scale (Enloe, 1993; Howell, 2018).

Karim and Beardsley's work engages with mainstream peacekeeping scholarship, but despite the book's title suggesting otherwise, it pays scant homage to feminist theory (Karim and Beardsley, 2017). Like many quantitative studies on peacekeeping, it treats gender, and sex, as discrete and already given categories, and in some cases indirectly reifies binary ideas about sexed bodies. In the same vein, Pruitt provides important insights into the experiences of women peacekeepers' everyday lives in her study of the all-women squad initially deployed by the Indian Central Reserve Police Forces to Liberia from 2007 and continually until 2013 (Pruitt, 2016). Pruitt's account is principally concerned with gender relations in peacekeeping and is less interested in other axes of identity and difference which may inform women peacekeepers' accounts—although Pruitt is careful to situate their labor in the context of the political economy of women, peace, and security more broadly. Pruitt's study is primarily interested in women's role as a specific all-women squad and what analyzing their experiences can tell peacekeeping scholars, among others, about how gender becomes instrumentalized in global labor projects like those of peacekeeping. It was clearly influential on Karim and Beardsley's subsequent study, in which they make a compelling case for the inclusion of women in peacekeeping based on a logic of equal rights and opportunity. They show through their empirical study that the barriers to women's participation in peacekeeping are rooted in a combination of bias and discrimination at the state level, and reinforced by limitations placed on women once deployed (Karim and Beardsley, 2017). Heinecken and Wilén make some similar observations, demonstrating that where women are deployed, they are expected to take on "feminine" tasks and to bear the invisible burden of helping to ameliorate gender inequities, beyond what is expected of male peacekeepers (Heinecken, 2015; Wilén, 2020). Though they provide valuable insights on the challenges faced by women peacekeepers, these studies nevertheless take for granted gender as the primary axis by which to understand peacekeepers' lives and their respective places within the peacekeeping industry. Notably, none of these studies pays particular attention to the role of geopolitics (and the global color line as discussed in Chapter 2), or the politics of the gendered body, which in turn underpin ideas about effectiveness and inclusion. This is where critical concepts like intersectionality, along with some brief reflections on my own research, can help challenge these more exclusionary trends in the scholarship.

Martialing the Line: Embodied Peacekeeping

In the course of fieldwork in peacekeeping missions, I have noticed a visible increase in the presence of women peacekeepers. In 2006 and then again in 2012 and 2013 I conducted fieldwork in several peacekeeping missions (UNMIL, MINUSTAH, and UNMIK) where I interviewed and spent time with women peacekeepers. In Liberia (UNMIL), I spent most of my time with an all-women contingent of militarized police from the Central Reserve Police Forces (CRPF) of India. I also spent time observing and speaking with women officers in the Ghanaian, Nepalese, and Philippines Armed Forces as well as among Dutch, Swedish, and Norwegian police peacekeepers. And I observed the work of a woman close protection officer working as a civilian/private security contractor. My analysis of the role of women in peacekeeping has been informed by my desire to analyze multiple power relations within these militarized and neoliberal environments.

My findings suggest a number of themes that are particularly relevant to discussions about the distinct experience of women soldiers[4] in the context of postconflict environments. Interviewing Indian women peacekeepers made clear that recent deployments of all-women squads rely on unit cohesion and collective deployments in order for women soldiers to "fit" into such militarized settings. In Liberia, these women peacekeepers worked in a collective group (Formed Police Unit, FPU), had specific and limited contact with local people, and were never dispatched for duties where they were required to act as sole agents. Thus, even when they provided close protection services for the president of Liberia (as they sometimes did), they did so in groups of four to eight individuals. The importance of collective and group solidarity was evident in their everyday working activities. Soldiers prepared food together, lived in communal but sex-segregated barracks, and carried out group training and exercise rituals daily. They also collectively shared in worship and leisure activities. Only the most senior-ranking woman officer traveled on her own but always chauffeured by a male driver in a private vehicle.

One evening I was invited to dinner in the officer's dining hall and joined some other invited guests. These guests were civilian or military police officers working in other sections of the mission and not part of a contingent or collective group. One of the guests approached me, as he had heard from the commanding officer that I had previously conducted fieldwork in his hometown of Trivandrum, in the state of Kerala, India. As we chatted, I mentioned that I had been speaking with a junior woman officer in the contingent who was also from Kerala, and I asked him whether he had had a chance to speak his native tongue (Malayalam) with her, in light of the fact that the contingent's working language was predominantly Hindi or English. He emphatically dismissed the notion that they might have conversed, for he was adamant that it was not appropriate to speak with someone of the opposite sex, and of a junior (and subservient) rank as well—despite his civilian status.

It was at this moment that I realized how pervasive were the "sex" segregation norms within the living spaces of these women peacekeepers. Despite the narratives of progress appropriated by senior officers to elevate India's contribution of women peacekeepers to global gender equality standards, many patriarchal norms persisted within this national contingent. Women's presence in the militarized space of the peacekeeping mission provided only limited possibilities for challenging "internal" patriarchal codes and gendered expectations of women and men. But externally this was also emphasized. Police peacekeepers from Turkey regularly referred to the Indian squad as "the ladies" instead of as colleagues or even by their rank, which was always visible by their uniform epaulettes. Despite the norms that circulated, women peacekeepers stressed the importance of their collective, not individual, identities and narrated how their presence in the mission enabled them to represent their country and make their contribution to their nation.

Women peacekeepers emphasized their psychological and moral skills (as "good women who didn't drink") but still had to work on their physical skills of strength and endurance. In this way, they had to continually make corporeal investments, as the ideal military resource is the "manly" body. Indian women peacekeepers were highly trained in weaponry work and spent considerable time training their bodies as "cyborgs"—where they became hybrid body-machines/body-weapons (Masters, 2005). Exercise regimes, military drills, and a disciplined ethos pervaded daily routines. The peacekeepers who participated in a medal parade ceremony which I observed spent the majority of the ceremony demonstrating their embodied prowess with displays of martial arts and mastery of weaponry (i.e., blindfolded loading and reloading of handguns). The Master of Ceremony of the parade announced a long list of soldiers' achievements including membership of various Olympic teams (in previous years) such as high jump, judo, and gymnastics. Morning and evening religious rituals of eating and/or fasting and meditation also contributed to a fashioning of themselves as pious warriors who did their work from a moral and spiritual passion; as such, they needed to discipline their bodies for national duty.

Importantly, spatial restrictions were imposed on the Indian women by their militaries. As a result of sex segregation and patriarchal norms, these peacekeepers were subject to disciplinary regimes which held different consequences for women than for men. While the all-male squad in a nearby region was also subject to restricted movement, there was no corresponding discussion about their "respectability" among senior officials, as in the case of the all-women squad. Over the years, senior-ranking officers were keen that their deployment of women and claims to be pioneers of gender equality in peacekeeping missions could not be challenged either within the mission or back home. Essential to protecting the reputation of the nation and the continuation of the women's deployment was the "respectability" of the peacekeepers, who could not be seen as engaging in "Western" habits of freely roaming the urban and humanitarian contexts. Their bodies became the sites upon which these discourses were inscribed.

Two discourses were appropriated to frame and justify these prohibitions and their attendant regulation of women peacekeepers. First, peacekeepers' safety and security in "hostile" contexts was of utmost importance. Force protection, however, is not the unique purview of Indian peacekeepers, as most national militaries (and especially contingents) are concerned about troop fatalities. But the imperative of force protection prevalent in peacekeeping missions is taken up (rather conveniently) by the Indian state. Despite living within a fortified aid landscape (Duffield, 2001; Smirl, 2015), the domestic concerns of India are transposed onto the peacekeeping context. In this way, patriarchal norms about the separation of men and women in public spaces are produced and reproduced. Gender regimes from the national context influence the particular constellation or assemblage of patriarchal expectations in the mission. The regulation of these peacekeepers occurs through contradicting some of the "positive" effects of deploying a critical mass of women within such androcentric settings. As a visibly recognizable and present collective, these women become both hypervisible and simultaneously invisible. While they go to great lengths to slip into corners and to "disappear" from sight, in terms of numbers they are a minority and therefore numerically conspicuous. While their presence challenges who can rightfully occupy militarized spaces, the controlled sequestering of some women peacekeepers can have the effect of invisibility. And although their presence is potentially challenging to dominant versions of militarized masculinities, it takes the form of a same-sex bloc rather than a critical (and politicized) mass.

In contrast, the accounts shared by Ghanaian women peacekeepers were not suggestive of a hyperinvestment in their bodies as resources for martial labor. Instead, these women officers viewed their martial labor as equivalent to that of their men colleagues. With "equalizing" rotation, Ghanaian peacekeepers did not have an overly sex-segregated set of expectations placed on them. All peacekeepers had to participate in all the duties associated with camp life and professional military work. Exercise regimes focused on group sports rather than individual body work such as weight lifting. According to the peacekeepers, there were times when women officers were asked to assist senior-ranking officials in welcoming formal guests, but importantly, there was less restriction on women soldiers socializing with other men soldiers or going off base. Even so, one officer shared her nostalgia for freer movement, stating that "back in Ghana, I'm able to come and go as I please." In the camp, all officers had to gain permission to leave and go into local markets, but they did not have to travel in same-sex groups. Given the low numbers of women staff, this scenario would not have been possible in any case, even if desired. While Indian women peacekeepers could not travel alone into the city, Ghanaian women peacekeepers had fewer restrictions on their freedom to travel alone into public spaces.

Ghanaian peacekeepers were heavily invested in their national identities vis-à-vis the peacekept. For most, their education and professional military training provided a route to upward mobility at home in Ghana and allowed to them to make a claim for themselves as distinct from and superior to Liberians. Their daily routines were not centered on embodied exercise regimes in the same way as the Indian peacekeepers. Instead, the Ghanaian officers consistently emphasized their superior cultural and educational backgrounds. Part of this was related to making a good impression on me as the researcher. For these officers, admission into prestigious European master's programs was an avenue for promotion in or exit from the military, and they continually attempted to distance themselves from the more manual aspects of military labor. Ghanaian women peacekeepers found the manual aspects of the military a reflection of limited choices that arise from lower socioeconomic backgrounds. Joanna was keen to demonstrate that her work involved a number of philanthropic projects with local communities; she talked of how nursing enabled her to bring "good things" to those in need. Here the focus was not on the soldiering body or investments in bodily capital but on aspirational class goals and the accumulation of educational capital.

Ghanaian peacekeepers continually narrated the Ghana Armed Forces as an example of a gender-friendly military. The Ghana contingent reflected a less restrictive but asymmetrical gender composition as it provided more visibility to women officers in local communities and within the contingent. Women officers prepared food alongside their men colleagues and dined, celebrated, and worshipped with them, too. While many of the male officers shared their belief that women were not as physically strong, there was a general consensus that women's place was, indeed, in the military. There was no critical mass of women peacekeepers, and those that were present did not have to endure other contingents' strict sex segregation within the physical spaces of living. Embodiment, at least in the conventional military sense of manufacturing cyborg bodies, played a less central role in their identities and their ideas about who can provide security, although clearly different forms of body work were taking place within this contingent's space. Women officers were often experts in health and were tasked to dispense medicine and care for the bodies of fellow soldiers and local populations. In the philanthropic work of the women staff, their own bodies were downplayed and muted, whereas their contribution to security was to help care for and repair other bodies. For example, they contributed to furthering knowledge about health and reproduction (midwifery training courses) and provided technical skills for local youth (computer training classes) to ensure the security of local populations. As a result of this, I suggest that this form of investment and identity work may mean that certain military cultures provide the necessary background to enable women's more likely transition into, and inclusion within, peacekeeping.

With an increasing number of senior women figures in peacekeeping missions (Landgren, 2015), the desire for women bodyguards may be on the rise. This is because women peacekeeping leaders have shown a different perspective on gender equality and may be interested in increasing the diversity of those in traditional security roles and in having officers of the same sex, as the duties of close protection require a certain level of closeness with those they are tasked to guard. The one protection officer that I spoke to, Philomena, although not strictly a private security contractor, worked much more as a lone agent providing security services for mission leaders. However, she had no sooner arrived in the mission when she was required to take leave, as she had allegedly failed to meet the exacting fitness requirements of active-duty security officers. One of her male colleagues shared with me his feelings about close protection officers and their need to continually invest in and maintain certain types of bodies. His own investments were evident as he spent hours each evening (when not on duty) working out in the UN gym. In his opinion the true signifier of an army's professionalism was in the ability to adhere to rigorous physical regimes, whether woman or man (his Israeli experiences were given as evidence).

In Liberia, most peacekeepers engaged in significant body work, passing the time as well as fashioning themselves to display their fleshy armor in the form of visibly muscled bodies. One Nordic woman police peacekeeper, who was a martial arts expert in Thai boxing, was known because of a notorious match against a colleague. Katrina had grown tired of the men "instructing" her in the gym and boxing setting and suggested a match between herself and another colleague trained in martial arts. Katrina herself was almost six feet tall and was used to dealing with "macho" cultures in gyms. During the grudge match, which it was said was reminiscent of Billy Jean King and Bobby Riggs, the woman officer "won points" but eventually succumbed to the superior physical strength of her opponent. Her opponent was upset at his victory and blamed Katrina for inciting the match, stating that he "never hits women." With visible bruises (a black eye), Katrina wore her defeat in an "honorable" fashion, according to numerous peacekeeper accounts, as many saw her defeat as a badge of courage. Additional, possibly apocryphal, stories circulated about how, while spending a day at the beach, "brave" Katrina had been mugged, during which her handbag and camera were stolen, an event that left her slightly shaken. Collegial shock and dismay were expressed in relation to this highly skilled and respected soldier who showed that she was vulnerable, despite having battled a man in the ring just weeks earlier. Clearly Katrina also symbolized patriarchal fears over women soldiers' presence in military settings; women soldiers are often represented as exceptionally vulnerable and susceptible to patriarchal forms of crime and violence. Despite her being exceptionally physically and mentally "tough" by patriarchal standards, her mugging confirmed for peacekeepers the "dangers" of the mission as well as the perpetual vulnerability of women officers. These examples show that women who work alone or in a small group may indeed have to rely more heavily on their individualized skills, whether embodied or cognitive. They cannot simply utilize the collective capital that comes from being part of a contingent—something that women officers often benefit from in regard to successful security work and experiences, as is seen in the case of the Indian women squad.

What I want to stress in this section is that by prioritizing gender and gender alone, peacekeeping scholarship has enabled what Belkin might refer to as a foil (Belkin, 2012). That is, gender becomes the distractor—it becomes the foil by which the complexity of forms of oppression and other structural inequalities are "deprioritized" or obscured altogether. In addition to this, gender becomes the foil for the category of embodied sex (Tudor, 2021). In all the examples from my research it was evident that there was a patriarchal anxiety about mixing differently sexed bodies in particular spaces, and this exists alongside a deep investment in believing that men and women are fundamentally so biologically different that no matter what equality measures are in place, there is always a perceived greater risk to those embodied as female/woman. This means that as embodiment becomes a benchmark around which to assess martial suitability, already marginalized women and men face further marginalization. In addition, the sex-gender binary becomes sedimented, feminists argue for integrating women who can be socially "the same" as men, and androcentric militaries still believe that integrated women need to be kept separate from and secured by the "real" male soldiers.

This is why returning to critical scholarship is so vital: it provides the theoretical tools with which to disrupt contemporary discussions about gender and peacekeeping. These tools are already given to us in the work of feminist, antiracist, and antimilitarist thinkers who argue for taking seriously multiple, interlocking, and intersectional systems of power. Consequently, these tools allow scholars to reexamine moral and political questions about whether peacekeeping should exist at all.

The Coloniality of Gender: Machine Masculinities, SEA, and the Infantilization of the Peacekept

In this chapter, I have shown the ways in which gender, when understood through a more complex lens such as intersectionality, can allow attention to the variety of subject positions and lived experiences afforded in peacekeeping spaces. In doing so, I provide an epistemic account of peacekeeping from the perspective of those positioned in these multiple ways. I also demonstrate the ways in which gender is itself not a fixed category, and how its pairing with the category of sex can both sediment patriarchal expectations as well as act as a foil for the maintenance of other "desire industries" (Agathangelou and Ling, 2003). In this final section I examine some of the problematic representations of the subject of sexual exploitation and abuse in peacekeeping. While this subfield of research and analysis now comprehensively examines causes and consequences, it has done so almost exclusively with a primary focus on gender—at the expense of looking at processes of racialization, colonialism, and capitalism (Henry, 2013). Current policy responses to SEA are bereft of a sufficient accounting for unequal global relations of power—that is, of geopolitics and the histories of colonialism (Henry, 2019). By turning back, yet again, to the critical interventions of earlier scholarship on peacekeeping, I suggest that by drawing on intersectionality and related concepts, I might challenge a singular focus on or privileging of gender as analytical unit, which narrows the possible analyses of and challenges to sexual relations in peacekeeping contexts.

Here, I turn to Lugones and the concept of the "coloniality of gender," or what she terms the "modern/colonial gender system" (Lugones, 2008). This is developed from Quijano's concept of the coloniality of power, which is essentially a structural analysis of global racial capitalism (Quijano, 2007). Within Quijano's theory of the coloniality of power are already incorporated the categories of gender, heterosexuality, and race. But Lugones argues that it is not enough to subsume gender, race, and class within this system, because it obscures to some extent the ways in which women of color/colonized women were subjected to this power in very specific ways. Lugones reconceptualizes the logic of the "intersection" and argues that it is only when gender and race are understood as "intermeshed" that women of color are actually seen (Lugones, 2008, p. 4). More importantly, Lugones argues that Quijano's understanding of gender is overly "biologized as it presupposes sexual dimorphism, heterosexuality, patriarchal distribution of power and so on," thus relegating gender to the "organization of sex" (Lugones, 2008, pp. 5–6). Moving onward, Lugones argues that gender is a colonial tool that imposes an oppositional/binary sexed system which determines who can be women and who can be men. Drawing on the work of Oyéronké Oyewùmí, Lugones shows how colonization involved the classification and ranking system of "races" as well as the inferiorization of Black women and women of color (Oyewùmí, 1997). Lugones challenges readers to understand the place of gender before and after colonialism and asks: who was able to occupy the category of woman? Were colonized women afforded such privileges? Both of these key points are relevant to earlier discussions in this chapter and for the subject of sexual exploitation and abuse because they reveal the investments in the sex-gender binary system (sex as biological and gender as social) and investments in ideas about peacekept women (who are most often racialized) as outside of the category of the human (Tudor, 2021).

Lugones's theorization of the coloniality of gender continues some of the work of intersectionality for thinking about women peacekeepers and their position as simultaneously privileged and marginalized in terms of peacekeeping power relations, but now in regard to thinking through the topic of SEA. In my chapter on SEA (Henry, 2013), I suggest that drawing on critical race and postcolonial feminist theories enables a different understanding of sexualized power relations in peacekeeping environments, although it does not prescribe a magic solution to how SEA should be addressed in policy and practice terms. The UN understands sexual exploitation and abuse to take place between peacekeeping men and beneficiary/peacekept women (although the official narrative is much more expansive and inclusive) (Henry, 2013; Westendorf, 2020). A number of assumptions are embedded within the official policies and paperwork—mainly that peacekeepers are in a position of social and economic privilege and power. While this may be the case in general, it is not necessarily so in regard to Global South peacekeepers. Peacekeepers have a range of privileges afforded them—some have their own UN passports that are issued to allow them easier travel to and from mission sites—but they are still bound by the social and economic conditions of the global economy. The second assumption is that women beneficiaries are not in a social and economic position to exercise "true" choice and are therefore vulnerable to various forms of exploitation. Essentially the UN understands that there is no (sexual) scenario between a peacekeeper and a local person that is not imbued with power and inequality. One would think that the UN is invested in a metacritique of peacekeeping as a colonial practice—but alas, no such luck! Instead, the UN views these relationships as evidence of gross gender inequality rather than sexual imperialism; in fact the assumption that peacekeepers can go home, whereas local people cannot, is based primarily on the peacekeeper as a Global North individual with economic privileges which allow them to return home easily. Consequently, the UN adopts a hardline approach invested in viewing gender as part of a system which relies on biological sex as fixed, and assumes from these fixed positions a certain amount of naturalized or associated power and agency (or lack of it).

What is wrong with this particular perspective on a pernicious problem? If local women in the postconflict setting are being exploited by peacekeepers, surely there is reason to object, reason to mandate against such actions. One of the problems with the current approach to combatting SEA is that gender does not work on its own in regard to conditions of exploitation. While the policies and guidance on SEA account for inequalities of income and gender, they do not fully account for the ways in which geopolitics and the global color line contribute to intersecting forms of oppression; all those subject to the power of the peacekeeping mission are potentially victims of exploitation. The peace industry itself is premised on replicating the capitalist system that Quijano outlines and Lugones critiques. There is no innocent peacekeeping context filled with a few "bad apples"; the entire foundation of peacekeeping is predicated on the exercise of patriarchal, racial-colonial, and military power. This links back to arguments I put forward in Chapter 1, where I discuss peacekeeping as an epistemic project. Consequently, if we think about what is left out when gender appears on its own, as a foil, or as a system which sediments sex, then what do we think about SEA?

First, I argue that it is necessary to look at the range of sexual relationships going on in peacekeeping missions. Sexual intimacy or sexual violence are not only a by-product of gender—they also arise out of the complex matrix of power that characterizes multidimensional peacekeeping. However, to say that all relationships in a peacekeeping setting are unequal does very little in the way of drawing attention to specific systems of power, such as those made evident by legacies of colonialism, military occupations, and neoliberal economic development policies. And which sexual relations, if any, are free from power relations, more broadly? While some recent scholarship has made links between conflict-related sexual violence and SEA (MacKenzie 2023; Nordas and Rustad, 2013; Westendorf, 2020), little of the literature attempts to consider the perspectives of those selling sex, for example. It may be that many individuals do not identify their relationships with peacekeepers as nonconsensual and therefore do not claim (or want) a victim status. On the one hand, SEA is a form of sexual imperialism that is facilitated by the UN and its policy of having male-dominated forces as the primary agents of peace (Harrington, 2010). However, this interpretation means that structures override individual choices—because the structures of patriarchy accommodate exploitative conditions. Alternatively, taking a sex worker–centered approach would ascribe more agency to individuals selling sex or in consensual relationships with peacekeepers. In this way, those involved would not be overly *biologized* or essentialized as quintessential victims. And these types of representation can slip very easily into the narratives of racial science, such as that women from certain regions in the world "mature sexually" at a younger age (Higate and Henry, 2004). Furthermore, a sex worker–centered approach would challenge the colonial infantilizing of both women and men in the Global South as incapable of consenting to relations, even if the economic conditions they find themselves in mean that choices are not as free as Global North conditions might suggest (Mwapu et al., 2016; Doezema, 1999).

Second, the assumption that sexual relations are structured by the gender system alone eclipses the politics of geography. Why are certain peacekeepers deployed to some missions and not others? Where peacekeepers come from does matter. However, Razack's ideas once again make evident that not all peacekeepers are equal and that there is the global color line to consider (Razack, 2004). Yet, paradoxically, Razack suggests that where peacekeepers come from is irrelevant to the possibility of exercising power in the context of the "colonial script" (Razack, 2004). What Razack argues instead is that it is the peacekeeping space (as a stage) that allows the enactment of colonial scripts. This is why she notes that the specific troop-contributing country of the peacekeeper is not particularly important in terms of the exercise of power. In my research with Nigerian peacekeepers posted to Liberia it was clear that the specter of SEA and reputational smears on national contingents were of considerable concern to military leaders. When visiting one Nigerian battalion, the questions I asked were concerned with the general work of Nigerian peacekeepers, yet the contingent commander continually assured me—without my having made any reference to the issue—that his men did not fraternize with the local people and that none were in anyway involved in SEA. Immediately after the interview and visit, another peacekeeper from a different national contingent, who had facilitated our meeting, commented on the Nigerian commander's curious "obsession" with refuting—unsolicited—the possibility that his men might be implicated in any wrongdoing (Henry, 2015). Whether peacekeepers from the Global South engage in SEA or other forms of misconduct is not simply a matter of the exercise of patriarchal power; it depends on whether peacekeeping is understood as a project that involves the perpetuation of multiple forms of power.

Third, the literature on SEA often assumes that the only sexualities that on-duty peacekeepers inhabit are predatory, exploitative, dangerous, and so on. A Twitter campaign launched in 2015 aimed to challenge peacekeepers' violations of the peacekept and drew attention to those seen as sexual "predators" in light of what were seen as unsatisfactory responses by the UN.[5] Since, in the eyes of the UN, there is no room for a mutually consenting and beneficial relationship between a peacekeeper and a local person, the logical extension from activists may be that all forms of military masculinity led to sexual predation. This, I suggest, contributes to a view of gender (and subsequently sex) that reproduces essentialist and problematic understandings of sexual behavior. The slide into essentialism explains why the "predatory" label can be so easily attached to peacekeepers in the first place, in its implicit assumption that there is something unrestrained that is either inherent to the military or to masculinity, and that predisposes male peacekeepers to participating in gendered violence or exploitative relationships. While Wood's groundbreaking article on the variations in sexual violence in war was not written with peacekeeping contexts in mind, it is worth noting that Wood contests any idea that sexual violence is a manifestation of natural biological needs (Wood, 2006).

In the gender training that peacekeepers undergo, they are taught that consent is irrelevant to the context and that power relations are always asymmetrical (Holvikivi, 2021). That is, structural conditions trump individual consent and choice. The dismissal of consent and choice leads, I argue, to particularly problematic ideas that assume a similarity between male peacekeepers and machines—that they are either driven by biological "necessity" or masculine "excess" (hard wiring), which requires prohibitive measures to keep this always potentially violent sexual behavior in check. Like robots, peacekeeping men are incapable of agential decision-making. I refer to these as "machine masculinities," where male peacekeepers are viewed more as objects of masculinity (with their own programming!), rather than as subjects who belong to a politicized category or group: men (McCarry, 2007). Harking back to earlier work reminds us of the need to consider structural power along with the multiple systems of oppression at work. As Whitworth argues, peacekeeping men often feed into and/or devolve sex industries in peacekept countries (Whitworth, 2004).

Of particular relevance here are the earlier discussions of martial masculinities such as those begun by Enloe, Whitworth and Cockburn and Žarkov, which placed masculinity and masculinities under considerable scrutiny. Was masculinity itself (and therefore patriarchal power) at fault for various forms of gendered and racialized violence, or was this an outcome of the military environment and culture? While the debates on military and militarized masculinities expanded from the early 2000s onward, I argue that the vibrancy of debate stalled by 2015 (Henry, 2017). The early scholarship, for example, explored how military cultures shaped the performance of particular masculinities in peace contexts (Cockburn and Žarkov, 2002; Whitworth, 2004). This literature was critical of the seamless transitions between valorized warrior masculinities and the placement of conventionally trained soldiers in situations of complexity and postconflict trauma. This work did not take the concept of military masculinity for granted; rather it was seen to be shifting, fluid, contingent, and often times paradoxical. In some scholarship there are arguments made about the role of military masculinity as causal of gender-based violence (Patel and Tripodi, 2007). A question previously asked to challenge homogenizing narratives about masculinity can be found in a joint article, where we asked in what ways some peacekeeping men "opt out" of SEA and through what means they do this (Higate and Henry, 2004).

Fourth, and finally, why can agency not be ascribed to the peacekept as much as it can be imputed to any Global North person? This question forces scholars to think critically about the differential experiences of Global South women peacekeepers and of those who are the beneficiaries of peacekeeping practices. It is difficult to deny the deeply problematic conditions that are grounded in transnational ideas about appropriate gender lines in postconflict settings (Jennings, 2014). However, it is important to pay attention to structural inequalities along the lines of the peace-war continuum, because the peacekept do not experience life inside of a spatial vacuum. And it is not enough to look at gender alone outside of these complex systems of inequality and power that form the backdrop to peacekeeping contexts. If some among the peacekept make claims of SEA-based victimhood, then this is important to recognize, but it is also vital to listen to those who view themselves differently—perhaps as agential sex workers or even as individuals who have been exploited by virtue of the social and economic transformations brought on by the mission itself. How do the peacekept construct, negotiate, navigate, and view themselves in the complex peacekeeping spaces they inhabit?

Turning back to the coloniality of gender (and echoing Razack's important work on peacekeeping as a colonial project), I argue that SEA is a logical outcome of the peacekeeping project rather than an "unintended consequence" (De Coning et al., 2017). This is because peacekeeping is invested in a geopolitical view of postconflict spaces as in need of intervention, akin to colonial attitudes called out in a variety of early peacekeeping scholarship (Pouligny, 2006; Paris, 2001; Zisk Marten, 2004; Razack, 2004).

Conclusion

I began this chapter with reflections on the complexity of conversations and relations established between myself and my research participants in peacekeeping missions. Women peacekeepers do not experience the peacekeeping landscape only along the single axis of gender. Acknowledging the diversity of their positioning and experiences means taking seriously the intersectional nature of everyday life for those women and men who are geopolitically marginalized but tasked to participate in peacekeeping practices. Taking intersectionality seriously in regard to women peacekeepers allows a more critical take on their integration into peacekeeping missions and reveals some of the limitations imposed on them by a system that prioritizes white and Global North being, perspectives, heteropatriarchal norms, and militaristic values. Challenging its singularity prevents gender from becoming a foil for obscuring the ways in which peacekeepers from the Global South enter the mission as already marginalized individuals who must prove themselves the martial equal of their Global North counterparts. Women peacekeepers manage their identities as women out of place in the peacekeeping mission by actively fashioning themselves along a number of lines, constructing their bodies and identities to maximize their agency and status within their national military institutions. In this way, they are not just women, encumbered by a "faulty" biology and the wrong kind of body that they must work to compensate for in some way, or the inherent possessors of a set of cultural skills that make them more operationally effective than was previously recognized. Rather, they are engaged in constructing themselves as militarized individuals, fit for purpose, and in no way confined by the limits of their bodies. In this way women peacekeepers challenge the idea of sex and gender as being anything but fixed or singular. Finally, I turned to the subject of sexual exploitation and abuse in peacekeeping missions. The dominant peacekeeping scholarship on SEA tends to marginalize the perspectives of postcolonial scholarship more broadly. Peacekeeping is foundationally racist, sexist, and militaristic, and as a result,

SEA must be approached from multiple theoretical vantage points if it is to be permanently erased as just another weapon of war that takes women, young girls (and indeed, some men and young boys too) as its casualties. To view SEA as a form of sexual imperialism makes it possible to understand why it is that Global South women have often been the objects of sexual and gender-based violence before, during, and after conflict. At the same time, it is unproductive and dismissive of local peacekept women's agency to assign them a status not dissimilar to that of children, as the feminist and colonial logic sometimes portrays them; rather, they are agents able to make rational choices including whether to be (or not to) in sexual and romantic relationships with peacekeepers. The global inequalities that precede peacekeeping missions do not suddenly disappear when peacekeepers arrive, and in some cases, they may be intensified, no matter how good or altruistic peacekeepers' intentions may be. I suggest that these global inequalities that serve to obscure common humanity can be better addressed when peacekeeping and other scholars come to a critical engagement with concepts such as intersectionality or the coloniality of gender, and are willing to invoke them within their theorizing and embodied praxis.

CHAPTER 4

Where's the Peace? The Martial Politics of Peacekeeping

> I will
> not dance to your drummed
> up war. I will not pop
> spin break for you. I
> will not hate for you or
> even hate you. I will
> not kill for you. Especially
> I will not die
> for you. I will not mourn
> the dead with murder nor
> suicide. I will not side
> with you nor dance to bombs
> because everyone else is
> dancing. Everyone can be
> wrong. Life is a right not
> collateral or casual. I
> will not forget where
> I come from. I
> will craft my own drum.
> —Suheir Hammad, "What I Will"

> Raise the stars of our nation, raise
> the Brit's Union Jack,
> put the dread right behind us—for
> there's no turning back.
> Not there for the fighting, not there
> for the fall,
> we are the friend of no one—and the
> enemy of all.
> . . . We are the Peacekeepers.
> —Mike Subritzky, NZATMC–AP Lima
> 1979, Kiwi Peacekeepers

Introduction

I open this chapter with an offering to readers of two very different genres of poetry, chosen for the sense they convey of the varying perspectives of those in proximity to war and peace. Here, I echo the arguments introduced at the beginning of the book: that peacekeeping is an epistemic project which sets out to construct particular knowledge about war and its aftermath, and that in doing so, it makes recourse to certain narratives about gender, race, and militarization. Though they emerge as the creative sentiments of two very different cultures, both poems are representative of the diverse range of views that surround peacekeeping. The first poem speaks to those who refuse to be a party to militarism as an ideology, while the second resembles a paean to those who advocate for and perhaps mythologize the role of militaries in pursuing moral justice. In the first poem, Hammad addresses an imagined audience of perhaps like-minded pacifists, and advocates for resisting militarism, violence, and war. The reader is called on to think about the destructive effects of conflict and of the martial culture of soldiering.

Subritzky's (full) poem takes a different tack, asking of readers that they experience war vicariously by placing themselves in the "boots" of a Kiwi peacekeeper—that they *martialize* their thinking to experience at a remove the social and physical landscape of a place besieged by war. Martial symbols and values are invoked, enveloping the backstage peacekeeper in a cloak of honor, masculine strength, and moral fortitude. In their different messages about war and peace, the poems show the ways in which stories about the military and war can be told in extremely polarized ways. Subritzky views war as a conflict taking place away from his home; both the perpetrators of war and the violent consequences of conflict exist in spaces beyond his New Zealand home. Its perpetrators are others (Africans, Russians), but its violent consequences are felt "over there" (Rhodesia, Lima). Hammad, quite differently, disrupts the naturalization of war by demonstrating what resistance to war might look like, not merely witnessing its atrocities as a bystander or supporter of war thinking. Resistance to militarization requires a challenge to the normalization of war (the image and cacophony of the beating drum rings both martial and monotonous bells). More importantly, both poems help to unveil that there is no "pure" response to supposedly organic and inevitable processes such as war. In this sense, what we learn about peacekeeping through peacekeeping scholarship is shaped by which narratives are foregrounded and which ones become persuasive (or not) in framing peacekeeping as innocent, benign, or natural.

The poems also remind readers of the ways in which the everyday can be a source of epistemic insight into the lived realities of martial practices such as peacekeeping—which might not appear so transparently in the problem-solving literature. A defining piece of writing on the ways in which the military (and security) slips into everyday life and discourse is Cohn's 1987 article on defense intellectuals (Cohn, 1987). In this important work, Cohn sets out to show the techniques through which defense "talk" invokes various versions of masculinity, through recourse to what she refers to as "technostrategic discourses." These discourses provide a way of speaking about nuclear weapons that does the work of minimizing their martial and destructive power. Cohn unveils the investments that defense intellectuals make when narrating their work that make invisible the pain and suffering that weapons have the capacity to inflict. For example, defense intellectuals infantilized the bomb (by patting it like a small child or pet), sexualized and feminized various aspects of scientific detail concerned with the weaponry (using rape metaphors to talk about what they imagined the bomb would do to enemies), and in some cases usurped maternal power by suggesting that masculine design was akin to giving birth (Cohn, 1987).

Following on from this work, Enloe's groundbreaking feminist study on the politics of militarization and women's lives provides the foundations for extending this early feminist scholarship on militarization (Enloe, 2000). Enloe demonstrates the ways in which gender is the ground on which both ideologies and practices of warfare are constructed and enacted. In a fascinating introduction, Enloe uses cultural products such as a Star Wars–themed can of soup and the figure of Carmen Miranda to illustrate how military ideas permeate ordinary and somewhat innocuous parts of culture (Enloe, 2000). Enloe changes the optics of critical approaches by doing much of the same linking of perspectives from the margins when she looks at the militarization of sweatshops, the impact of bases on civilian women, and the sexual politics of women's lives under military occupations (Enloe, 2000, 1993, 1989). While best known for its centering of women's lives, Enloe's early work was concerned to lay bare the ways in which race and ethnicity worked to divide or unite those in militaries in Malaysia (among other countries in East Asia) (Enloe, 1978, 1983). Interested in how "difference" functions inside nations and their militaries to either seduce citizens into accepting military service as a natural patriotic duty or to create a foundation for resisting co-optation and incorporation, Enloe's work began with a curiosity about the "micro-details of empire" (Lutz, 2006). What Enloe's intervention in the field does is to put gender relations at the center of discussions of war and thereby provide the basis for arguments made by others about gender being foundational in war and causal in militarization (Sjoberg, 2014; Cockburn, 2010). This work takes a slightly different tack than work which has sought to examine the way in which gender features as part of telling a different war story (Goldstein, 2001) and has essentially been the catalyst for a rich and evolving subfield of international relations. However, the roots of arguments like Cohn's and Enloe's can also be found in the work of Cockburn. Cockburn's work pays homage to standpoint theory; like Enloe, who starts with objects in the domestic household, Cockburn begins from where women are standing. Cockburn argues that analyses of war, militarism, and peacekeeping begin from the lives of the marginalized (especially women) because they experience such processes in distinctively unequal ways to men (Cockburn, 2008). What Cockburn adds is to situate women's experiences on a continuum; drawing on the continuum concept from studies on violence against women, Cockburn argues that the continuum is also about the spectrum of war and peace (Kostovicova et al., 2020; Cockburn, 2004). All of these scholars contributed to my own understanding of militarization and militarism as not only about gender or gender relations but about multiple and intersecting lines of oppression that are not always immediately discernible or acknowledged.

In conceptualizing militarization, or the "step-by-step process" by which ideas of the military and military might are driven deep down into the soil, Enloe points to the everyday, quotidian ways in which such ideas become psychically, socially, emotionally, and mythically embedded and reflected in society (Enloe, 2000). It is the very taken-for-grantedness of this ordinariness or everydayness that is the major contribution that scholars such as Cohn, Enloe, and Cockburn have made in politicizing both gender and militarism (the ideology of the military as a good and necessary thing). In her formative and well-cited chapter, Enloe sets the scene for thinking about how militarization creeps into daily life in times of peace, while Cockburn tracks the many ways in which experiences of insecurity, violence, and war provide the basis for those on the margins to organize for peace and against war (Enloe, 2000; Cockburn, 2008). Following on from conceptualizing militarization and militarism as structural, Howell builds on this important work by suggesting that perhaps a more accurate account of the power of the military might be to understand martial politics as the default position of the state (Howell, 2018). Howell argues that there is no useful distinction between the "before" and "after" of militarization because the foundations of the state are intrinsically martial. In the example of policing in the Canadian context, Howell demonstrates how settlers used martial force to oppress and discipline Indigenous people in a variety of spaces—a colonial pattern that still finds fertile ground in the present. Throughout this chapter, I draw on these two significant conceptualizations of militarism/militarization (as ideological, structural, and processual) and martial politics (as discursive, political, and epistemic) to show how earlier feminist critiques of militarization as patriarchal and colonial aligned with critical race theory's attention to the global color line and enabled a broadening and strengthening of these challenges to contemporary peacekeeping scholarship. Paying attention to the everyday experiences of those on the margins, whose standpoint offers an epistemic break in peacekeeping thinking, provides an important intervention in the literature: it allows a return to thinking about what a world *without* peacekeeping might look like, especially if it is concluded that peacekeeping is an extension of patriarchal, colonial, and martial power (Wegner, 2023).

But what do war and militarization have to do with peacekeeping in the first place? And why is it important to think through peacekeeping with some of these early writings in mind? Peacekeeping, as outlined in the first chapter, is a process and project instituted in the aftermath of World War II, and in the years since then it has peaked in relation to a number of different types of conflict. For example, peacekeeping missions were established in the period after Partition in India; in 1974 in Cyprus, now known as the "frozen" conflict on a divided island; the genocidal wars in the Balkans and Rwanda led to long-established military and civilian missions; from the early 2000s missions were established across the Mano Region in West Africa; and in the Americas, Haiti became the site for a universally detested mission where civil violence and political instability resulted in the first free Black republic becoming occupied by foreign forces yet again. As much as some scholars and activists would like to think about peacekeeping's raison d'être as fundamentally about "keeping peace," peacekeeping operations have always followed on the heels of armed violence and thus do not "break" war patterns, as might be commonly perceived. Even if they symbolically mark the end of this violence, peace support operations are intimately tied to armed conflict and violence in a variety of ways, only one of which is the actual deploying of national militaries to provide law and order (Sloan, 2011). It is this "attachment" to militarism and martial politics (Stavrianakis and Stern, 2018; Howell, 2018; Millar, 2023) that has been widely criticized in feminist critical military studies, geography, international relations, anthropology, and history. Yet this attachment to all things martial persists as somehow natural to postconflict settings and has become a mainstay of contemporary peacekeeping studies.

I suggest that the body of early critical work provides not only a gateway to thinking about the gendered and racialized logics of peacekeeping and other humanitarian work (Razack, 2004; Whitworth, 2004) but an avenue for extending critiques of martial projects more broadly (Cockburn and Žarkov, 2002; Mazurana et al., 2005). An example here is the dearth of scholarship on peacekeeping that examines the extent to which diverse notions of peace are achieved in contexts of increasing militarization and the fortification of military powers. Thus this chapter explores where and how critical conceptualizations of the martial in peacekeeping can be remembered and argues for an explicit antimilitarist stance in peacekeeping studies.

Unpacking the Military in Peacekeeping

What constitutes peacekeeping in the wake of insecurity, armed violence, conflict, and war? As Mazurana, Raven-Roberts, and Parpart outline in their book, peacekeeping consists of a complex range of formal and informal activities (Mazurana et al., 2005, p. 18). According to the authors, peacekeeping takes shape in one of three ways: as observer missions, peacekeeping operations, or peace enforcement operations; they are usually staffed (at leadership levels) to reflect military and humanitarian goals as set out by the United Nations Secretary General. Observer missions tend to mostly involve civilian personnel and military observers, while peace support operations include multinational forces under the "command" of the

United Nations and are focused on armed units as a deterrent to violence, as well as providing direct forms of protection. They derive political legitimacy by securing *consent* from the warring parties to be present as a peacekeeping force; to act in ways that promote the *impartiality* of that force; and commitment to use force only in *self-defense*. Peace enforcement operations allow for "direct action" against those viewed as threats to peace, including when peacekeepers become the subjects of attack and other acts of aggression. Typical examples here include postwar Bosnia and Herzegovina, East Timor, and Haiti, where "safe areas" were often created to maximize the protection of civilians (and peacekeepers!) (Williams, 2020).

Peacekeeping is by no means simply a martial activity that operates in a top-down manner or as a seamless operation to bring about peace and stability in a former conflict zone (Enloe, 1993). At its core, peacekeeping centers military objectives; it does so by allocating the bulk of peacekeeping labor to those individuals with martial skills and to those countries with national military capabilities in both technology and personnel. Cultural references to peacekeeping often invoke the iconic blue helmets and blue berets worn by peacekeepers under the UN auspices; these items are essential military equipment worn as both protection and identification (Pruitt, 2016; Higate and Henry, 2009). When I teach a week on gender, race, and peacekeeping to my postgraduate students, I ask them to think of images that come to mind when the word "peacekeeper" is mentioned, and they almost unanimously mention the blue helmets, although students from former conflict zones may also reference the blue berets or the white UN-branded tanks and other martial equipment that scholars such as Rubenstein and Ben-Ari and Elron have written about in their respective analyses of martial symbols (Rubenstein, 1993; Ben-Ari and Elron, 2001). As a regular exercise during the first week of my course, I ask students to bring in an item they feel adequately reflects militarization, an object that can speak to the everyday and that is associated with militaries or the martial culture. One year, a student who had previously worked with the UN in Afghanistan decided to attend the first class not just with the requisite object in hand but with an entire ethnographic-inspired experience. The student had donned an UN-blue burka and had ridden the Underground from her student digs, observing the reactions of her fellow commuters and passengers as she approached the university. Wearing the burka all the way into class that morning, she observed that the UN coloring and marking of the burka clearly confused those around her. Her own conclusion was that by customizing the burka in the exact shade of blue used by the UN, the burka had become militarized, too—although it is clear that the militarization of the burka has a long history (Ridouane, 2019).

In the early days of fieldwork, I carried out in Liberia, Haiti, Kosovo, and Cyprus, I was struck by the power of the symbols of the UN. In Haiti, martial branding (bold UN letters) gave to UN planes and helicopters a certain aura of authority, enhanced security, and safety (Smirl, 2015). On one stormy day, my UN-planned flights from Port-au-Prince were canceled and I had to take a commercial carrier, which went ahead despite bad weather warnings. Among civilian peacekeepers there was a sense that because the UN flights were "official" and flown by military or former military pilots, there was less danger and risk involved in using these forms of transportation, and some advised me to be careful taking the commercial carrier. This logic of basic security and safety extended to the "rugged" features of SUVs and other private vehicles. UN vehicles were equipped for uniformity and functionality; they appeared basic in appearance but were renowned for being highly durable and reliable. Thus most peacekeepers had access to vehicles manufactured by Toyota, specifically designed for particular terrains and purposes. Internally these vehicles would have some "basic" features and finishes and there would be an expectation that they would be used on rough, difficult, and varied road conditions, that is, they would be specified for four-wheel drive (Loftsdóttir and Björnsdóttir, 2010). The cars were bulky in shape and size and often a little difficult to maneuver for peacekeepers who did not have experience driving larger vehicles, as may have been the case for Global South peacekeepers, who would likely not have had access to personal vehicles of this type. This became a political issue in regard to the retention of women peacekeepers in missions, who were sometimes deemed to lack sufficient "basic" driving qualifications upon arrival. In the past some women officers had failed the deployment driving tests and had had to return home (Karim and Beardsley, 2017). Some countries introduced predeployment training in driving for women soldiers to combat this "barrier." In Haiti, a woman peacekeeper from West Africa, "Mariam," recounted to me how she became more and more excluded from the male martial community because she did not feel confident driving the UN vehicle and consequently was "left behind" when French and Canadian police officers would travel into the town to frequent local restaurants and cafes. In these ways the martial is part and parcel of the culture of peacekeeping and is often the most dominant and persistent symbolic form in a mission. And it is one that has very clear gendered and racialized effects.

It is not only the UN symbols that dominate the peacekeeping landscape (Higate and Henry, 2009, 2010). The bulk of peacekeeping labor is military in nature and undertaken by a range of troop-contributing countries that deploy traditional military units. In my own fieldwork I came across military contingents from the air force (Ukraine and Philippines), the navy (Chile and Argentina), and the army (Nepal, Ghana, Pakistan, and Nigeria), as well as a range of police forces and formed police units (India, Thailand, and Bosnia). Peacekeepers from these countries engaged in office administration and clerical work; manual activities including engineering and large-scale infrastructural repairs; and training, shadowing, and mentoring in the security sector. Military peacekeepers continually mentioned prior military service and training as if to emphasize that they knew nothing outside of martial "time" (Henry, 2015). Regardless of the presence of civilian peacekeepers, military spatial and temporal practices took primacy.

I was particularly struck by the pervasive martial ethos and culture while conducting my fieldwork among Indian police and Bangladeshi military in Liberia. In the former, I found that there were clear demarcations of "appropriate" leisure spaces within which some semblance of "civilian" behavior was expected. On a number of occasions, I was invited to India House to dine with officers during their large evening meal service. As mentioned in Chapter 3, I was often confused by the ways in which martial expectations were abruptly introduced into ostensibly social/leisure spaces. I shared earlier the example of the engineer who had firmly reminded me of the no-fraternization policy during evening meals. I was always informed of the proposed schedule of events when invited; thus, I was given the option to attend puja/prayers before the evening meal, which was followed by chatter and watching televisions programs cabled in from India.

Meals were prepared and served on a martial timetable. On a visit to a Nigerian battalion in Liberia, the conversations and tour of the base took up more time than anticipated, with the result that I and my police peacekeeper host arriving late to a lunch invitation extended by the neighboring Bangladeshi battalion. At almost 3 P.M., my host and I were quite famished, and the battalion commander had instructed the cooks to keep all the dishes warm in anticipation of our arrival in the mess hall. We were both quite embarrassed and apologetic, and quickly realized that we could not rush through our meal to catch up on lost time. Instead, we needed to demonstrate our appreciation for the food, sampling every dish and in large quantities! After we made our way through the meal, we were asked to join the commander for tea. Feeling quite full and overheated by the mid-afternoon temperatures, I realized that military time goes along with rank and ritual. Thus, we could not turn down any of these invitations as it would not only be impolite in a cultural sense, but it would be disrespectful to the schedule of those at the top of the military hierarchy. Sitting with the commander and having tea while the rest of the contingent cleaned up the entire canteen later than their usual schedule, thanks to our late arrival, enabled me and my host to indirectly valorize the culture of martiality; even with its wonderful hospitality, we were participants in normalizing the military as a site of intimacy, regularity, and sustenance. We enabled the military hierarchy to be enforced in uncomfortable ways for those of lower ranks. Harking back to Enloe's can of soup, it was evident that everyday activities can be so deeply militarized that it is difficult to challenge the inequalities that exist within these institutional spaces.

The martial side of peacekeeping is also characterized by an allegiance to various other scientific and social practices. For example, a Nigerian engineering battalion tasked with maintaining vehicles and other heavy equipment also took a side gig as occasional teachers at the local high school in Monrovia, providing some relief to overworked teachers by delivering a few physics and math classes. While shadowing these soldiers, I noticed that the teaching did not explicitly draw on their identities as soldiers but instead laid great emphasis on how science had afforded them the opportunity to choose their preferred martial duties and to potentially forge a career outside the military. Considered as scientific and logistic experts rather than low-ranking "grunts," as one officer remarked, this exempted them from more physically arduous labor.

Women soldiers from Ghana also used their medical and nursing skills to help local communities and to gain respectability within their home communities. Emphasizing their public health qualifications rather than their martial skills enabled the Ghanaian peacekeeping women to gain the confidence of local women, who might otherwise not trust uniformed personnel. However, their medical training in a soldiering institution did play a role, for their martial work allowed them to claim an elevated status relative to that of local people (Henry, 2012, 2015). For example, Ghanaian women officers believed that the culture of their own militaries reflected more gender equality and "progressive" thinking than Liberian culture(s) and that this distinguished them from local women, who they believed to be "subservient to their menfolk." Undoubtedly, the military had provided them with a level of expertise and education that shielded them from some of the problems endured by local populations (such as the difficulty of finding paid unskilled work). The struggles of the peacekept were exacerbated by the structural inequalities of the postwar economy and the changes in the political economy of the peacekeeping era. In this way, soldiers used their martial capital strategically to shape their own complex soldiering identities as superior.

Even time spent with civilian peacekeepers invoked martial ideas and values. Suddenly immersed in a highly militarized zone, one human rights officer told me of how the presence of UN soldiers around him brought flashbacks of his time growing up in Rwanda. Other civilian personnel complained to me about the "brutishness" of so many military men around them. At social functions and in the bar scene, civilian peacekeepers were pitted as "soft" in comparison to overt performances of traditional forms of militarized masculinities—hard drinking and partying (Henry, 2015). Outside Monrovia, a Czech peacekeeper told me that he was on the verge of "formally" requesting that "more women be sent" to the region, as the contingent felt that living in all-male spaces was causing a great deal of tension and stress. This was a call to break the monotony of a macho-military context, although notably the request was not for the deployment of women soldiers but rather for civilian women peacekeepers, who would not be subject to the rigid and disciplinary military culture and ethos. Military culture did not always reflect this stereotypical view of male "excess." Some troop-contributing countries expected their police and military to behave more like "honorable" civil servants, as I document in my article which discusses drinking cultures among peacekeepers from northern Europe (Henry, 2015). But even the idea of the "civilized" performances of honorable civil servants had overtly disciplined connotations, resembling Foucauldian ideas of the military, hospital, and school atmosphere of surveillance rather than an innocent humanitarian ethos (Chandler, 1999).

Schedules and rituals followed the end goal of maintaining a soldier for fitness and fighting, despite working in an explicit "peace" setting. Sport was incorporated into the military day, and from 3 P.M. onward, most militarized peacekeepers were expected to engage in some individual or group sporting activity. While this helped to pass the time in the mission, it was encouraged by national militaries as it kept soldiers occupied and in "fighting" shape. But it was not only sport that confirmed militaristic thinking. Among the Uruguayan and Ghanaian peacekeeping battalions I spent time with, it was apparent that rotating duties were based on evenly spreading the labor, such that each soldier stepped into every role and took up all tasks uniformly, regardless of gender or ethnic background. All the

Ghanaian peacekeepers had to do a laundry shift—washing the military fatigues/uniforms and making sure that they were pressed accordingly. Uruguayans all took a shift working in the makeshift/mobile bakery container, most times competing to produce the best *medialunas* on base. Despite the seemingly ordinary, domesticated, and perhaps civilian aspects of these activities, they were tied into militarized and disciplinary schedules (Hyde, 2016). These activities contribute to a militarization of the mind (Maringira, 2015) and the body (Higate and Henry, 2009; Dyvik, 2016; Henry, 2015; Holmes, 2019; Kylin, 2012; Väyrynen, 2018). In this sense, to return to the work of Cockburn and Enloe, the process of militarization is driven deep into the psyche of individuals and society through these everyday rituals that are either consciously or unconsciously derived from military ideology, practice, and values. And to take on Howell's contributions is to argue that this process never begins from a pure or innocent civilian starting point. Rather, militarization is an ongoing construction and production. What is important to acknowledge here is that, while Fetherston and Nordstrom point out that there is no simple "switch" inside a soldier's helmet that can enable a natural shift to a peace-promoter (Fetherston and Nordstrom, 1995), militarization never leaves peacekeeping as a space and practice.

What these insights do is to remind the peacekeeping scholar that peacekeeping does not become militarized from one moment to the next, in the Enloe sense; nor does it replicate what Howell refers to as martial politics like a traditional state might, in a seamless and unending way. Rather, what feminist and critical race scholars writing about militarization and militarism teach us is that peacekeeping is actively and deeply invested in military values, ideologies, symbols, and cultural practices as well as military labor (as discussed in Chapter 3). These investments arise primarily through the process by which military men come into being—that is, through gendered and racialized nation making, to draw on Razack's account of how violence is inherent to peacekeepers' formation (Razack, 2004; Basham, 2018, 2013; Welland, 2017).

Despite the pervasiveness of colonial forms of martiality in peacekeeping, there is no one martial norm that permeates all mission environments. As noted in Chapter 3, Global South peacekeepers often experienced questioning of their legitimacy when among European soldiers, for example. Multiple martial standards and cultures exist within missions and there is often contestation over which set of norms holds the higher value; this is intersected by the multiplicity of "cultures" that crisscross the space (Duffey, 2000; Higate and Henry, 2009; Rubenstein, 1993). In my article "Parades, Parties and Pests" (Henry, 2015), I outline the ways in which peacekeepers from some TCCs perpetuated certain peacekeeper ideals of working and partying in equal measure, and that this ethos sometimes helped to sustain conventional forms of masculine performance (Wegner, 2021). In fact, peacekeeping, like other martial contexts, requires actors (peacekeepers) to perform various identities continually and repetitively, from the macho warrior to the empathetic and capable caretaker (Henry, 2012, 2015; Welland, 2015). Either way, these performances always refer forward and back to all that is martial. Thus, even in informal spaces within the mission, militarization pervades and persists in structuring the everyday. That is the everyday nature of peacekeeping—what keeps peacekeeping ticking is martiality itself. Without the martial, peacekeeping would not, and could not, exist.

Histories of Martial Violence in Peacekeeping

In the previous sections I have highlighted the ways in which peacekeeping is symbolically, spatially, and temporally dominated by all things martial. I do this primarily by highlighting everyday incidences of the martial as observed or narrated to me by peacekeepers in my ethnographically inspired research in Haiti, Liberia, and Kosovo. Ironically, my analysis above tends to portray the martial as somewhat benign in itself. At times the symbols, routines, and schedules of peacekeepers I observed did appear very ordinary—so much so that in my initial queries, at the beginning of fieldwork, many were suspicious of my interest in their experience of the "everyday." Several peacekeepers later told me that they thought I was an investigator sent by the UN to spy on them! However, I want to neither romanticize nor vilify individual peacekeepers by rank or by nationality. In the reception of the book *Insecure Spaces* (Higate and Henry, 2009), there was often a sedimentation of stereotypes about groups of peacekeepers. For example, during presentations of the book, my coauthor and I had to continually reject racist and colonial generalizations about Bangladeshis being "actually quite small" and about Nigerians being quite "bullish" that would come from our audiences when we would share our analysis of the *perceptions* of the peacekept or peacekeepers. Rather, I argue that it is the martial nature of peacekeeping as an institution, organization, structure, and epistemic project that is important to grasp.

In this section, I initially turn to Razack's genealogy of peacekeeping violence in order to outline how the seemingly mundane aspects of peacekeeping can mask inequalities and forms of violence that are engendered by peacekeeping's martial foundations. In her book, Razack recaps incidents of peacekeeper violence against local civilians ranging from sexual abuse of minors to the torture and murder of the "peacekept" (Razack, 2004). Reading Razack's account of the white supremacist/racist foundations of peacekeepers' presence in a multitude of missions provides the opportunity to examine the links between martial-colonial politics/practices and peacekeeping. Razack argues that peacekeepers enacted routine violence in Somalia, Haiti, Bosnia, and Kosovo, and in particular, names Belgian, Italian, and Canadian troops as implicated (Razack, 2004, p. 53). In her analysis of peacekeeper violence, she reveals a number of discourses prevalent among advocates of peacekeeping as a "force for good." For example, Razack illustrates how peacekeepers and peacekeeping nations maintained a belief that peacekeepers' enactments of violence stemmed from their fractious irritation with daily living amid the "heat and dust" of Somalia; from their aversion to the "uncivility" and "barbarity" of local people (invariably Africans, Muslims, etc.); and from the combat training that they had undergone emerging (almost surprisingly!) in these tense postconflict environments—the latter a sort of inherent automated response, similar to problematic arguments made about sexual violence as a "natural" weapon of war (Baaz and Stern, 2013). Instead, I argue that peacekeeping embodies the gendered, racialized, and martialized tendencies of mastery as the norm rather than the exception.

Cockburn and Žarkov also outline some of the problems of peacekeeping in their analysis of the impact of male-dominated deployments in Bosnia in the late 1990s (Cockburn and Žarkov, 2002). The epistemic focus of their project is to unearth perspectives from below and to unpack the gendered and racialized tropes that work to cover over the unequal power relations between structures of peacekeeping and those who are supposed to benefit from the presence of such forces. In a chapter by de Leeuw, it is evident that TCCs construct themselves along "hard" or "soft" military lines when it suits their particular agenda; in this case the Dutch military constructed themselves as helpless in the face of ethnic conflict and genocide (de Leeuw, 2002; Sion, 2006). Like Razack's accounts of the centering of the peacekeeper as a deflection away from too trenchant examinations of racialized and other forms of violence (Razack, 2003, 2007), de Leeuw demonstrates how militaries are adept at explaining away either acts of violence (even in peace contexts) or the opposite—that is, *not* acting in a way that promotes peace, in the face of armed violence against civilians (Henry and Higate, 2016). I discuss the peacekepts' accounts of their feelings of alienation from peacekeepers, precisely because the latter extended their martial prowess into areas that fostered insecurity for the peacekept—aligning with gangs, perpetuating sexual exploitation, or even adopting a noninterventionist stance and refusing to thwart violence committed by gangs against civilians (Henry and Higate, 2016). In that chapter we referred to this as "scarce protection, abundant predation"; these spatial practices of providing minimal care to the peacekept and allowing increasing violence by local militias and gangs to persist clearly have martial roots. Allowing violence to occur was indeed a common occurrence in missions; mandates around the protection of civilians became a priority from 2000 onward. Peacekeeping was originally founded on ideas of maintaining peace through acts of neutrality, albeit through the paradoxical threat or deterrent of force (Ruffa, 2014). Maintaining borders or cease-fires was traditionally the main raison d'être, though, as explained above, peacekeeping allows for a reasonable use of force in the line of defense. However, these defense arguments are almost always used to justify violence, and by way of recourse to racist stereotypes. When Canadian peacekeepers explained their actions to a military court back at home, they defended their use of arbitrary detention and torture as a "natural" response to the racialized and "inferior" and inherently "violent" Africans (Razack, 2004).

In another case, Dutch peacekeepers stationed in and around Srebrenica scrawled misogynist and racist graffiti aimed specifically at Bosnians over posters in their makeshift barracks, plainly violating established protocols of neutrality and denigrating those who had already been victimized (Rošul-Gajić, 2016). The graffitied and other defaced posters were spotted by women's organizations working with women in different areas throughout the region.[1]

Feminist scholars such as Cockburn and Žarkov have long drawn attention to how ideas about race and gender are deeply imbricated in the rhetoric of war and warfare, and their edited collection goes further, revealing the continuities between martial cultures of war and the "postwar moment" when the establishment of peacekeeping does not serendipitously eradicate all of the inequalities that existed prior to the war (Cockburn and Žarkov, 2002). Their account, along with others, demonstrates that processes of militarization run deep, whatever the intentions of well-meaning humanitarians; the martial politics that are central to the functioning of many states do not simply "disappear" when those states deploy their militaries for international peacekeeping efforts. Cases of sexual exploitation and abuse which have been documented by a number of scholars support Razack's arguments that peacekeeping violence is not an exception to the norm but a reflection of the norm (Jennings, 2014; Henry, 2013; Lee and Bartels, 2020; Nordås and Rustad, 2013). In Chapter 3, I discuss sexual exploitation and abuse and demonstrate how prevalent ideas about gender in peacekeeping settings can alter the focus of peacekeeping reforms—for example, in committing to women peacekeepers as either a means for addressing gender imbalances (the commitment is never at parity levels/50 percent) or reducing incidents of sexual exploitation and abuse without a wider recognition of the challenges that women peacekeepers then face as a result of their deployment (Wilén, 2020). This same apparent concern for rectifying gendered harms can also simultaneously act as a foil for consolidating imperial power in peacekeeping governance structures. While I remain critical of approaches that assume that peacekept women are devoid of rational agency in deciding to engage (or not) in relationships with male peacekeepers, I do nevertheless also observe how the presence of military men continues to negatively impact social relations in mission sites. Investigations into children born from relationships between local women and peacekeepers in missions in Haiti and Democratic Republic of Congo reveal how young women who have been involved with military and police peacekeepers are socially stigmatized and experience increased poverty and a range of other exclusionary social effects (Lee and Bartels, 2020). The "rest and recuperation" "off-duty" culture of the military and the realities of the disruptions and altered socioeconomic and other relationships within the peacekept communities as a consequence of the presence of militarized peacekeepers—which are too often dismissed as "exceptional"—should be of central concern to those interested in combatting such gendered and racialized forms of harm (Henry, 2013, 2015). How these practices contribute to structural forms of violence and inequality can be found in the political economies that are established as a result of the presence of high numbers of military and other peacekeeping personnel (Jennings, 2014). Enloe points this out early on in her work on the connections between trade and military bases (Enloe, 1989); Cockburn highlights this nexus in her work with Hubic that explores women's agency in peacekeeping contexts (Cockburn and Hubic, 2002), and further extends this line of argument in her work on gender relations as causalities of war (Cockburn, 2010).

To illustrate these arguments further, I reflect on fieldwork in and among multinational peacekeepers in Liberia. Spending time with some police peacekeepers and humanitarian aid workers provided some insight into how the culture of militarism shapes the performances of multiple masculinities. On one occasion, I was invited to attend a barbecue with a small group of peacekeepers. During the barbeque the peacekeeper hosting the social gathering kept apologizing for his shortcomings as a host in the absence of his girlfriend. Later, in conversation, he told me of his sadness following the ending of his relationship with Maria, his former girlfriend, who had returned home to the Philippines. Maria had been working as a civilian peacekeeper and they had met via mutual friends in the mission. They had been living together for almost a year in "relative harmony," and Maria's return home had occurred just before my interviews with Adin. When I inquired what had happened to cause the breakup, he told me that there had been a falling out with some other members of his contingent; there had been a fight, a confrontation on a night of heavy drinking. According to what Maria told Adin, she had been working at her desk in the headquarters building when another member of Adin's contingent had come to visit a senior officer in an adjacent office. Greeting Maria, Bran reached out and held her name badge, which was hanging from an UN lanyard around her neck. As he did so he (deliberately) touched her chest/breasts. Maria immediately made clear her displeasure at his intrusive and unwanted touching, confronting the man loudly, and her angry remonstrances were heard throughout the office. Her abuser responded by accusing Maria of being overly sensitive and left quickly. By the evening, news of their encounter had circulated widely, and she returned home to the shared flat with Adin, visibly upset. The incident, while not strictly uncommon among the multiethnic Balkan contingents, definitely reflected prior grudges emerging once again. Divisions from the Yugoslav wars continually reemerged in these somewhat ordinary moments. At work are competing ideas about patriarchy and ownership of women's bodies—but also the endurance of codes of masculine and cultural honor that are supposed to reflect the "peaceful and harmonious" place that constitutes former Yugoslavia. Military memories resurfaced in a number of ways: from contests over women, a series of "face-offs" which ensued at various parties. These face-offs would usually come about at various "checkpoints" such as the entrance to private residences, parking lots of exclusive restaurants and bars, and the gates to beaches and parks (Henry, 2015). Face-offs did not occur at formal military checkpoints, where there could be professional misconduct repercussions for peacekeepers. However, these fewer formal checkpoints often triggered memories of war and engendered a violent and aggressive stance between peacekeeping men and local security men. Sometime after Maria's departure from the mission, another civilian peacekeeper became interested in Adin, but before things could progress, Bran "stole" the new love interest. When I asked Adin what had happened, he told me that in resentment at the dishonorable behavior of Bran, he simply reimagined wartime in the mid-nineties as a way to remember that the "past is never simply in the past."

In the course of my fieldwork I observed the different performances of masculinity among peacekeepers; some men represented themselves in a manner that appeared less militaristic, as antiwar, nonviolent, peace-loving individuals, while others presented themselves as stereotypical warriors. Bojan was a "traditional soldier" by his own admission. As Emir continually reiterated to me, "I never hate, because I see what it did to my country." Others performed more stereotypical—normative—forms of masculinity. On one evening, Milos, a member of the (unnamed Balkan) contingent, became inebriated and started to "bring out the skeletons" when no one wanted to talk either about the "war" or the recent "stealing" of women, or to engage him in a physical confrontation. A "brotherhood" of military and policemen rushed to his side. Milos was quickly bundled away, so that his aggression would not be allowed full expression or spill over in ways that might eventually embarrass himself or others and/or undermine his macho status. Safely outside and in a fit of anger he dramatically ripped his shirt in two (in the manner of the Incredible Hulk), performing his version of hegemonic masculinity among his mostly male audience. When Milos returned to the party wearing a completely different shirt it was clear that most of the party goers assumed he had been in some sort of physical altercation. Perhaps the act of ripping his shirt was itself a coping mechanism (and possibly a good antitoxic way to deal with his frustrations) in response to the stresses of living under military masculine cultural expectations. And of further note, the examples I provide are very much to be understood within the contest of heteronormative, patriarchal cultures, both inside and outside the context of the national military. However, while all these acts can also be understood within the context of distinct cultural expectations, they are all recuperated by the military at large. What I mean by this is that any transgressions of gender, sexuality, and culture that soldiers are engaged in are redeemed or saved by the military institution itself. In this sense, the power of the military supersedes transgressive behavior and ultimately provides a safety net in the peacekeeping context.

I end this section with a brief anecdote about how violence is both absent and present in the peacekeeping setting. On the one hand I have argued that violence is foundational to the martial character of peacekeeping—it is a logical extension of the militarization and martial politics that underpin the establishment of missions. Thus, it is not just that such forms of violence are inevitable, but that they are built into the very fabric and design of peacekeeping by virtue of form and function. However, at the same time, peacekeepers themselves seem ill-prepared to deal with violence outside of their own bodies and organizations. On one of my final fieldwork trips to Liberia, I spent time with Filipino peacekeepers in order to understand some of their daily routines and the work they were doing to build sustainable gardens in and around their bases. At the end of my tour and stay with the battalion, I was given a lift back to my hotel in a vehicle among a convoy of small jeeps with personnel from the contingent. There was a lane leading from the base, an open abandoned area of land about one hundred yards from the road and adjacent to the entrance to a roundabout and busy set of intersections. As the convoy drove toward the busy road, I spotted a mound in the center of the open area of land. Through puddles of muddy water (it had been raining very recently) and various bits of debris and strewn litter, we drew closer to the mound, and I could see that it was a bent shape, the outline of a black plastic bag wrapped around and closed with duct tape at one end. It looked very much like a body, a corpse, discarded at the headquarters of one of two TCCs' base camps. As it registered in my mind that I might possibly have been observing a corpse, I looked up and met the eyes of a soldier sitting opposite me in the back of the open jeep. He and I mouthed the words at the exact same time: "Is that a body?," we half whispered simultaneously. For a moment, the two of us sat in silence; it did not appear that anyone else on the jeep had noticed the corpse-like bundle. Finally, I broke the quiet, and suggested that the soldier alert the security office at the UN Headquarters so that they could send out the relevant teams to investigate. After making a brief phone call to his superiors, we sat in silence again.

Reflecting back on this episode reminded me, too, of an interview I had with a peacekeeper from Serbia, Drag. He had confided to me how much he dreaded going to his work each day, and how, within the first weeks of his arrival in Monrovia, he had to come realize how unsuited he was for peacekeeping duties. Drag shared with me that he had previously worked as a border control officer and was relatively senior in age and rank, but as the father of a nine-year-old daughter, he had thought that peacekeeping work might help to provide a better life for her in an increasingly competitive economy in the Balkans. He worried about his daughter and her mother, both left back at home in Serbia, and the impact his absence would have on them. But his hopes for a career as a peacekeeper soon evaporated. Within the first month of his new role, he was accompanying a group of international and national police officers to help investigate the aftermath of election-related violence. When the two teams arrived at the scene, they found the body of a man, who had been beaten to death, lying on the road. He recounted how he had been visibly shaken; despite his military training and having experienced the war in former Yugoslavia, he had never actually seen a dead body before, at least not in the line of duty. While some of the team members had experience in homicide divisions, Drag had felt "out of his depth." After this incident, he had trouble sleeping and requested late-night shifts in a rat-infested old warehouse where surveillance equipment had been set up by the policing command. He told me that to pass the time, he took as many shifts as he could and tried to avoid being rostered into any work schedule that necessitated his having any contact with local police or the local population.

I bring up these fieldwork moments, because along with my earlier analysis, informed by feminist and critical race scholarship, they expose readers to the militaristic underpinnings of everyday peacekeeping labor and practice. They lay bare too the ways in which military values and ethos run through every aspect of peacekeeping. However, this does not always mean that peacekeepers are themselves conscious of this process, or are simply agents who carry out the "dirty" military work of their nations. Rather, the imperative to be "fit for duty," or to be prepared to deal with war and its sometimes equally violent aftermath, does not necessarily chime with the lived realities of peacekeepers from the Global South. Seen in this light, the Filipino peacekeeper's surprise at encountering death, despite being a part of an institution that is trained in pursuing death, seems beyond ironic.

I end on the reflection that both the peacekept and military peacekeepers are wholly unprepared to deal with various forms of violence. I believe that an analysis of militarization and racialized martial politics needs also to account for the counterexamples, the oppositional or unexpected reactions of peacekeepers to the effects of war, everyday insecurity, and structural violence. Here I am thinking specifically of how Japan has engaged in peacekeeping from a very different yet totally invested perspective (Frühstück and Ben-Ari, 2002; Fujishige et al., 2022). When Japanese peacekeepers (police) have been sent to peacekeeping missions, they have found it very difficult to deal with incidents of violence among beneficiary populations (Fujishige et al., 2022). In some instances, Japanese police had never previously encountered the level or scope of violence that the national police they were expected to support or deal with. Their discomfort at managing these violent encounters became the basis for the Japanese government to rethink the deployment of security personnel and shift operational strategy instead to providing alternative ways of supporting missions, for example, to operational logistics. This disavowal of violence and working with violence also reflects Japan's own investment in the national self-image of peace. To conclude, then, is to argue that there is no simple expression of military power when it comes to peacckeepers themselves. Peacekeeping is a lot of "fumbling and stumbling," as Goran, a Croatian peacekeeper, told me. Understood in this way, peacekeeping as process is revealed as both militarized and already martial, a project that is never pure or complete.

Conclusion: Remilitarizing Martial Peacekeeping

While I have argued that this book is primarily an engagement with peacekeeping scholarship, it is important to think about some of the backdrop of global governance that I believe has been highly influential on the development and progression of this scholarship. In 2017, a report emerged titled *Improving Security of United Nations Peacekeepers: We Need to Change the Way We Are Doing Business*, led by Lieutenant General (Retired) Cruz (and hereafter known as the Cruz Report) and commissioned by the United Nations to assess the future of peacekeeping operations (Cruz et al., 2017). The bulk of the report argues for a more "proactive" stance toward threats to peace; it actively calls for what I believe is a "retro" version of androcentric military command, which values physical prowess in terms of "manpower" and techno-strategic weaponry and technologies. Strikingly, at no point does the report address the socioeconomic consequences or impact of the presence of foreign militaries on peacekept populations. A word search of the report finds not a single instance of the terms "women," "female," or "gender," and perhaps more importantly, references to "sexual exploitation" are similarly absent. Instead, there are frequent mentions of issues of "abuses," "threats," and "risks," but these relate solely to the numerous challenges that apparently confront peacekeepers. I argue that, fundamentally, this report represents a remilitarizing of peacekeeping. It recenters military thinking as the starting point for peacekeeping operations and advocates a reinforcement of traditional and aggressive military principles, as if peacekeeping is akin to a war setting.

The Cruz Report marks a watershed moment in policy terms because it argues for "returning" to traditional state military orientations in humanitarian and postconflict settings. It uses the military deaths that Williams discusses as justification for taking a more "robust" stance vis-à-vis the peacekept (and "belligerent" parties) and to justify an increase in expenditure and focus on military means to peacekeeping ends (Williams, 2020). The arguments put forward in this report seem not to pose an obstacle to a range of research and scholarship, as is evident in the work of Hultman, Kathman, and Shannon, who draw on large data sets to demonstrate why peacekeeping "works" (Hultman et al., 2019; Howard, 2019). While in general, scholars do not "endorse" the report, they do however engage with its general recommendations without recourse to much earlier criticism. From Razack's warning that violence against host populations follows peacekeeping wherever it goes, to Whitworth's account of the gendered power relations that structure militaries before they are deployed, there is a plethora of critical interventions that point to the problems of a military-centered approach to fostering peace and development in postconflict contexts.

However, the Cruz Report and scholarship that argues similarly contribute to the normalization of militarism and militarization (Williams, 2020; Cruz et al., 2017; Hultman et al., 2019; Howard, 2019). I argue for returning to the work of scholars who insist on the importance of analysis that uncovers and unpacks the gendered, racialized, and martialized basis of peacekeeping—work that is vital in providing an alternative to contemporary militarized forms of peacekeeping. But why is this approach to peacekeeping a problem in the first place? Duncanson demonstrates that militaries can be "forces for good," a view with which Paris agrees, arguing that overall, peacekeeping missions do more good than harm (Duncanson, 2013; Paris, 2004). Peacekeeping "saves lives," even if operations and missions are beset by a number of problems (Hultman et al., 2019). By exploring a range of empirical examples from my fieldwork and revisiting some of the earlier interventions of feminist standpoint scholars, postcolonial critics, and antimilitarist activists, it becomes evident that there is no good theoretical or empirical reason to continue to normalize the military in peacekeeping. There is no reason why antimilitarist and anticolonial thinking cannot inform our analyses of "the underbelly" of peacekeeping missions and what can be done to approach these processes differently. If one follows the arguments of scholars such as Enloe, Whitworth, Cohn, and Cockburn, peacekeeping itself stems from an already heavily gender-skewed martial foundation; this is not in dispute, judging from the sheer volume of work by feminists. If we again turn to scholars such as Žarkov; Mazurana, Raven-Roberts, and Parpart; and Razack, we can see that a plethora of incidents of violence, aggression, and dehumanizing treatment toward the peacekept (and sometimes other peacekeepers) originates in the unchecked power of macho, Global North, military cultures. These cannot easily be categorized or dismissed as "exceptional" or the actions of a few "bad apples" (Razack, 2004) when considered against the backdrop of ideology and cultures of military institutions; they contribute to the reproduction and maintenance of a range of inequalities through emphasizing and valorizing androcentric, colonial, and warrior practices. When we pay attention to these critical analyses, it is possible to advocate for a different path for peacekeeping. It is also morally necessary, considering all of the problems that remain, to consider seriously the end of militaries in peacekeeping.

CHAPTER 5

For the Peacekept: Decolonizing, Demilitarizing, and Degendering Peacekeeping

Humanitarian interventions occur in response to what now we call "humanitarian crises," but who is "human" worthy of protection, and what constitutes a "crisis" requiring response are both matters of perception. Someone counts as "human" in political and social life only if others recognise him or her as such. Something is a crisis only if it flies in the face of what we agree is acceptable. Thus, what constitutes a humanitarian crisis is always a function of the normative fabric of political life and standards of acceptable behaviour in the world.
(Finnemore, 2008, p. 198)

The dynamics of war and violence are firmly situated "out there"—in specific Third World regions, countries and localities—and with "their" problems. Thus, the larger, global economic and political dynamics, and more specifically, the role of the West in the economies and politics of Third World countries and the wars unfolding in these countries, are often absent.
(Žarkov, 2008, p. 2)

Introduction

This chapter synthesizes the critical analyses that I have drawn on throughout previous chapters in order to examine what such interventions can offer to the project of reimagining and ending peacekeeping. I argue that because peacekeeping is a knowledge project, it is possible to intervene in the production of this knowledge so that those learning about peacekeeping come to know it in ways that are different and more judicious. I explore this "knowing differently" in more detail in the final chapter. Having reviewed all the lost opportunities to draw on critical theories of gender, race, and the military for peacekeeping, I now want to think through how different the body of peacekeeping scholarship might look if it were to engage with some of the more conceptually politicized commitments that I suggest are lacking within more mainstream work. This requires interventions into the epistemic project of peacekeeping, necessary to successfully challenge how the peacekept are simultaneously imagined and affected by practices of peacekeeping that renders them as liminal subjects rather than agential humans at the center of thinking, policy, or practice. That said, my intent is not to "rehabilitate" the peacekept and merely reconfigure them as corrected objects of global governance, aid experimentation, neoliberal development, or humanitarian rescue fantasies. Nor do I want to "re-center" the peacekept in order to elevate their own perspectives as equally benign and/or innocent in the same manner that peacekeeping is generally represented. Rather, I show how studies from the late 1990s to the mid-2000s (Zisk Marten, 2004; Pouligny, 2006; Cockburn, 2008; Cockburn and Žarkov, 2002; Ramsbotham and Woodhouse, 1996; Richmond, 2004; Mac Ginty, 2016; Autesserre, 2014) draw attention to the importance of understanding peacekeeping through the perspective of the peacekept, and how this epistemic opportunity is foreclosed by continued allegiances to militarism, neoliberal development objectives, Global North thinking, patriarchal organizational cultures, and racialized hierarchies and geopolitics—all of which persist in peacekeeping policy, practice, and scholarship.

Decolonizing Peacekeeping

I have argued throughout that peacekeeping is an epistemic project grounded by its colonial (among others) foundations in both ideology and practice. I have shown also that few studies have developed critiques of peacekeeping that acknowledge the politics and histories of military-humanitarian interventions and the legacies of racial hierarchies implanted by colonial administrations for the more ordered management of recalcitrant, oppressed, and colonized peoples. In particular, I have demonstrated in earlier chapters how peacekeeping reproduces colonial relations through particular policies and practices that maintain socioeconomic, cultural, and moral hierarchies between the institution of humanitarian governance and the peacekept. Studies by Zisk Marten and Pouligny already pointed to the importance of focusing on what local populations experience from their location at the sharp end of humanitarian interventions (Zisk Marten, 2004; Pouligny, 2006). This is where standpoint theory can be meaningfully reintroduced—scholars like Enloe and Cockburn had been arguing for many years that those who experience war followed by peacekeeping operations must be consulted and listened to when humanitarian operations are designed and planned (Enloe, 2000; Cockburn, 2008). And of course, who is listened to in any given postconflict context is always contingent on socioeconomic hierarchies and local and global relations of power.

To be fair, the processes of peacekeeping necessitate a series of consultations with local populations, global governance institutions, and the international and humanitarian organizations which implement and oversee peacekeeping policies and practices. I have no wish to deny or dismiss the genuine efforts made to engender participatory and consultative processes. What I do want to argue is that contemporary and mainstream peacekeeping scholarship does not readily acknowledge the contingent nature of peacekeeping spaces, nor does it accommodate alternatives to the conventional patriarchal, colonial, and martial approaches that have made up historical interventions to date. My research shows that it is epistemically impossible to step outside the histories of colonialism that form the backdrop of peacekeeping missions. There are extreme inequalities among the range of actors brought together in peacekeeping contexts, and the duality of the peacekept and the peacekeeper obscures how some among them are able to exercise power, or are made subjects to that power. Inevitably this has meant that, overall, the peacekepts' position within the nexus of these relationships renders them continuously vulnerable and insecure, and their own knowledge systems are relegated to the margins of peacekeeping scholarship, policy, and practice. This does not negate the ways in which the peacekept attempt to take up positions of autonomy and to exercise agency in the face of such modes of power. However, it is this agency that is continually resisted by peacekeeping narratives or else recast as a form of petulance or stubborn childishness.

A few examples serve to show some of the ways in which the peacekept are marginalized in the scholarship. First, the very term and concept of "the peacekept," as I outlined in Chapter 1, is itself a critical and political categorization. Few studies use this term, partly because scholars are reluctant to employ a term so overtly politicized, and because of the connotations of objectification and passivity (Fisher and Wilén, 2022). The peacekept, by simple definition, are "kept" by something or someone, thus emphasizing a one-way direction of power. While "the peacekept" can be interpreted as a patronizing and objectifying term, I use it, as Clapham does, to draw attention to the ways local people are *acted on* by peacekeeping organizations and peacekeepers (Clapham, 1998). This highlights the consistent and unequal relations between those who act on behalf of the UN and those that are acted on, as host-nation citizens. To highlight these inequities is to challenge the normalizing rhetoric of host and guest or beneficiary and benefactor, terms that do not do justice to the complex nature of peacekeeping as a set of relations. I use the term and concept of "the peacekept" not to obscure the myriad of ways that those living and working in peacekeeping sites resist the forms of governance they face spatially and temporarily, but to reveal the instrumentalist and strategic ways they are invoked in various problem-solving texts.

Peacekeeping involves a number of competing demands and practices. For example, military peacekeepers are often under directives from their commanders to avoid "fraternization" with local populations. This is a common military edict that has been used primarily to avoid male soldiers paying for sex or becoming involved in sexually exploitative relations with local women (Jennings, 2016, 2019; Fetherston, 1994; Harrington, 2010). Historically, some nation-states have accommodated fraternization in very specific ways, as evidenced in and around US military bases in South Korea (Moon, 1997; Yuh, 2002), and there have been long-term consequences of such state-sanctioned forms of sex work (Koester, 2020; Whitworth, 2004). The idea is that military personnel are to concentrate on the tasks that support peacekeeping goals; to be disciplined by following orders; and to avoid social interactions that could bring disrepute onto the forces. Policies that mandate against fraternization are principally concerned with managing soldiers' activities and behavior to preserve the "good" reputation of the sending military, rather than grounded in concerns about securing the protection of local populations. However, in peacekeeping operations there are a number of elements of such mandates that necessitate interaction with local people. Think back to the Pakistan battalion soldiers—discussed in Chapter 2—who became involved in medical outreach and humanitarian aid and relief for local children. Providing resources such as food or medical education invariably requires interaction with local populations and can sometimes necessitate complex forms of cooperation. In some cases, militaries have invoked a further policy: a "no sex" rule that forbids sexual relations between soldiers and members of the peacekept population while deployed to the mission (Jennings, 2010; Narang and Liu, 2021; Harrington, 2021). Few feminist scholars have engaged with these informal or national military-level policies, an elision that reflects both the general absence of attention to colonial relations of power that are embedded within sexually exploitative relations between peacekeepers and the peacekept, and the prioritizing of gender as the primary axis of oppression in discussions of sexual exploitation and abuse within the peacekeeping scholarship (see Chapter 3).

On the other hand, peacekeepers regularly managed relations at the local level in ways that reinforced colonial forms of power. As I discussed in Chapter 2, women peacekeepers from Global South nations were not subjected to the prohibitions against interaction with local women—in fact, on some occasions it was actively encouraged, as happened when the women of the Indian peacekeeping force gave Bollywood dancing lessons to local women. That the women—both peacekept and peacekeeper—were sometimes given freer rein to socialize reflects the patriarchal heteronormativity that undergirds dominant understandings of sexuality and sexual relations within peacekeeping rhetoric. In other words, there appeared to be no consideration given to the possibility that women socializing together might lead to sexual relations—exploitative or otherwise—between women; there was an overriding assumption that sexual exploitation and abuse occurred only in the context of heteropatriarchal norms.

Peacekeeping men managed domestic and security arrangements in their accommodations, too, thus replicating inequalities in their interactions. While in Haiti, Roberto, a peacekeeper, shared how he "helped" his housekeeper to be a more "responsible" person. He told me how Haitians were unable to understand the concept of saving and that they regularly gave away the wages they received on payday. To help disrupt this practice, Roberto paid the housekeeper's monthly salary into a bank account that he set up in her name. When speaking with NGO staff who were working with local communities to support the promotion of women's small business enterprises, I was told that women often incurred debts to family members in order to run operations, and when they received any payments had to quickly repay these debts that they had acquired from a variety of donors. From month to month, they were often running on a deficit; thus they were not "choosing" to "spend" their money "foolishly," as was assumed by many peacekeepers I spoke with, but adopting a rational strategy to stay afloat in their pressured economic circumstances. Repaying debt quickly meant that women entrepreneurs would be more likely to secure other loans if caught short again in the future. The narrative of the peacekept as childlike minors bereft of budgeting and money management skills was commonly heard from peacekeepers keen to show themselves as financially literate and superior. Ironically, these sorts of financial slights against the peacekept did not apply in relation to sexual and romantic relationships, where peacekept women were seen as shrewd, materialistic, and savvy when it came to managing their "wealth."

Peacekeepers often offered evidence of the peacekepts' supposed proclivity to avoid work. Bruno, for example, complained about the "naps" the local UN staff would take while on duty in the headquarters building. He and friends would take the lift to the top floor where there was an open rooftop space, which UN peacekeepers would regularly visit for cigarette breaks. Bruno and his friends were upset when local UN staff began sleeping on the steps leading to the rooftop terrace. Local staff would lie on either side of the final section of the steps, and "fully stretch out as if they were at the beach." Even though they themselves visited this rooftop space for their cigarette breaks, the peacekeepers regarded the sight of the "open sleeping" of local UN staff as an indication of their laziness, reinforcing their beliefs that Liberians lacked a sufficiently "strong" work ethic. Thus, even when I asked questions of peacekeepers that aimed to elicit their personal experiences, peacekeepers would proffer, unsolicited, their racist and colonial opinions of the peacekept, against whom they compared themselves in favorable terms.

As I briefly discussed in my article on peacekeeper's contradictory positionings (Henry, 2015), Dan, a peacekeeper from Eastern Europe stationed in Liberia, recounted his distrust of the ability of local people to provide him with good customer services. For instance, he would take the suits that he was required to wear for some aspects of his work to be dry-cleaned at a shop near his flat. He seized on a discussion of what he regarded as the poor quality of service he received from the locals as an opportunity to share with me his opinions on the standards of living among the peacekept, and his wish to sever ties with local people rather than make connections for social reproductive labor (Rashid, 2021). Dan repeatedly complained that there was no concept of customer service, that Liberians did not take pride in their work and needed to "grow up" and "make something of themselves." When Dan became dissatisfied with his previous housekeeper's work, he fired her and set about purchasing a washing machine so that he could do his own laundry. He also bought a large purchase of sundry supplies so that he could clean his entire flat, using his more "robust" cleaning methods which "Africans" appeared incapable of grasping or applying. When I enquired what sort of wage, he was initially paying his housekeeper, his response was that "it does not matter, it could be a million dollars but the result would be the same!" These narratives of the peacekept as slovenly and lazy workers were common among peacekeeping officers who lived in privately rented accommodation. Notably, peacekeepers who were responsible for all internal cleaning and property security (for example in containers, barracks, bases, or military compounds) did not seem to have these kinds of interactions with local people and so did not express the same level of hostility and disdain toward the peacekept.

During one of my fieldwork trips, I was staying in an apartment complex and would sometimes get a lift home with a group of peacekeepers living in neighboring apartments. I would meet them next to the gate of the headquarters building as my access inside the UN building was limited. On the journey home, I would ask the peacekeepers about their days, and we would often stop at the supermarket to replenish supplies. As they knew that I did not have a car this was a hugely helpful gesture, especially when I needed to purchase containers of filtered water and other heavier items. As we would enter the gates of the small residential compound, there would invariably be a group of local security guards and other laborers. On one occasion, when we arrived, the security guard was sitting in the courtyard, together with a group of his friends. Seeing this, Drag became upset, as he had not seen the security guard when leaving for work that morning, and he asked him where he had been. Half apologetically, the security guard explained that he had been very hungry, for he had not eaten at all the previous day, and overcome with weakness, had gone home to get food. Drag did not entirely believe the security guard's explanation and roundly suggested that he be more disciplined about his work. Later, Susanne, one of the American women peacekeepers who lived in the apartment above Drag's, came outside and offered the security guard some of the food she had made that evening. Drag witnessed this act of kindness from his window, and later admonished Susanne that it was a bad habit to listen to the "made-up stories" of "lazy" locals, for it would encourage them to "beg" for food. He concluded his diatribe with the warning that she was being "scammed."

Thinking through critical interventions by scholars interested in standpoints, intersectionality, coloniality, color lines, racial hierarchies, militarist thinking, and martial technologies of power has allowed me to observe social relations in everyday peacekeeping life. This has served as a constant reminder of the need to keep critical theories with me as I interpret the practices and actions that I witnessed. Consequently, I argue that acting as agents of the UN, peacekeepers actively construct knowledge about peacekeeping processes and practices; about their own and others' identities; and about the peacekept as subjects in "need" of reform, transformation, rescue, and intervention. In doing so, peacekeepers act out a range of patriarchal, colonial, and military identities and desires (Agathangelou and Ling, 2003) as well as reflect, through their action and words, the epistemic foundations of peacekeeping more broadly. While some of these peacekeeping men and women may themselves have been subject to systems of colonialism, they nevertheless contributed to the maintenance of these "colonial scripts" (Razack, 2004).

Revisiting a range of theoretical framings and foci of writing has enabled me to interpret new empirical observations and material from a different epistemic standpoint. Honoring feminist, postcolonial, and antimilitarist debts by crafting a lens through which to better see and understand the political conditions of marginal peacekeepers and the peacekept has allowed an alternative to peacekeeping to emerge. The space to consider what alternatives exist for peacekeeping has to be partially derived from reading "against the grain" (Hall, 1980). Thus, to decolonize peacekeeping is to come to know it via critical theories that "reverse the gaze," challenge multiple forms of oppression, and consider nonviolent forms of futurity.

Demilitarizing the Military: Toward Abolition

> To paraphrase Audre Lorde, whilst militarization may not be a tool in the master's armoury, it is also not what we need to dismantle the master's house. Abolitionist futures are much more than de-militarized ones. They demand not merely a defunding of the police, but also a divestment from the arms, surveillance, and security industries, a radically transformative organization of the global economy, and far-reaching reparative justice for colonial violence and settler colonial erasure.
> (Manchanda, 2022, p. 4)

Postcolonial and feminist scholars have argued that militarization and martial-colonial politics are a consistent feature of peacekeeping (Razack, 2004; Whitworth, 2004; Cockburn and Hubic, 2002; Mazurana et al., 2005). In fact, the martial basis of peacekeeping is so endemic that it influences how civilian peacekeepers act toward the peacekept, as I demonstrated earlier. However, power breeds resistance—even among those who have themselves been militarized.

Members of the military and police forces leveraged their "martial habitus" as a means of gaining access to multicultural working spaces, such as those of peacekeeping (Henry, 2015; Duffey, 2000). Military peacekeepers relied on their previous martial training and education and played up these resources when in the missions. But many were looking for alternatives to the military, especially because there was such a heavy "body" cost. That is, they were ambivalent about remaining in the military any longer than absolutely necessary. For many, being in any "forces" required physically arduous work, and the rigorous and inflexible institutional regimes did not permit them much choice in how they managed their everyday lives.

Tellingly, many of the peacekeepers with military and police backgrounds that I met were often in the process of seeking independent security positions; such roles were coveted for they released the post holders from their bonds of obligation to their national forces. Although they had to rely on their bodies as resources (in the form of making themselves into fortified physical specimens) to obtain positions in the first place, they were able to garner significantly better wages and benefits without being tied to the "drudgery" of military labor. A close protection security officer working in the offices of the special representative of the secretary general, for example, would benefit from UN employment in more ways than the traditional deployed soldier. Many of these close protection positions were desired by peacekeepers, who lived with the knowledge that their traditional deployment would come to an end after the stipulated maximum of three years. For some peacekeepers, the prospect of returning to the grueling—and less well remunerated—daily routines of military and police work regimes evidently held little appeal, and some leveraged their positions to try to secure more permanent work offering better pay, benefits, and conditions. As Bruno termed it, the "deployment game" created a great deal of competitive tension inside and outside the mission and was the cause of corruption as members of particular units jostled to secure promotion back at home. Once deployed, police officers realized that a mission appointment could facilitate considerable improvement in their financial status. Therefore they pursued whatever avenues they could to influence the recruiters' decision-making at national headquarters and at the UN offices in New York. Bruno spoke of his awareness that bribes were commonly paid to ensure that certain applications would sit at the bottom of the pile or would be conveniently missing when the short list was presented to senior officials at the UN.

A senior police peacekeeper demonstrated to me the levels of corruption among his own national forces. He had requested a "sample" of newly deployed peacekeepers to appear before him at headquarters and, conducting a second informal interview, had asked them a series of questions to establish their "competency." Afterward, the officer concluded that it was highly likely that the new peacekeepers had not composed their own introductory application letters as, according to him, "they could not speak English at all." He suspected that many among the newly deployed must have known people in positions of authority who were able to ensure that their generic letters of application—doubtless written on their behalf by others—were approved.

Aside from financial reasons for wanting employment in private security type of arrangement, many experienced the working conditions within the military as particularly difficult for a number of reasons. Police peacekeepers from across the missions consistently shared one grievance, and that was that as a result of the masculinist ethos of the organizations in which they worked, professional working relations were always under considerable strain. Militarized workers were required to perform certain versions of body-centered masculinity (Masters, 2005; Mäki-Rahkola and Myrttinen, 2014; Bennike and Stoltz, 2022). While attending a post–medal parade lunch, I noted the performance of different masculinities on show and the subtle hierarchies of masculinity in play. Ukrainian peacekeepers represented their nationalities through the wearing of formal ("traditional") civilian dress, which they wore to welcome guests to lunch. Senior commanding officers from other military contingents sat at the head table, where they participated in the triple toast with small plastic glasses of vodka. As toasts were raised at every table, a few peacekeepers of different nationalities turned to me to see whether I was indeed drinking the vodka or had replaced it with a nonalcoholic drink. It was a moment in which the peacekeepers were themselves weighing me up in terms of where I might be positioned along religious and national lines, but also with some curiosity as to how "macho militarized" I was as a woman researcher immersed in peacekeeping settings. As Evasdottir candidly writes in her ethnography of Chinese archaeologists, drinking contests often form part of the hazing requirements for field researchers to be fully accepted (Evasdottir, 2004). And importantly, as Whitworth shows in her book, the culture of such organizations encourage competition, and these cultural aspects cannot adequately enable soldiers to make the "helmet switch" to peace that Fetherston rightly suggests is necessary for peacekeeping (Fetherston, 1994; Whitworth, 2004; Fetherston and Nordstrom, 1995).

Military organizations help shape the identities of future peacekeepers, but many of these workers long for an escape from the very martial habitus that they have crafted and strategically appropriated for themselves (Henry, 2015). Raj lamented to me several times how much he wished that he could secure a job outside the security sector, for the nature of his work meant that he had missed several important family occasions (for more on these effects see Rashid, 2021, 2020; Chisholm 2022). He questioned whether the widespread justification of military duty as service for the "motherland" was sufficient compensation for the lost moments with his children and parents (Rashid, 2020). In his opinion, he was required to have a "manly" occupation, but the strings that came attached to his role within the global peacekeeping labor force were not too dissimilar to "those who work in the Gulf" and other overseas workers. Despite his high-ranking status in the mission and at home, Raj was disappointed that he had not been able to convert this into the dividends he had expected.

Being in the peacekeeping mission with its strong military culture and presence also brought back traumatic reminders of past events. In Haiti, military and police peacekeepers would carry weapons—handguns and pistols—as part of routine duty. This was quite different from the operational practice of arming peacekeepers at checkpoints or along boundaries and green zones. Sandra was anxious about carrying a handgun but argued that it was necessary, "especially" in Haiti. She had taken an advanced hostage course in preparation for her deployment to Port-au-Prince and felt that her previous experience of working in a relatively affluent neighborhood in the US had not fully "prepared" her for the level of policing that peacekeeping in Haiti would entail. As it turned out, during the months preceding our interview, there had been a record number of kidnapping cases in Port-au-Prince, and this was a constant conversation and topic among peacekeepers. Thus, peacekeepers who would, at home, perform their duties in safe, air-conditioned office environments were now regularly exposed to danger in unfamiliar environments where their presence was not always welcome. For some, the on-the-ground realities of the peacekeeping mission rudely contrasted with their imagining of the peace operations for which they had had to successfully compete. For example, on one of his first peacekeeping postings, Adin was unexpectedly attacked by a group of thieves and struck repeatedly on the back of the neck with a large cutlass. He recovered in hospital and was given a short reprieve to return home, but then continued his duties as normal. Whenever he behaved erratically, other contingent members would whisper in hushed tones that he was to be afforded certain leeway in consideration of this most traumatic event. However, most of the peacekeepers among the officer ranks had reached senior positions and thus "avoided" having to be in "dangerous" situations, though they were not entirely invulnerable; many of their roles entailed carrying out duties in small groups or pairs, and traveling to and from their accommodations alone, and hence they risked being targeted by hostile, armed criminals. Juan told me how he always kept his pistol with him or in the glove compartment of his UN vehicle; he stated openly that he feared being raped and that the weapon was his only means of protecting himself from this potential crime. Bruno had begun his career as the equivalent of a street cop and had worked his way up through a number of departments, including some time in counterterrorism intelligence. He retained vivid memories of wartime, which would be recalled in certain emergency situations. Loud noises startled him; even the pealing of church bells on Sunday in Port-au-Prince served to remind him that he was not "in paradise," after all. Conversely, for Adin, the sound of the call to prayer in Monrovia was a welcome distraction from his indentured military existence.

What these candid moments showed me is that peacekeepers who had applied for deployment as a means to achieving the fruits of a "good life" nevertheless held contradictory feelings about their belonging to the military, even though it allowed them opportunities to improve their financial standing. They were proud that their earnings helped to elevate their families back home and could potentially liberate them from what they regarded as physically depleting martial work (Berlant, 2011, pp. 191–222; Rashid, 2020; Chisholm, 2022). Through listening to peacekeepers narrate their ambivalence toward military institutions and military labor, I reveal the limitations of attachments to the military as a way of life and thus advocate for an antimilitarist stance. Those beholden to martial institutions who find a way to strategically position themselves in and against the power of militarism are themselves testament to the problems with the martial domination of peacekeeping. It is the work of antimilitarist feminists such as Enloe and Cockburn that has inspired this deeper exploration of the limits of a military-centered life.

Enloe's entire corpus asks scholars to take seriously the lives of those on the margins, while Cockburn's continually returns to the importance of viewing war and peace from the perspective of those who experience it and where they stand. Both these perspectives call into focus the peacekept and their erasure from mainstream peacekeeping scholarship at the expense of an obsession with improving peacekeeping "effectiveness." Antimilitarist, feminist work on masculinities and peacekeeping facilitates a pacifist standpoint, which although not derived directly from Black feminist theory, has its foundation in some similar interventions, epistemically and politically speaking. And in synthesizing the work of Black feminist scholars writing on standpoint and intersectionality, I argue that taking up these critical perspectives allows for a rethinking of what peace might look like if, for example, abolitionist arguments about defunding the US police were taken seriously and drawn on in the peacekeeping context (Namakula, 2022; Walcott, 2020). Crenshaw's intersectional work on understanding the ways in which Black women in the US are erased from accounts of white supremacist police violence and brutality is instructive for peacekeeping scholarship, which often naturalizes militarized interventions as benign—at least for the peacekept (Crenshaw et al., 2015; Williams, 2020). If the very foundations of the security sector and martial power are colonial in nature, then no amount of training the peacekeepers and adapting policies and practices can ameliorate the violence of such responses (Basham, 2018). Linking back to Lugones's writings on the coloniality of gender, it is important to consider how the rhetoric of the Global North has served to marginalize Global South soldiers and the peacekept within peacekeeping practices through the reproduction of colonial racial tropes that deem them not fully human. Peacekeeping and humanitarian ideology does not assign all peacekeepers equality of status, nor does it consider those receiving peacekeeping beneficence to have the capacity to act as rational, agential subjects (Razack, 2004). Patriarchal-colonial-martial power is reproduced through and in peacekeeping spaces, and these structures of oppression and exclusion are in turn iterated within the peacekeeping scholarship. Postcolonial and critical race scholarship's contributions to abolitionist perspectives offer different ways of thinking about interventions in humanitarian contexts. Rather than pursue foundationally racist, sexist, and militarist practices, peacekeeping's past critical interventions might be used as the basis for abolishing peacekeeping in its current formation.

Degendering Peacekeeping

I have argued, along with other scholars, that peacekeeping is an epistemic project which constructs knowledge about sexed and gendered relations, among others. While many scholars have taken the view that peacekeeping requires reform in order to correct its gender imbalance, I suggest that by turning to earlier critiques of the gendered and racialized politics of peacekeeping, it is possible to think of peacekeeping as the ultimate reproducer of inequalities of gender and sex. Similar to Belkin's suggestion in *Bring Me Men* (Belkin, 2012), I argue that single-axis gendered analyses can mask a multitude of foundational and epistemic problems and obscure or elide a range of systems of power. I have shown in Chapter 3 how peacekeeping is androcentric in its ideology and male-centered in its organization. It is also steeped in colonial ideas about the particular contexts and specific people who are considered in need of or would benefit from intervention, adaptation, and rescue—a civilizing mission for the twenty-first century—as I discuss in Chapter 2. Employing a "manly" means to achieve these ends has prioritized military solutions to problems that originate in theories of humans as essentially and inevitably conflictual (Kaplan, 1994). Drawing on Enloe and others, Kaplan argues that binary and oppositional ideas of "self and other" run parallel to prevailing philosophies about race and nation, men and women, and nature and culture. Essentially, the epistemic basis of militarism is a belief and commitment to hierarchies as the organizing principle of human society. Early work by Enloe and Cockburn drew on these sentiments to expose the gendered nature and effects of military endeavors which center hegemonic masculine norms (Enloe, 1993; Cockburn, 2008). But there was also an element by which gender was "fixed" in discussions by virtue of the need to pay attention to the silences—the points in time where women were not given credit for their contributions or where women were the victims of war-specific crimes because of the pervasiveness of beliefs about women as culture keepers. This has meant that the binary of sex and gender remains untroubled in peacekeeping thought. Embedded in patriarchal peacekeeping are these very same binary notions of sex and gender, masculine and feminine, and self and other, as demonstrated in the quote at the start of this section and Whitworth's sentiments: "Basic military training helps to nurture the exaggerated ideals of manhood and masculinity demanded by national militaries. But this transformation is most effectively accomplished through the denigration of everything marked by difference, whether that be women, people of colour, or homosexuality. It is not by coincidence that the insults most new recruits face are gendered, raced and homophobic insults: young soldiers are learning to deny, indeed to obliterate, the 'other' within themselves" (Whitworth 2004, pp. 242-243). Because of this oppositional ideology in peacekeeping, gendered analyses always remain limited in what they can offer as an antidote to martial interventions. And to reiterate Shepherd's warning about gender critiques—the point is not to "make war safer for women" but to challenge the racial, gendered, and militarized basis of the war system (Shepherd, 2016).

I draw on an example of a situation that was narrated to me during my first fieldwork trip to Liberia. My colleague and I were speaking with Agatha, a prominent nun who had been working to develop nursing education in and around Monrovia. Agatha told us how long she had been stationed in Liberia and of the many peacekeepers she had seen come and go in that time. She recounted an incident where a young woman[1] (aged fifteen) had been living with a Nigerian soldier-peacekeeper in a house in a small village outside of town. The peacekeeper was due to return home for a period of time. When some civilian peacekeepers discovered her age, they informed on the officer, who quickly and quietly returned home without a word to the girl. The young woman was very angry and came to the nun seeking advice and support. She told Agatha that she was now financially destitute, complaining that it was due to the interference of others that she was now in a no-win situation. According to Agatha, some community members had known about the situation but had chosen not to intervene or "meddle" in a matter that was not their business. However, following her abandonment by the officer, the young woman became the object of stigma, either because the matter of her cohabiting sexual relationship with the Nigerian officer had been widely exposed, or because the news that she had been living in an adult sexual relationship had somehow filtered back to her natal home, where she was in disgrace and no longer welcome. Now she was homeless and all alone. Agatha was sympathetic to the young woman's plight and offered the view that although she was underage, her adolescence and maturity made the situation quite complex; exiled from her family home and being still in high school, she was unable to afford to live independently. As it turned out, the officer had been in negotiations to give her tuition fees for school, but the offer had vanished in the wake of his abrupt departure.

This incident reminded me of Zalewski's argument around the subject of gender and its conceptual inflexibility (Zalewski, 2010). What work does gender do in these situations other than to act as a lens to tell us about the power discrepancies between men and women in a given situation? How does it remedy structural inequalities or enable us to think about the situation of this young woman as bound by more than gender? The above scenario demonstrates the limits of thinking with a singular category like gender. In this instance a simple observation about gendered power relations fails to take into account the young woman's intersectional situatedness. She is not just a young woman in need of rescue from sexist exploitation; rather she is a subject who is trying to strategically position herself in order to maximize her own security and needs. A gendered analysis of peacekeeping keeps intact the very distinction between sex and gender and presumes peacekept women to be perpetual victims and in need of saving. Again, Lugones's insistence on the coloniality of gender comes to mind when thinking about what is applied to white Global North women peacekeepers and what is applied to those peacekept women; the latter seem to be exempt from the category of human (Mohanty, 1984). Drawing on intersectionality and standpoint theory here offers the opportunity to deprioritize or decenter gender and to examine instead the ways in which geopolitics, class, and sexuality help to structure the young woman's experiences of discrimination and struggle.

Women from the Global South working in peacekeeping missions face similar, yet unique challenges, as I outlined earlier. On the one hand, many were prohibited from moving about the mission with the same freedom of movement enjoyed by their male colleagues. In this way, the all-women squad of police peacekeepers from India became the object of conversation among the police peacekeepers working at headquarters in Monrovia. When the commander of the group would arrive and walk through the communal and open offices toward the office of the head of police, most of the peacekeeping men sitting at their desks would stare, snicker, and whisper among themselves; moreover, they insisted on referring to the women peacekeepers as one homogenous block: "the ladies." On one occasion, when I shared the advanced weapons training background of these women, a Balkan peacekeeper became agitated and reeled off a list of his "marksman" qualifications. Another peacekeeper sitting at a nearby desk supported his statement, informing me that only a few police are given a "sharpshooter" role, for which they have to prove themselves skilled and accurate marksmen in order to gain this special status. The Indian women peacekeepers might be qualified, but he lessened their achievements by suggesting that they had earned their qualifications in a not particularly "good"—that is, Global South—military. When I asked the sharpshooter whether he was able to share with me the details of his skills in the training he was involved in, he was clearly disgruntled that his skills were not being put to use, for he was mostly doing paperwork and shifts that required him to watch a screen most of the night. His resentment of the women peacekeepers developing an "exceptional" reputation for their specialist skills was evident when he tried to demonstrate his own advanced proficiencies and they were ignored in favor of women with "far less training."

Drawing on the early work by Whitworth, it is apparent that ideas of "appropriate" and "real" military masculinity persist despite the presence of women peacekeepers; in fact, military masculinities are still constructed in opposition to the denigrated feminine (Whitworth, 2004). In addition, a hierarchy of national militaries was continually referred to by peacekeepers that often echoed the global color line (Razack, 2004). Thus, while gendered analyses make visible the inequalities along lines of feminine and masculine, they also often reinforce patriarchal ideas about femininity and masculinity. Sex and gender become sedimented and a liberal idea of feminism is then implemented to address these gaps and inequalities. However, the global color line, intersectionality, and standpoint enable a wider analysis of the role of capitalism and global labor chains as determining which women and which men are able to be peacekeepers (Manchanda, 2022).

Challenging these patriarchal, racist-colonial, and martial attachments can also take place in relation to ideas about multiple masculinities. While Global South militaries are seen as offering up expedient and physical prowess en masse, it is evident that the UN itself capitalizes on idealized laboring bodies and male-dominated national militaries, and does little to challenge these patriarchal practices. On an earlier fieldwork trip, I and a research colleague visited the Bangladeshi battalion outside of Monrovia. Upon arrival we were told that the battalion base commander would like to see us after our visit with peacekeepers around the base. At some point a lower-ranking soldier suddenly came to us and relayed that the commander was ready to meet with us. We entered a portable cabin and patiently waited. We spent about thirty minutes waiting and were growing a bit frustrated with our compressed time schedule, for we needed to travel back to Monrovia before darkness fell. Suddenly the door to the cabin opened, and bathed in the sunlight was the commander. We were slightly taken aback by the commander's uniform, as it was quite common for those deployed to missions to wear field uniforms when not attending formal ceremonies or events. The commander was wearing military dress of a type that we were not accustomed to seeing. He had donned sunglasses, jodhpur-type trousers, and knee-high boots and carried a horsewhip, which he waved in the air, instructing his assistants to clear the path for him to enter, and for his full rank and status to be acknowledged by everyone in the room. All the soldiers present stood to attention, and I and my colleague wearily stood up to join in the collective acknowledgment, despite our lack of military qualifications. I do not recall what the broader topic of our conversation was, only that the commander was very keen to establish his authority, demonstrate his many achievements, and to emphasize the subservience of the command beneath him—which these soldiers obliged. He asked us about our own qualifications and geographic origins and nationalities. On the car journey back to Monrovia, we tried to make sense of this gendered and martial performance that seemed to us to be bordering on the parodic. We discussed whether the uniform itself was a hangover from the colonial era and whether we thought he had appropriated it with subversiveness or compliance. As discussed in earlier sections of this book, colonial and gendered stereotypes and Orientalist images of South Asian peacekeepers traveled extensively and were evident not only in the words of the peacekept, but had to be resisted in our own observations. We had to challenge our own tendency to read these performances as colonial and gendered mimicry or a form of blind acceptance of, in this case, British versions of martial warrior superiority. What was evident about the commander's performance of masculinity was that it was intended for us as foreign researchers and not for the eyes of the peacekept. Many of my observations that I have written about in this book demonstrate the gap that often exists between the everyday activities of peacekeepers and the everyday lives of the peacekept. Far away from these colonial performances of mimicry, the peacekept continue to live and die.

Challenging the fixity of gender requires an examination of how gender features in peacekeeping practices and how it is maintained by peacekeeping scholarship (Holvikivi, 2023). While it is true that in the making of martial gendered identities certain ideas about embodied gender and biological sex become sedimented, it is the performances of peacekeepers that makes the compelling case that gender alone is insufficient for analyzing how power works. Nevertheless, gendered ideas form the basis for how peacekeeping works. It is not disconnected from what we know about war making and the use of soldiers as its main agents (Cockburn, 2010). As Cohn and Ruddick argue: "The practice of war entails far more than the killing and destroying of armed combat itself. It requires the creation of a 'war system,' which entails arming, training, and organizing for possible wars; allocating the resources these preparations require; creating a culture in which wars are seen as morally legitimate, even alluring; and shaping and fostering the masculinities and femininities which undergird men's and women's acquiescence to war" (Cohn and Ruddick 2004 p. 4). Scholars interested in challenging the gendered basis of peacekeeping need to think beyond the binaries and to think about the multiple systems of oppression and how they impact peacekeepers and the peacekept.

The Gaze of Peacekeeping

> Focusing the gaze on the local realities somewhere there, far away, looking at the African and Balkan 'warlords' and their greed and cruelty, not only exonerates the West from its involvement in essentially global—not

> local—processes, but also makes invisible two important aspects of these processes: one is the growing militarization of global economies (as well as governance); another is what one might call the genderedness of these processes (Žarkov, 2008, p. 4).

I suggest that critical interventions in the peacekeeping scholarship provide the footing for thinking outside masculinist, martial-colonial ideologies and toward an abolitionist-inspired alternative. But why has the scholarship not thoroughly explored options outside of patriarchal, militarized, and colonial frames? This is because, as an epistemic project, peacekeeping reflects Enlightenment values, which are steeped in ideas about Europe (and subsequently the Global North) as the "superior" center of civilization, culture, and morality (Howell and Richter-Montpetit, 2019, 2020). Thus the construction of the "other" has not only produced Global South peacekeepers as suspect but the peacekept have been framed as objects of rescue and transformation. This occurs at the same time as the knowledges of the peacekept (as agents) has been firmly sidelined, at best, or worse, erased. Engaging with mainstream scholarship it is possible to discern how scholarship has reinforced dual aspects of the gaze: (1) it objectifies and appropriates the peacekept as a means to patriarchal-colonial-martial ends; (2) it epistemically positions the knowledge systems and values of the Global North as innately superior, and therefore morally and politically justified in assigning itself as the global police, and thereby obscures and delegitimizes any resistance that emerges from the peacekept to challenge peacekeeping power.

During my first field research trip to Haiti, my colleague and I spoke with Yvette, a doctor working for a local charitable organization in Port-au-Prince. She was Haitian-born but had been educated abroad, after which she had returned to work in Haiti, driven by a conviction that it was her duty to support her country and people affected by the conflict. She acknowledged her privilege and narrated how stressful life was for the majority of Haitians, many of whom were still suffering the widespread effects of trauma, when they came to her seeking medical treatment and health advice. For example, she had been mapping increasing rates of high blood pressure, diabetes, insomnia, and varying symptoms of post-traumatic stress disorder, as well as psychosomatic effects of living in situations of armed and criminal violence. These conditions—which included hair loss, skin irritations, and general fatigue and depression—and the generally poor state of health of Haitians have been extensively documented by a number of scholars; yet again, those writing on peacekeeping pay scant to no attention to these important accounts and the wider experiences of the peacekept (James, 2008, 2010a, 2010b; Maternowska, 2006; Farmer, 1996). Yvette's daily experiences and encounters with sick and traumatized Haitians who sought her help at her clinic—which was located near the "red zone" (Lemay-Hébert, 2017; Higate and Henry, 2009)—meant that her own stress levels were also considerably high. It was her understanding that the general levels of insecurity experienced by Haitian citizens had been exacerbated by either the overreaction or underreaction of military peacekeepers to gang-related violence (Henry and Higate, 2016). Yvette recounted her own recent violent experience when she had been kidnapped as she was about to enter her car outside the clinic. She believed that her mature age had possibly reminded the kidnappers of their own mothers and that she had been able to exploit this, for she was able to convince them to release her quickly. Yvette complained that she had been kidnapped in broad daylight, in front of the military peacekeepers who were stationed at a checkpoint near her clinic. She was also upset because when she went to speak with them about the insecurity in the area, she was astonished to discover that there was not one among the contingent's members able to speak to her in French. "Why," she asked, "did the UN think it was acceptable to send anglophone soldiers?"

Yvette's experience with peacekeepers demonstrates how the peacekept's experiences can expose some of the problematic ways in which peacekeeping is organized and operationalized. Peacekeeping troops are traditionally populated by a particular nation which offers its national forces to the UN Secretary General. Thus the UN relies on member states "volunteering" their militarized personnel, a factor that has previously been used to explain the low numbers of women peacekeepers (Narang and Liu, 2021). The UN does not select which national forces are put forward for peacekeeping operations, with the result that it has no control over the linguistic capabilities troops bring with them to the mission space. The imperative to get "boots on the ground" as quickly as possible overrides considerations about cultural, linguistic, or other sources of difference; in situations of conflict, the UN's primary mandate is to ensure that peacekeeping missions are swiftly and easily established and populated with military personnel whose presence acts as a highly visible, physical deterrent to ongoing violence. In essence, by martially commanding or occupying spaces under the authority of the Security Council, peacekeeping institutions legitimate the military-centered response to humanitarian "problems." While soldiers are being organized transnationally, smaller numbers of civilian personnel are recruited and dispatched. This peacekeeping design continually places the peacekept passively—as objects that require securing. That is, the peacekept become the referent object of the peacekeeping project. Here, the key thrust of my argument is that the peacekept, as imagined in the Global North peacekeeping gaze, remain excluded from European ideas of autonomous or agential subjects because the peacekept can only be understood through this viewpoint. Instead, the gaze reflects the epistemic centeredness of peacekeeping, all with its colonial, patriarchal, and martial roots.

Yvette's encounter with non-French-speaking peacekeepers was not an isolated instance. Among the Uruguayan battalion that I spent time with during fieldwork in the city of Cap-Haïtien, there was only a single officer with a fluent command of French. This officer was the main liaison between the battalion and other peacekeeping personnel outside of the contingent. The language barrier served to isolate the battalion from the local community in many respects, although there were attempts to find and attend local events and to befriend civilian peacekeepers who also spoke French and Spanish. In this case, the peacekept were also doubly disadvantaged as many did not—or would not—always speak French (the language of their former oppressors) and preferred to use Kreyol, although they almost all could understand French speakers, while the reverse was not the case. At the peacekeeping mission in Monrovia, the Indian women peacekeepers took the initiative to learn French and established and built bridges with local women where possible. By contrast, in Haiti, Uruguayan women peacekeepers were treated as their rank dictated and as such had very limited opportunity to interact with or to affect the peacekept in the everyday sense. Notably though, the fact that the Indian women peacekeepers had to navigate with limited mobility meant that their interactions with the peacekept were generally confined to formal and organized events.

Often the peacekept existed as seemingly mere photo opportunities for the UN newsletter. One woman's activist in Buchanan, in Liberia, told me that she had been featured on a number of UN posters and advertisements (some of which proudly hung in the large *palava* hut (village meeting space) that had been constructed through UN funding), but that concrete support for her community was conspicuously vanishing. Enloe, Razack, Cockburn and Žarkov, and Whitworth all demonstrate that the distance and proximity of peacekeepers to local populations is a site for scrutiny and analysis—and I argue this extends well beyond the physical presence of peacekeepers and to the lines of connectivity that feature in relation to economic support. What forms of coloniality, martiality, and gender structure the interactions that are made possible in a peacekeeping mission? "Miriam" refused to wait around for "long-term funding" and was committed to her community and doing work for survivors of gender-based violence because, as she stated, "Who else is going to do it?" Thus, while I highlight the ways in which the peacekept were "kept," there was also the inertia of countless grassroots organizations and ordinary citizens moving postconflict life forward.

Another example is drawn from fieldwork in Liberia. We traveled with Haile, a senior civilian peacekeeper, to a town that had a defunct steel manufacturing plant. Haile was responsible for enabling a large steel company's representative to come to Liberia in order to see whether they could establish a significant investment. In this case the UN civilian peacekeeper was responsible for analyzing what the potential "costs" would be for the community. Would an appropriate school be established for the children of workers? Would there be a negative environmental impact causing damage to property or harm to public health? In conducting the analysis Haile recounted all the benefits a private corporation could potentially bring to the area and to the lives of the peacekept. His job was to provide a list of possible obstacles (rights violations) and to help "smooth" the process for this foreign company to establish itself in the community. Haile was dismissive of consultation with the local community, whom he considered "too ignorant" to fully understand the impact of any such investments. He grew frustrated with having to answer local people's concerns about the amount of money that would be available for income, compensation, or fees for clinics, schools, and other institutions that were to be set up. Haile saw the peacekept as an "obstacle" in and of themselves, who could potentially sabotage their own futures by "scaring" off the company seeking to invest in the manufacturing plant and, by extension, in their community. He talked about the people of the community as infantile, their vision for the future stymied by long years of conflict, and unprepared to invest in their own futures through their own hard work. He bemoaned that the peacekept (not his term) had become exceptionally "dependent" on UN systems and other aid packages, a dependency that reinforced representations and discourses of the peacekept as objects of programs and policy. Yet, notwithstanding his views on the nation's dependence on foreign aid, Haile believed that foreign investors such as private corporations represented the only viable development solution to the long years of regional instability and insecurity in the region. He believed that increasing regional wealth would have a positive effect and smooth over all the inequalities that resulted from the "war."

Conclusion

> A decolonial feminist praxis requires that those from the imperialising/colonising side take heed of the anti-

colonial desires and directives of the colonised, rather than focusing on one's own liberation or telling the colonised how they need to liberate themselves.
(Shigematsu, 2015)

In synthesizing the previous analysis, I argue that by turning to critical scholarship, peacekeeping can be known by another name. In doing so, I suggest that the logical conclusions of engaging in critical race and postcolonial feminist accounts of the limits of gender as a single category provide a map to undoing gender as it is currently conceptualized in peacekeeping scholarship. This is not to dismiss scholarship that has drawn attention to gender and to men's and women's lived experiences, but to argue for taking the multiplexity of categories of difference and systems of oppression into greater account in the way peacekeeping knowledge is produced. This entails unpacking gender and its binary corollary of sex in order to see the ways gender can be used by institutions of power to distract from imperial desires that make themselves visible when the gaze is reversed. In deconstructing the fixing of gender and sex, it is possible to view the peacekept in more complex ways while at the same time recognizing the structural conditions under which they are situated in peacekeeping environments and their attempts to pursue the good life—perhaps in intention not so different from the Global South peacekeepers who are subject to the global color line.

A decolonial critique of peacekeeping does not have to implicate individual behaviors of peacekeepers. It is not to say that peacekeepers are all Global North military men, bent on exploiting the peacekept and erasing Indigenous knowledge systems. Rather, it is to say that peacekeeping is an epistemic project that centers Global North knowledge, reinforces geopolitical inequalities, and perpetuates an organizational system founded on violence. As such the foundations of peacekeeping enable colonial relations to persist in peacekeeping, rather than recede, over time. The critical work by a range of scholars, and the examples I provide from fieldwork, point to the endurance of colonial-style relationships rather than a move toward more mutually empathetic cooperation (Sylvester, 1994).

In this chapter I have also put forward an abolitionist alternative. This stems from the antimilitarist and peace work of feminist scholars and activists. In speaking from the perspective of those women who have experienced war and its devastating effects, scholars such as Cockburn, Žarkov, and Enloe insist that militarism cannot be pacified when soldiers are the main response to humanitarian crises. And Howell's account of martial politics shows that the martial has always and forever been present—there is no peace as long as it is allowed to be present.

Viewing peacekeeping as an epistemology could help to politicize the category of the peacekept, draw attention to the ways in which they are positioned within peacekeeping practices, and challenge the existence and operation of such humanitarian interventions. By turning to the work of critical theories it is possible to revitalize peacekeeping scholarship: to demand that scholars contributing to it actively position themselves in the field; and to demand that they are held to account when they consciously or unconsciously uphold colonial, martial, and patriarchal ideas within their capture of peacekeeping and the possible avenues for change in those contexts. If such critical theories are put to work, then the analysis shifts away from blaming local populations for the failure of a peacekeeping mission and provides the space to analyze how systems (racial, gender, and martial) keep some parties and actors in a perpetual state of marginality and powerlessness. This chapter examines what it would mean to decolonize, demilitarize, and degender the UN and its peacekeeping practices. What would it mean to challenge peacekeeping as an epistemic project, a field of study, and a site of empirical research? By drawing on the critical theories I discuss throughout and on my own empirical research, this chapter demonstrates that the marginality of the peacekept in peacekeeping is entirely congruent with its epistemic and political foundations.

CHAPTER 6

Toward Archives and Ends

The film *Quo Vadis, Aida?*, directed by Jasmila Žbanić and released in 2021, provides a critical reflection of what I have argued throughout this book—namely that peacekeeping is founded on problematic ideologies of gender, race, and the military. It is 1995 and Aida, the main protagonist of the film, provides translation services to Dutch military peacekeepers stationed near Srebrenica, in what is now Bosnia and Herzegovina. Despite her attempts to save her family members, Aida alone survives the genocidal events that take place in the presence of a United Nations peacekeeping mission during the Yugoslav conflict. Specifically, what the film demonstrates are the ways in which multiple forms of militarized masculinity and allegiance to military goals and institutions are foundational to the perpetration of gendered and racialized forms of violence. Importantly, this violence is enacted precisely after a peacekeeping mission has already been established, and when there is a widespread expectation of peace. However, as the film shows, peacekeeping is not a panacea for militarized conflict, nor is it the neutral humanitarian practice it often purports to be. The film captures how, despite the intentions of individual peacekeeping men, violence was inflicted on those who were under the watch of blue-helmeted, armed soldiers. As I have argued, peacekeeping is not innocent—it is a moral, political, and epistemic project that reflects global inequalities and systems of oppression, marginalization, and exclusion rather than one that evolves simply in response to conflict scenarios. This book sets out the multiple ways in which peacekeeping institutions enable the production of knowledge about those subject to peacekeeping policies and programs—the peacekept—and how the knowledges produced often replicate the relations of power found in the contexts of patriarchy, apartheid, segregation, and colonial rule. This analysis provides a new archive of knowledge about peacekeeping and potential alternative paths to peace. In addition, the book highlights the intentional identity work that peacekeepers engage in so that they themselves will be seen as worthy warriors, equipped with the relevant skills and capacities to take up peacekeeping tasks in a militarized market economy.

In the introductory chapter I outlined the ways in which peacekeeping has been written about to date, highlighting some key critical interventions in a literature which is most often concerned with changing how peacekeeping functions rather than challenging why and how it was established in the first place. However, within this scholarship can be found a collection of critical texts that interrogate the foundations of peacekeeping practice—namely feminist, postcolonial, and antimilitarist analyses. By returning to this critical body of work, I argue that peacekeeping can be repoliticized. Here the foundations of peacekeeping ideology and practice can be challenged, especially in regard to processes of racialization, coloniality, gender, and militarization that often are sidelined by attempts to measure operational effectiveness or efficiency. Through my years-long ethnographically inspired fieldwork, I use examples from my research to highlight the legacies of colonialism, militarism, and patriarchy, in particular, through accounts by peacekeepers and local people living and working in peacekeeping missions. I expose how theories such as intersectionality and standpoint allow for a broader understanding of the challenges that women peacekeepers face, and the limits of accounts that see sexism as the primary form of oppression in a given context. These concepts also allow for an accounting of global inequalities in labor, such that a global color line can be discerned when it comes to peacekeeping. This huge disjuncture in the peacekeeping labor provided by Global South troops, and women among them, reflects divisions of labor on a global scale. With the burden of military labor comes disproportionate military death—of course borne by those already positioned in geopolitically unequal ways. Who dies in the course of providing military service? Which peacekeepers' lives are expendable? Clearly, peacekeeping is not innocent.

When examining the contributions of feminist scholars, it is evident that peacekeeping has been a predominantly male military enterprise. In any analysis paying attention to gender alone, binaries are reinforced, problematic concepts like operational effectiveness are reproduced, and incidents of sexual exploitation and abuse end up acting as a foil for imperial activities. This is where an intersectional and postcolonial analysis can offer an important corrective. The legacy of gender and peacekeeping scholarship is a lack of in-depth analysis of other axes of difference and interlocking systems of oppression. In general, the ways in which women who have been victims of sexual violence in peacekeeping missions, or those who work in the sex industry, have been portrayed in peacekeeping scholarship, suggests a replication of colonial archetypes and relations.

And importantly, this links with cultures of martial masculinities and the obsession with military solutions to postconflict and peacekeeping problems. While feminist scholars have debated whether militarization creeps into everyday life or whether it was always at the heart of the state or global governance organizations, peacekeeping has both embraced its martial roots and called for an increase in war capabilities and technologies. In this way, some peacekeeping scholarship has been complicit with military industries and economies and subsequently has enabled geopolitical inequalities to be reinforced. Because peacekeeping has gained a somewhat noble status despite ongoing media exposés of sexual misconduct, abuse, and exploitation—as well as examples of inaction that have resulted in a large number of preventable deaths (as depicted in the film mentioned above)—its ideological roots in patriarchal, martial, and colonial thinking have been underscrutinized.

In synthesizing the examples and analysis of patriarchal, colonial, and martial peacekeeping practices, I suggest what decolonizing, degendering, and demilitarizing peacekeeping might mean for peacekeeping scholarship. In committing to decolonization I ask readers to think critically about how single-axis analyses mask the wider political effects of peacekeeping on the peacekept. The UN's investment in gender goes beyond a feminist commitment; it also contributes to maintaining rigid versions of gender and sex that reify gender roles and norms that suit instrumentalist martial ends. For example, the arguments that women's integration into peacekeeping does not compromise operational effectiveness contributes to a normalization of martial institutional cultures and related professional standards. That peacekeeping men's potential "operational ineffectiveness" is never measured says something about the ongoing epistemic inequalities built into peacekeeping. Can the "mediocre man" syndrome (Besley et al., 2017) be applied here? Finally, I point to issues around demilitarization and draw briefly on abolitionist perspectives more generally. When Crenshaw reveals how women killed by police in the US are regularly invisibilized, it is clear that calls for defunding the police might also be applied to peacekeeping settings where martial power has had disastrous consequences, such as documented by Razack in the context of Somalia (Crenshaw et al., 2015; Razack 2004).

Abolitionist Ends

Throughout the book I have made clear that abolitionist perspectives have seldomly been indulged in the peacekeeping scholarship. In coming to the rightful conclusion that abolition should be considered, nay, adopted, as the primary conceptual and political lens through which to view peacekeeping, it will not be a surprise that I have been inspired by the work of Black feminist theorists, critical race scholars, decolonial and postcolonial thinkers, and radical Marxist activists as well as Afropessimist, anti-carceral, and abolitionist advocates. Scholars such as Razack, drawing on critical race theories, along with Crenshaw and Davis, have argued for paying attention to the racialized and colonial roots of martial systems (Crenshaw 1989; Davis 1981). While Crenshaw and Davis focus on police and prison brutality against those on the margins, I believe that the work of such scholars provides a strong political basis for arguing against the continuation of peacekeeping, at least in its present form.

While abolitionists trace the movement's origins to eighteenth-century campaigns advocating the ending of the trade in slavery and enslavement in Europe and the Americas, it also owes a debt to the civil rights movement in the US (Davis, 1981; Crenshaw, 1989, 1990). It is well established from this literature that marginalized and racialized communities in the US are at greater risk from police violence (Combahee River Collective, 1995, 1983). When applied to the peacekeeping context, these perspectives provide the tools for thinking about the founding principles, epistemologies, and the subsequent wider structural framework within which the peacekept are situated. Thinking with abolitionist perspectives, then, means that acknowledging the marginality of the peacekept and the unequal relations between Global North governance designers and those deployed to discipline the peacekept, mirror colonial-style relations. To deny the legacies of colonialism in the present is to maintain the myth of some nations and regions as organically peaceful, developed, and disciplined.

In Razack's concluding chapter, she reorients the discussion away from the issue of how to "fix" peacekeeping (Razack 2004). This is a question that has been posed to me on a number of occasions. The framings are often "but if the military is an established institution, should we not make it less violent?" Or, "peacekeeping happens whether we like it or not, so shouldn't we make it better?" And even "people in conflict-affected countries *want* peacekeeping, so isn't withdrawing it a form of colonialism itself? How can we witness the disintegration of a country, and *do nothing*?" As I argued earlier, our affective attachments to rescue often obscure the foundationally problematic roots of peacekeeping and the legacies it engenders today. Subscribing to antiracism, decolonial feminism, and pacifism requires political commitment and moral judgements; I believe that to take abolition seriously requires making visible those cracks where militarization seeps in or has already taken root and become sedimented (Fanon, 1963). Black feminist theory can school scholars in peacekeeping and other fields to extend our critical lenses to those more mundane and presumably benign responses to global crises.

Archives

The book draws on many years of fieldwork, conversations, participant observation, and archival documents. In this final chapter I suggest that by navigating through the scholarship with a different viewpoint, it is possible to imagine a different peace future, one that does not need to uphold patriarchal, colonial, and martial frames. The problem-solving approach to peacekeeping continually asks the wrong question: "How can peacekeeping be made better?" Reforming peacekeeping will not attend to the issues of coloniality that persist, or the problematic framing of those women who sell sex to peacekeepers as quintessential victims of gender inequalities, for example. And will the foundations of peacekeeping be interrogated and studied as a means to an alternative future? This would require giving up the Global North's privileged gaze, the investments in and attachments to ideas that if women were integrated, then peacekeeping could be so much better, and the insidious and dangerous idea that more military might will protect vulnerable peacekeepers in the face of new security challenges. But the way to overcome the incessant loop of continually tinkering with peacekeeping as practice, as reflected in the scholarship, is to make an epistemic journey back in time—that is, to *pay "citational and intellectual debts"* to scholars such as Enloe, Žarkov, Razack, Whitworth, Mazurana et al., and Cockburn (Madhok, 2020). The second way is to continue to speak to the coloniality ever present in peacekeeping scholarship. This is evident in the ways in which narratives around duty to nations continually romanticize peacekeeping service. This framing of peacekeeping fails to account for the unequal division of peacekeeping labor in which individuals become the "speaking commodities" of the UN (Moten, 2003; Jones, 2015). It is Global South men and women—those racialized in global politics as inferior—who bear the burden of peacekeeping duty and death. The third way is to imagine what peace might look like without militaries and militarized bodies. Why has peacekeeping scholarship been so wedded to militarism? Drawing on the melancholic responses of a range of peacekeepers, I provide evidence that the military itself is an institution that provides contradictory experiences. Finally, if the peacekept were recentered it would become increasingly clear that military solutions are not sustainable in postconflict societies. Without massive infrastructural change and social transformation, the peacekept cannot determine their own paths toward peace. And this is not to romanticize the peacekept, either, but instead to imagine alternatives that do not replicate the models of coloniality that have already existed and created widespread inequality.

Ultimately, because peacekeeping is an epistemic project it needs to be understood through critical concepts and theories. What better way to reimagine and repoliticize peacekeeping studies than to return to key contributions that have been epistemically marginalized? What of the work of feminist scholars that pointed to the male domination of peacekeeping? What of the critiques of peacekeeping as that which replicates colonial violence? And what about the scholars advocating for less military and more civilian focus? Or those suggesting that our investments in the martial cannot be separated from patriarchal and colonial logic? Can peacekeeping be demilitarized any more than it can be decolonized? Peacekeeping studies is a critical repository of knowledge about gender, race, and the martial. It tells us a great deal about the endurance of systems: patriarchy, racism and colonialism, and militarization. The ways in which these systems of power continue in contexts where peace is supposed to prevail. It is only by revisiting this critical history that we can move meaningfully toward a just and political end goal: the abolition of peacekeeping.

Quo Vadis, Aida? demonstrates that, in fact, in its attempts to remain committed to martial mandates, the UN actually enabled Serbian forces to continue to kill men and boys who could and should have been protected. The UN forces did not remain the neutral harbingers of peace they believed themselves to be. In the previous chapters, I have tried to demonstrate that peacekeeping is not a naturally peaceful response to war but an epistemic project that judges who should provide peace and who should be protected. The mainstream scholarship continues to reproduce colonial ideas about nations; about the character of war, conflict, and humanity; and about workers from the Global South and their capacities to hold up martial power in the name of individual social and national political mobility. Unfortunately, as rich as the literature on peacekeeping is, mainstream scholarship is dominated by approaches that do not pay sufficient attention to the patriarchal, colonial, and martial relations that are produced and sustained by peacekeeping as an institution, organization, industry, and practice. This book questions whether we can come to know peacekeeping differently, and consequently think of the prospect of peacekeeping's end.

NOTES

Chapter 1

1. Approximately 193 member states make up the United Nations as part of the General Assembly. They are granted membership by the General Assembly and on the recommendation of the Security Council (Berridge and Lloyd, 2012).

2. Economic and Social Research Council New Security Challenges Programme Grant (RES-223-25-0061).

3. The *peacekept* generally refers to those individuals who are nationals of the postconflict country (or countries) where a peacekeeping mission has been established and are the beneficiaries of peacekeeping programs, policies, and, in some cases, ultimate power. The term is first used by Clapham in *Being Peacekept* (Clapham, 1998).

4. It is important to note that there are a number of works preceding this period (from 2002 on) that do offer critical perspectives on peacekeeping. I have not included an exhaustive list but have focused on some formative texts that remain consistently ignored in contemporary peacekeeping studies. This curious omission is what I seek to address, and to understand why certain critical approaches remain less co-optable yet are compelling in political terms. Some of these texts that I have not summarised in this chapter but remain important include N. J. Wheeler, *Saving Strangers: Humanitarian Intervention in International Society* (Oxford: Oxford University Press, 2000); O. Ramsbotham and T. Woodhouse, *Humanitarian Intervention in Contemporary Conflict: A Reconceptualization* (Cambridge: Polity Press, 1996); F. Debrix, *Re-envisioning Peacekeeping: The United Nations and the Mobilization of Ideology* (Minneapolis: University of Minnesota Press, 1999); J. W. Burton, *Violence Explained* (Manchester: Manchester University Press, 1997); M. Duffield, *Global Governance and the New Wars: The Merging of Development and Security* (London: Zed Books, 2001); and M. Duffield, "NGO Relief in War Zones: Towards an Analysis of the New Aid Paradigm," *Third World Quarterly* 18, no. 3 (1999): 527–542.

5. Relia and Miha are pseudonyms as are all named participants throughout.

6. MINUSTAH fact sheet, https://peacekeeping.un.org/en/mission/minustah (accessed 27 December 2022).

7. https://ebolaresponse.un.org/liberia and https://peacekeeping.un.org/en/story-of-unmil-book-ebola-counties (accessed 27 December 2022).

8. Civilian peacekeepers are hired through a specific UN-run recruitment process and do not have any standing or professional affiliations with militaries.

Chapter 2

1. Thanks to Jenny Tan and Cecily Jones for this suggested framing.

2. D. Millhon, "Thai Restaurant Thrives in War-Torn Kabul," ABCNews.go.com, 16 July 2003 https://abcnews.go.com/International/story?id=79453&page=1 (accessed 29 December 2021).

3. S. Boseley, "Why Haiti's Cholera Epidemic May Last for Years," *Guardian*, 12 November 2010 https://www.theguardian.com/world/2010/nov/12/cholera-haiti (accessed 4 January 2022).

4. Peacekeepers from Eastern Europe often self-identified as white but also simultaneously described themselves as coming from the second world.

5. Currency estimates in US dollars.

6. Medal parade ceremonies are places where military and police peacekeepers receive medals from the UN's Special Representatives, commending their service and duty.

7. https://www.reuters.com/world/africa/islamist-militia-kills-malawian-peacekeeper-east-congo-un-2021-05-10/ (accessed 4 January 2022).

8. https://www.nytimes.com/2006/01/08/world/americas/chief-of-un-troops-in-haiti-is-found-dead-in-hotel-room.html (accessed 4 January 2022).

9. Lavalas supporters are those that generally backed Aristide's bid for leadership of Haiti.

Chapter 3

1. I use "women" and "men" and sometimes "female" and "male" throughout the book to encompass and include those that self-identify by using either term.

2. Although some of the peacekeepers I spoke with are from Eastern Europe, I classify them alongside peacekeepers from countries such as Nepal, Bangladesh, Nigeria, Ghana, and the Philippines. While this is problematic in terms of racialization, their inclusion within the category is primarily based on their socioeconomic situatedness and dependence on this form of transnational income.

3. See also C. B. Davies, "A Black Left Feminist View on Cedric Robinson's Black Marxism," *Black Perspectives*, 10 November 2016, https://www.aaihs.org/a-black-left-feminist-view-on-cedric-robinsons-black-marxism/; and C. L. R. James, "The Revolutionary Answer to the Negro Problem in the United States," 1948, https://www.marxists.org/archive/james-clr/works/1948/revolutionary-answer.htm.

4. When referring to soldiers I include any security sector forces including police, probation, fireservice and coastguard.

5. Kinouani, G. *Open Democracy* November 2016 https://www.opendemocracy.net/en/author/guilaine-kinouani/ (accessed 30 July 2021).

Chapter 4

Epigraph: Suheir Hammad, "What I Will," http://www.youtube.com/watch?v=LFbE8RBhSDw.

Mike Subritzky, NZATMC—AP Lima 1979, Kiwi Peacekeepers: https://www.angelfire.com/wa/warpoetry/Michael.html.

1. https://srebrenicaisdutchhistory.com/content/uploads/2020/07/SrebrenicaisDutchhistory_manifest.pdf (accessed 30 July 2021).

Chapter 5

1. Agatha used the term "woman" and thus I use this term rather than "girl."

BIBLIOGRAPHY

Abrahamsen, R., *Disciplining Democracy: Development Discourse and Good Governance in Africa*. London: Zed Books, 2000.

Adebajo, A., *Liberia's Civil War: Nigeria, ECOMOG, and Regional Security in West Africa*. London: Lynne Rienner Publishers, 2002.

Agathangelou, A. and Ling, L. M., "Desire Industries: Sex Trafficking, UN Peacekeeping and the Neo-liberal World Order." *Brown Journal of World Affairs* 10, no. 4 (2003): 133–148.

Ahmed, S., *Living a Feminist Life*. Durham: Duke University Press, 2016.

Alexandra, K., "Peacekeepers' Privilege and Sexual Abuse in Post-conflict Populations." *Peace Review* 23, no. 3 (2011): 369–376.

Anzaldúa, G., *Borderlands/La Frontera: The New Mestiza*. San Francisco: Aunt Lute Books, 1987.

Autesserre, S., *The Trouble with the Congo: Local Violence and the Failure of International Peacebuilding*. Cambridge: Cambridge University Press, 2010.

———, *Peaceland: Conflict Resolution and the Everyday Politics of International Intervention*. Cambridge: Cambridge University Press, 2014.

———, *The Frontlines of Peace: An Insider's Guide to Changing the World*. New York: Oxford University Press, 2021.

Baaz, M. and Stern, M., *Sexual Violence as a Weapon of War? Perceptions, Prescriptions, Problems in the Congo and Beyond*. London: Zed Books, 2013.

Baker, C., *Race and the Yugoslav Region: Postsocialist, Post-conflict, Postcolonial?* Manchester: Manchester University Press, 2018.

Barkawi, T., *Soldiers of Empire*. Cambridge: Cambridge University Press, 2017.

Basham, V., *War, Identity and the Liberal State: Everyday Experiences of the Geopolitical in the Armed Forces*. London: Routledge, 2013.

———, "Liberal Militarism as Insecurity, Desire and Ambivalence: Gender, Race and the Everyday Geopolitics of War." *Security Dialogue* 49, nos.1–2 (2018): 32–43.

Bastick, M. and Duncanson, C., "Agents of Change? Gender Advisors in NATO Militaries." *International Peacekeeping* 25, no. 4 (2018): 554–577.

Belkin, A., *Bring Me Men: Military Masculinity and the Benign Facade of American Empire, 1898–2001*. New York: Columbia University Press, 2012.

Bellamy, A., Williams, P. and Griffin, S., *Understanding Peacekeeping*. Cambridge: Polity, 2010.

Ben-Ari, E. and Elron, E., "Blue Helmets and White Armor Multi-nationalism and Multi-culturalism Among UN Peacekeeping Forces." *City and Society* 13, no. 2 (2001): 271–302.

Bennike, K. and Stoltz, P., "Peacekeeping Masculinities, Intersectionality, and Gender Equality: Negotiations of Military Life and Civilian Life by Danish Soldier/Veteran-Parents." *NORMA* 17, no. 1 (2022): 5–20.

Berdal, M. and Ucko, D., "The Use of Force in UN Peacekeeping Operations: Problems and Prospects." *RUSI Journal* 160, no. 1 (2015): 6–12.

Bergman Rosamond, A. and Kronsell, A., "Cosmopolitan Militaries and Dialogic Peacekeeping: Danish and Swedish Women Soldiers in Afghanistan." *International Feminist Journal of Politics* 20, no. 2 (2018): 172–187.

Berlant, L., *Cruel Optimism*. Durham: Duke University Press, 2011.

Berridge, G. and Lloyd, L., *The Palgrave Macmillan Dictionary of Diplomacy*. New York: Springer, 2012.

Besley, T., Folke, O., Persson, T. and Rickne, J., "Gender Quotas and the Crisis of the Mediocre Man: Theory and Evidence from Sweden." *American Economic Review* 107, no. 8 (2017): 2204–2242.

Bridges, D. and Horsfall, D., "Increasing Operational Effectiveness in UN Peacekeeping: Toward a Gender-Balanced Force." *Armed Forces and Society* 36, no. 1 (2009): 120–130.

Carby, H., "'On the Threshold of Woman's Era': Lynching, Empire, and Sexuality in Black Feminist Theory." *Critical Inquiry* 12, no. 1 (1985): 262–277.

Carreiras, H., "Gendered Culture in Peacekeeping Operations." *International Peacekeeping* 17 (2010): 471–485.

Chandler, D., *Bosnia: Faking Democracy After Dayton*. London: Pluto Press, 1999.

Chisholm, A., "Marketing the Gurkha Security Package: Colonial Histories and Neoliberal Economies of Private Security." *Security Dialogue* 45, no. 4 (2014): 349–372.

———, *The Gendered and Colonial Lives of Gurkhas in Private Security*. Edinburgh: Edinburgh University Press, 2022.

Chopra, R., "Invisible Men: Masculinity, Sexuality, and Male Domestic Labor." *Men and Masculinities* 9, no. 2. (2006): 152–167.

Clapham, C., "Being Peacekept." In O. Furley and R. May, eds., *Peacekeeping in Africa*, 303–319. s.l.: Routledge, 1998.

Cockburn, C., "A Continuum of Violence: A Gender Perspective on War and Peace." In W. G. A. Hyndman, ed., *Sites of Violence: Gender and Conflict Zones*. Berkeley: University of California Press, 2004.

———, *From Where We Stand: War, Women's Activism and Feminist Analysis*. London: Bloomsbury, 2008.

———, "Gender Relations as Causal in Militarization and War: A Feminist Standpoint." *International Feminist Journal of Politics* 12, no. 2 (2010): 139–157.

Cockburn, C. and Hubic, M., "Gender and the Peacekeeping Military: A View from Bosnian Women's Organizations." In C. Cockburn and D. Žarkov, eds., *The Postwar Moment: Militaries, Masculinities and International Peacekeeping.* London: Lawrence and Wishart, 2002, 103–121.

Cockburn, C. and Žarkov, D., eds., *The Postwar Moment: Militaries, Masculinities and International Peacekeeping.* London: Lawrence and Wishart, 2002.

Cohn, C., "Sex and Death in the Rational World of Defense Intellectuals." *Signs: Journal of Women in Culture and Society* 12, no. 4 (1987): 687–718.

Cohn, C., and Ruddick, S. "A Feminist Ethical Perspective on Weapons of Mass Destruction." *Ethics and Weapons of Mass Destruction*, (2004), 405–35.

Cold-Ravnkilde, S. and Albrecht, P., "National Interests as Friction: Peacekeeping in Somalia and Mali." *Journal of Intervention and Statebuilding* 14, no. 2 (2020): 204–220.

Cold-Ravnkilde, S., Albrecht, P. and Haugegaard, R., "Friction and Inequality Among Peacekeepers in Mali." *RUSI Journal* 162, no. 2 (2017): 34–42.

Combahee River Collective, "Statement." In B. Smith, ed., *Home Girls: A Black Feminist Anthology.* New Brunswick, NJ: Rutgers University Press, 1983, 264–274.

———, "A Black Feminist Statement." In B. Guy-Sheftal, ed., *Words of Fire: An Anthology of African-American Feminist Thought.* New York: New Press, 1995, 231–240.

Collins, P. H., "Learning from the Outsider Within: The Sociological Significance of Black Feminist Thought." *Social Problems* 33, no. 6 (1986): 14–32.

———, *Black Feminist Thought: Knowledge, Consciousness, and the Politics of Empowerment.* New York: Routledge, 2002.

Courtemanche, G., *A Sunday at the Pool in Kigali.* Montreal: Canongate Books, 2004.

Crenshaw, K., "Demarginalizing the Intersection of Race and Sex: A Black Feminist Critique of Antidiscrimination Doctrine, Feminist Theory and Antiracist Politics." *University of Chicago Legal Forum* (1989): 139–167.

———, "Mapping the Margins: Intersectionality, Identity Politics, and Violence Against Women of Color." *Stanford Law Review* 43, no. 6 (1990): 1241–1299.

Crenshaw, K., et al. *Say Her Name: Resisting Police Brutality Against Black Women.* New York: African American Policy Forum and Center for Intersectionality and Social Policy Studies, 2015.

Cruz, C., Phillips, W. and Cusimano, S., *Improving Security of United Nations Peacekeepers: We Need to Change the Way We Are Doing Business.* New York: United Nations, 2017.

Cunliffe, P., *Legions of Peace: UN Peacekeepers from the Global South.* London: Hurst, 2013.

Davis, A., "Reflections on the Black Woman's Role in the Community of Slaves." *Black Scholar* 12, no. 6 (1981): 2–15.

Davis, K., "Intersectionality as a Buzzword: A Sociology of Science Perspective on What Makes a Feminist Theory Successful." *Feminist Theory* 9, no. 1 (2008): 67–85.

Dayal, A., *Incredible Commitments: How UN Peacekeeping Failures Shape Peace Processes*. Cambridge: Cambridge University Press, 2021.

De Coning, C., Aoi, C. and Karlsrud, J., eds., *UN Peacekeeping Doctrine in a New Era: Adapting to Stabilisation, Protection and New Threats*. London: Taylor and Francis, 2017.

De Heredia, M. I., "Militarism, States and Resistance in Africa: Exploring Colonial Patterns in Stabilisation Missions." *Conflict, Security and Development* 19, no. 6 (2019): 623–644.

de Leeuw, M., "A Gentlemen's Agreement: Srebrenica in the Context of Dutch War History." In C. Cockburn and D. Žarkov, eds., *The Postwar Moment*. London: Lawrence and Wishart, 2002, 162–182.

DeGroot, G., "A Few Good Women: Gender Stereotypes, the Military and Peacekeeping." *International Peacekeeping* 8, no. 2 (2001): 23–38.

Diehl, P., "Peacekeeping Operations and the Quest for Peace." *Political Science Quarterly* 103, no. 3 (1988): 485–507.

Doezema, J., "Loose Women or Lost Women? The Re-emergence of the Myth of White Slavery in Contemporary Discourses of Trafficking in Women." *Gender Issues* 18, no. 1 (1999): 23–50.

Du Bois, W. E. B., *The Souls of Black Folk*. 1903; repr., New York: Fawcett, 2003.

———, "The African Roots of War." *Atlantic Monthly* 115, no. 5 (1915): 707–714.

Duffey, T., "Cultural Issues in Contemporary Peacekeeping." *International Peacekeeping* 7, no. 1 (2000): 142–168.

Duffield, M., "Governing the Borderlands: Decoding the Power of Aid." *Disasters* 25, no. 4 (2001): 308–320.

Duncanson, C., *Forces for Good? Military Masculinities and Peacebuilding in Afghanistan and Iraq*. New York: Palgrave Macmillan, 2013.

Dyvik, S., "'Valhalla Rising': Gender, Embodiment and Experience in Military Memoirs." *Security Dialogue* 47, no. 2 (2016): 133–150.

Elson, D. and Pearson, R., "'Nimble Fingers Make Cheap Workers': An Analysis of Women's Employment in Third World Export Manufacturing." *Feminist Review* 7, no. 1 (1981): 87–107.

Enloe, C., "Police and Military in Ulster: Peacekeeping or Peace-Subverting Forces?" *Journal of Peace Research* 15, no. 3 (1978): 243–258.

———, *Does Khaki Become You? The Militarisation of Women's Lives*. Boston: South End Press, 1983.

———, *Bananas, Beaches and Bases: Making Feminist Sense of International Politics*. London: Pandora, 1989.

———, *The Morning After: Sexual Politics at the End of the Cold War*. Los Angeles: University of California Press, 1993.

———, *Maneuvers: The International Politics of Militarizing Women's Lives*. Los Angeles: University of California Press, 2000.

Evasdottir, E. E., *Obedient Autonomy: Chinese Intellectuals and the Achievement of Orderly Life*. Vancouver: UBC Press, 2004.

Fanon, F., *The Wretched of the Earth*. Middlesex: Penguin Books, 1963.

Farmer, P., "On Suffering and Structural Violence: A View from Below." *Daedalus* 125, no. 1 (1996): 261–283.

Fetherston, A. *Towards a Theory of United Nations Peacekeeping*. London: Palgrave Macmillan, 1994.

Fetherston, A. and Nordstrom, C., "Overcoming Habitus in Conflict Management: UN Peacekeeping and War Zone Ethnography." *Peace and Change* 20, no. 1 (1995): 94–119.

Finnemore, M., "Paradoxes in Humanitarian Intervention." In R. Price, ed., *Moral Limit and Possibility in World Politics*. Cambridge: Cambridge University Press, 2008, 197–224.

Fisher, J. and Wilén, N., *African Peacekeeping*. Cambridge: Cambridge University Press, 2022.

Frühstück, S. and Ben-Ari, E., "'Now We Show It All!' Normalization and the Management of Violence in Japan's Armed Forces." *Journal of Japanese Studies* 28, no. 1 (2002): 1–39.

Fujishige, H., Uesuigi, Y. and Honda, T., "The Evolution of Japan's Peacekeeping Policy, 1992–2012." In H. Fujishige, Y. Uesuigi and T. Honda, eds., *Japan's Peacekeeping at a Crossroads*. New York: Palgrave Macmillan, 2022, 39–60.

Goldstein, J., *War and Gender: How Gender Shapes the War System and Vice Versa*. Cambridge: Cambridge University Press, 2001.

Hall, S., "Encoding/Decoding." In S. Hall, D. Hobson, A. Lowe and P. Willis, eds., *Culture, Media, Language: Working Papers in Cultural Studies, 1972–79*. London: Hutchinson, 1980, 128–138.

———, "The Problem of Ideology: Marxism Without Guarantees." In K. Chen and D. Morley, eds., *Stuart Hall: Critical Dialogues in Cultural Studies*. London: Routledge, 1996, 24–45.

Haraway, D., "Situated Knowledges: The Science Question in Feminism and the Privilege of Partial Perspective." *Feminist Studies* 14, no. 3 (1988): 575–599.

Harrington, C., *Politicization of Sexual Violence: From Abolitionism to Peacekeeping*. London: Ashgate, 2010.

———, "United Nations Policy on Sexual Exploitation and Abuse: Problematizations and Performances." *Critical Social Policy* 42, no. 3 (2022): 469–489.

Hasanbasic, J., "Liability in Peacekeeping Missions: A Civil Cause of Action for the Mothers of Srebrenica Against the Dutch Government and the United Nations." *Emory International Law Review* 29 (2014): 415–450.

Heinecken, L., "Are Women 'Really' Making a Unique Contribution to Peacekeeping? The Rhetoric and the Reality." *Journal of International Peacekeeping* 19, nos. 3–4 (2015): 227–248.

Henry, M., "Peacexploitation? Interrogating Labour Hierarchies and Global Sisterhood Among Indian and Ururguayan Female Peacekeepers." *Globalization* 9, no. 1 (2012): 15–33.

———, 'Sexual Exploitation and Abuse in UN Peacekeeping Missions: Problematising Current Responses. In S. Madhok, A. Phillips and K. Wilson, eds., *Gender, Agency and Coercion*. London: Palgrave Macmillan, 2013, 122–142.

———, "Parades, Parties and Pests: Contradictions of Everyday Life in Peacekeeping Economies." *Journal of Intervention and Statebuilding* 9, no. 3 (2015): 372–390.

———, "Problematizing Military Masculinity, Intersectionality and Male Vulnerability in Feminist Critical Military Studies." *Critical Military Studies* 3, no. 2 (2017): 182–199.

———, "Keeping the Peace: Gender, Geopolitics and Global Governance Interventions." *Conflict, Security and Development* 19, no. 3 (2019): 263–268.

———, "On the Necessity of Critical Race Feminism for Women, Peace and Security." *Critical Studies on Security* 9, no. 1 (2021): 22–26.

Henry, M. and Higate, P., "Peacekeeping Power Practices and Women's Insecurity in Haiti." In M. Stephenson and L. Zanotti, eds., *Building Walls and Dissolving Borders: The Challenges of Alterity, Community and Securitizing Space*. New York: Routledge, 2016, 133–154.

Henry, M., Higate, P. and Sanghera, G., "Positionality and Power: The Politics of Peacekeeping Research." *International Peacekeeping* 16, no. 4 (2009): 467–482.

Higate, P. and Henry, M., "Engendering (In)security in Peace Support Operations." *Security Dialogue* 35, no. 4 (2004): 481–498.

———, *Insecure Spaces: Peacekeeping, Power and Performance in Haiti, Kosovo and Liberia*. London: Zed Books, 2009.

———, "Space, Performance and Everyday Security in the Peacekeeping Context." *International Peacekeeping* 17, no. 1 (2010): 32–48.

Holmes, G., "Situating Agency, Embodied Practices and Norm Implementation in Peacekeeping Training." *International Peacekeeping* 26, no. 1 (2019): 55–84.

Holvikivi, A., "Training the Troops on Gender: The Making of a Transnational Practice." *International Peacekeeping* 28, no. 2 (2021): 175–199.

———, "Contending with Paradox: Feminist Investments in Gender Training." *Signs: Journal of Women in Culture and Society* 48, no. 3 (2023): 533–555.

hooks, b., *Ain't I a Woman: Black Women and Feminism*. Boston: South End Press, 1981.

Howard, L., *Power in Peacekeeping*. Cambridge: Cambridge University Press, 2019.

Howell, A., "Forget 'Militarization:' Race, Disability and 'Martial Politics' of the Police and of the University." *International Feminist Journal of Politics* 20, no. 2 (2018): 117–136.

Howell, A. and Richter-Montpetit, M., "Racism in Foucauldian Security Studies: Biopolitics, Liberal War, and the Whitewashing of Colonial and Racial Violence." *International Political Sociology* 13, no. 1(2019): 2–19.

———, "Is Securitization Theory Racist? Civilizationism, Methodological Whiteness, and Antiblack Thought in the Copenhagen School." *Security Dialogue* 51, no. 1 (2020): 3–22.

Hull, G., Scott, P. and Smith, B., eds., *All the Women Are White, All the Blacks Are Men, but Some of Us Are Brave: Black Women's Studies*. New York: Feminist Press, 1982.

Hultman, L., Kathman, D. and Shannon, M., *Peacekeeping in the Midst of War*. Oxford: Oxford University Press, 2019.
Human Rights Watch, *Hopes Betrayed: Trafficking of Women and Girls to Post-Conflict Bosnia and Herzegovina for Forced Prostitution*. New York: Human Rights Watch, 2002.
Hyde, A., "The Present Tense of Afghanistan: Accounting for Space, Time and Gender in Processes of Militarisation." *Gender, Place and Culture* 23, no. 6 (2016): 857–868.
James, C. L. R., *The Black Jacobins: Toussaint L'Ouverture and the San Domingo Revolution*. London: Secker & Warburg, 1938.
James, E., "Haunting Ghosts: Madness, Gender, and Ensekirite in Haiti in the Democratic Era." In M. DelVecchio Good, S. Hyde, S. Pinto and B. Good, eds., *Postcolonial Disorders*. Los Angeles: University of California Press, 2008, 132–156.
———, *Democratic Insecurities*. Los Angeles: University of California Press, 2010a.
———, "Ruptures, Rights, and Repair: The Political Economy of Trauma in Haiti." *Social Science and Medicine* 70, no. 1 (2010b): 106–113.
Jenne, N. and Ulloa Bisshopp, F., "Female Peacekeepers: UNSC Resolution 1325 and the Persistence of Gender Stereotypes in the Chilean Armed Forces." *International Peacekeeping* 28, no. 1 (2021): 134–159.
Jennings, K., "Unintended Consequences of Intimacy: Political Economies of Peacekeeping and Sex Tourism." *International Peacekeeping* 17, no. 2 (2010): 229–243.
———, "Service, Sex, and Security: Gendered Peacekeeping Economies in Liberia and the Democratic Republic of the Congo." *Security Dialogue* 45, no. 4 (2014): 313–330.
———, "Blue Helmet Havens: Peacekeeping as Bypassing in Liberia and the Democratic Republic of the Congo." *International Peacekeeping* 23, no. 2 (2016): 302–325.
———, "Conditional Protection? Sex, Gender, and Discourse in UN Peacekeeping." *International Studies Quarterly* 63, no. 1 (2019): 30–42.
Jones, J., "Black Radical Masculinities in American Warfare: Reconfiguring Resistance in the Body of Muhammad Ali Towards Exile." *NORMA* 10, nos. 3–4 (2015): 265–280.
Kachtan, D., "'Acting Ethnic'—Performance of Ethnicity and the Process of Ethnicization." *Ethnicities* 17, no. 5 (2017): 707–726.
Kandiyoti, D., "Bargaining with Patriarchy." *Gender and Society* 2, no. 3 (1988): 274–290.
Kaplan, D., "Women as Caretaker: An Archetype Which Supports Patriarchal Militarism." *Hypatia* 9, no. 2 (1994): 123–133.
Kappler, S., and Lemay-Hébert, N. "From Power-Blind Binaries to the Intersectionality of Peace: Connecting Feminism and Critical Peace and Conflict Studies." In *Feminist Interventions in Critical Peace and Conflict Studies*. Routledge, 2021, 34–50.

Karim, S., "Re-evaluating Peacekeeping Effectiveness: Does Gender Neutrality Inhibit Progress?" *International Interactions* 43, no. 5 (2017): 822–847.

Karim, S. and Beardsley, K., *Equal Opportunity Peacekeeping: Women, Peace, and Security in Post-conflict States*. Oxford: Oxford University Press, 2017.

Kihara-Hunt, A., *Holding UNPOL to Account: Individual Criminal Accountability of United Nations Police Personnel*. Boston: Brill, 2017.

Koester, D., "Gendered Legacies of Peacekeeping: Implications of Trafficking for Forced Prostitution in Bosnia–Herzegovina." *International Peacekeeping* 27, no. 1 (2020): 35–43.

Kolbe, A. and Hutson, R., "Human Rights Abuse and Other Criminal Violations in Port-au-Prince, Haiti: A Random Survey of Households." *Lancet* 368, no. 9538 (2006): 864–873.

Kostovicova, D., Bojicic-Dzelilovic, V. and Henry, M., "Drawing on the Continuum: A War and Post-war Political Economy of Gender-Based Violence in Bosnia and Herzegovina." *International Feminist Journal of Politics* 22 no. 2 (2020): 250–272.

Kothari, U., "Authority and Expertise: The Professionalisation of International Development and the Ordering of Dissent." *Antipode* 37, no. 3 (2005a): 425–446.

———, "From Colonial Administration to Development Studies: A Post-Colonial Critique of the History of Development Studies." In *A Radical History of Development Studies: Individuals, Institutions and Ideologies*. London: Zed Books, 2005b.

———, "From Colonialism to Development: Reflections of Former Colonial Officers." *Commonwealth and Comparative Politics* 44, no. 1 (2006a): 118–136.

———, "Spatial Practices and Imaginaries: Experiences of Colonial Officers and Development Professionals." *Singapore Journal of Tropical Geography* 27, no. 3 (2006b): 235–253.

Kothari, U. and Wilkinson, R., "Colonial Imaginaries and Postcolonial Transformations: Exiles, Bases, Beaches." *Third World Quarterly* 31, no. 8 (2010): 1395–1412.

Kronsell, A. and Svedberg, E., *Making Gender, Making War: Violence, Military and Peacekeeping Practices*. New York: Routledge, 2011.

Kylin, C., "Blood, Sweat and Tears—Shared Bodily Fluids, Emotions and Social Identity in Swedish Military Context." *International Journal of Work Organisation and Emotion* 5, no. 2 (2012): 193–207.

Landgren, K., "The Lost Agenda: Gender Parity in Senior UN Appointments." *Global Peace Operations Review*, 14 December 2015.

Latino, A., "Chronicle of a Death Foretold: The Long-Term Health Impacts on the Victims of Widespread Lead Poisoning at UN-Run Camps in Kosovo." In S. Negri, ed., *Environmental Health in International and EU Law*. London: Routledge, 2019, 365–377.

Lee, S. and Bartels, S., "'They Put a Few Coins in Your Hand to Drop a Baby in You': A Study of Peacekeeper-Fathered Children in Haiti." *International Peacekeeping* 27, no. 2 (2020): 177–209.

Lemay-Hébert, N., "The Bifurcation of the Two Worlds: Assessing the Gap Between Internationals and Locals in State-Building Processes." *Third World Quarterly* 32, no. 10 (2011): 1823–1841.

———, "Resistance in the Time of Cholera: The Limits of Stabilization Through Securitization in Haiti." *International Peacekeeping* 21, no. 2 (2014): 198–213.

———, "Living in the Yellow Zone: The Political Geography of Intervention in Haiti." *Political Geography* 67 (2017): 88–99.

Loftsdóttir, K. and Björnsdóttir, H., "The 'Jeep-Gangsters' from Iceland: Local Development Assistance in a Global Perspective." *Critique of Anthropology* 30, no. 1 (2010): 23–39.

Lorde, A., *Sister Outsider: Essays and Speeches*. Berkeley: Crossing Press, 1984.

Lugones, M., "Structure/Antistructure and Agency Under Oppression." *Journal of Philosophy* 87, no. 10 (1990): 500–507.

———, "The Coloniality of Gender." *Worlds & Knowledge Otherwise*, 2, no. 2 (Spring 2008): 1–17.

Lutz, C., "Empire Is in the Details." *American Ethnologist* 33, no. 4 (2006): 593–611.

Mac Ginty, R., *No War, No Peace: The Rejuvenation of Stalled Peace Processes and Peace Accords*. London: Palgrave Macmillan, 2016.

Mackay, A., "Training the Uniforms: Gender and Peacekeeping Operations." *Development in Practice* 13, nos. 2–3 (2003): 217–223.

———, "Mainstreaming Gender in United Nations Peacekeeping Training: Examples from East Timor, Ethiopia, and Eritrea." In D. Mazurana, A. Raven-Roberts and J. Parpart, eds., *Gender, Conflict, and Peacekeeping*. Oxford: Rowman and Littlefield, 2005, 265–279.

MacKenzie, M., *Good Soldiers Don't Rape: The Stories We Tell About Military Sexual Violence*. Cambridge: Cambridge University Press, 2003.

Madhok, S., "A Critical Reflexive Politics of Location, 'Feminist Debt' and Thinking from the Global South." *European Journal of Women's Studies* 27, no. 4 (2020): 394–412.

Maertens, L., "From Blue to Green? Environmentalization and Securitization in UN Peacekeeping Practices." *International Peacekeeping* 26, no. 3 (2019): 302–326.

Mäki-Rahkola, A. and Myrttinen, H., "Reliable Professionals, Sensitive Dads and Tough Fighters: A Critical Look at Performances and Discourses of Finnish Peacekeeper Masculinities." *International Feminist Journal of Politics* 16, no. 3 (2014): 470–489.

Manchanda, N., "The Janus-Faced Nature of Militarization." *Critical Military Studies* (2022): 1–5.

Maringira, G., "Militarised Minds: The Lives of Ex-combatants in South Africa." *Sociology* 49, no. 1 (2015): 72–87.

Massey, D., *Space, Place and Gender*. Cambridge: Polity Press, 1994.

Masters, C., "Bodies of Technology: Cyborg Soldiers and Militarized Masculinities." *International Feminist Journal of Politics* 7, no. 1 (2005): 112–132.

Maternowska, M., *Reproducing Inequities: Poverty and the Politics of Population in Haiti*. New Brunswick, NJ: Rutgers University Press, 2006.

Mazurana, D., "Do Women Matter in Peacekeeping? Women in Police, Military and Civilian Peacekeeping." *Canadian Women's Studies* 22, no. 2 (2003): 64–71.

Mazurana, D., Raven-Roberts, A. and Parpart, J., eds., *Gender, Conflict, and Peacekeeping*. London: Rowman and Littlefield, 2005.

McCarry, M., "Masculinity Studies and Male Violence: Critique or Collusion?" *Women's Studies International Forum* 30, no. 5 (2007): 404–415.

McClintock, A., *Imperial Leather: Race, Gender, and Sexuality in the Colonial Contest*. London: Routledge, 1995.

Millar, K., *Support the Troops: Military Obligation, Gender, and the Making of Political Community*. Oxford: Oxford University Press, 2023.

Minh-ha, T. T., *Woman, Native, Other: Writing Postcoloniality and Feminism*. Bloomington: Indiana University Press, 1989.

Mohanty, C., "Under Western Eyes: Feminist Scholarship and Colonial Discourses." *Boundary 2* 12 (3) (1984): 333–358.

Moon, K., *Sex Among Allies: Military Prostitution in US-Korea Relations*. New York: Columbia University Press, 1997.

Moraga, C. and Anzaldúa, G., *This Bridge Called My Back: Writings by Radical Women of Color*. Watertown: Persephone Press, 1981.

Moten, F., *In the Break: The Aesthetics of the Black Radical Tradition*. Minneapolis: University of Minnesota Press, 2003.

Mwapu, I. et al., "Women Engaging in Transactional Sex and Working in Prostitution: Practices and Underlying Factors of the Sex Trade in South Kivu, the Democratic Republic of Congo." 2016.

Namakula, E., "Rethinking United Nations Peacekeeping Responses to Resource Wars and Armed Conflicts in Africa: Integrating African Indigenous Knowledge Systems." *Journal of Aggression, Conflict and Peace Research* 14, no. 4 (2022): 320–333.

Narang, N. and Liu, Y., "Does Female Ratio Balancing Influence the Efficacy of Peacekeeping Units? Exploring the Impact of Female Peacekeepers on Post-conflict Outcomes and Behavior." *International Interactions* (2021): 1–31.

Newby, V. and Sebag, C., "Gender Sidestreaming? Analysing Gender Mainstreaming in National Militaries and International Peacekeeping." *European Journal of International Security* 6, no. 2 (2021): 148–170.

Nordås, R. and Rustad, S., "Sexual Exploitation and Abuse by Peacekeepers: Understanding Variation." *International Interactions* 39, no. 4 (2013): 511–534.

Olsson, L. and Tryggestad, T., *Women and International Peacekeeping*. London: Frank Cass, 2001.

Otto, D. and Heathcote, G., "Rethinking Peacekeeping, Gender Equality and Collective Security: An Introduction." In Heathcote, G., and Otto, D., eds., *Rethinking Peacekeeping, Gender Equality and Collective Security*. London: Palgrave Macmillan, 2014, 1–20.

Oyewùmí, O., *The Invention of Women: Making an African Sense of Western Gender Discourses*. Minneapolis: University of Minnesota Press, 1997.

Paris, R., "Echoes of the *Mission Civilisatrice*: Peacekeeping in the Post-Cold War Era." In E. Newman and O. Richmond, eds., *The United Nations and Human Security*. London: Palgrave Macmillan, 2001, 100–118.

———, "International Peacebuilding and the 'Mission Civilisatrice.'" *Review of International Studies* 28, no. 4 (2002): 637–656.

———, *At War's End: Building Peace After Civil Conflict*. Cambridge: Cambridge University Press, 2004.

Patel, P. and Tripodi, P., "Peacekeepers, HIV and the Role of Masculinity in Military Behaviour." *International Peacekeeping* 14, no. 5 (2007): 584–598.

Pouligny, B., *Peace Operations Seen from Below: UN Missions and Local People*. Bloomfield, CT: Kumarian Press, 2006.

Pruitt, L., *The Women in Blue Helmets. Gender, Policing, and the UN's First All-Female Peacekeeping Unit*. Berkeley: University of California Press, 2016.

Puechguirbal, N., "Gender Training for Peacekeepers: Lessons from the DRC." *International Peacekeeping* 10, no. 14 (2003): 113–128.

Pugh, M., "Peacekeeping and Critical Theory." *International Peacekeeping* 11, no. 1 (2004): 39–58.

Quijano, A., "Coloniality and Modernity/Rationality." *Cultural Studies* 21, nos. 2–3 (2007): 168–178.

Ramsbotham, O. and Woodhouse, T., *Humanitarian Intervention in Contemporary Conflict: A Reconceptualization*. Cambridge: Polity Press, 1996.

Rashid, M., *Dying to Serve: Militarism, Affect and the Politics of Sacrifice in the Pakistan Army*. Oxford: Oxford University Press, 2020.

———, "Precarious Attachments: Soldiers and Erasures of the Feminine in the Pakistan Military." *International Feminist Journal of Politics* 24, no. 4 (2021): 1–20.

Razack, S., *Looking white people in the eye: Gender, race, and culture in courtrooms and classrooms*. University of Toronto Press, 1998.

"From the 'Clean Snows of Petawawa': The Violence of Canadian Peacekeepers in Somalia." *Cultural Anthropology* 15, no. 1 (2000): 127–163.

———, "Those Who 'Witness the Evil.'" *Hypatia* 18, no. 1 (2003): 204–211.

———, *Dark Threats and White Knights: The Somalia Affair, Peacekeeping, and the New Imperialism*. Toronto: University of Toronto Press, 2004.

———, "Stealing the Pain of Others: Reflections on Canadian Humanitarian Responses." *Review of Education, Pedagogy, and Cultural Studies* 29, no. 4 (2007): 375–394.

Rehn, E. and Sirleaf, E., *Women, War and Peace*. New York: UNIFEM, 2002.

Rich, A., "Notes Towards a Politics of Location." In R. Lewis and S. Mills, eds., *Feminist Postcolonial Theory: A Reader*. New York: Routledge, 2003, 29–42.

Richmond, O., "UN Peace Operations and the Dilemmas of the Peacebuilding Consensus." *International Peacekeeping* 11, no. 1 (2004): 83–101.

Ridouane, A., "Post-9/11 Masculinist Incursions in Iraq and Afghanistan: Women's Bodies as Bullets in Imperialist Agendas." *Digest of Middle East Studies* 28, no. 1 (2019): 70–88.

Robinson, C., *Black Marxism: The Making of the Black Radical Tradition*. Chapel Hill: University of North Carolina Press, 1983.

Rošul-Gajić, J., "Women's Advocacy in Postwar Bosnia and Herzegovina. Implementation of UNSCR 1325 on Women, Peace and Security." *Journal of International Women's Studies* 17, no. 4 (2016): 143–159.

Rubenstein, R., "Cultural Aspects of Peacekeeping: Notes on the Substance of Symbols." *Millennium: Journal of International Studies* 22, no. 3 (1993): 547–564.

———, *Peacekeeping Under Fire: Culture and Intervention*. Boulder: Paradigm, 2008.

Ruffa, C., "What Peacekeepers Think and Do: An Exploratory Study of French, Ghanaian, Italian, and South Korean Armies in the United Nations Interim Force in Lebanon." *Armed Forces and Society* 40, no. 2 (2014): 199–225.

———, *Military Cultures in Peace and Stability Operations: Afghanistan and Lebanon*. Philadelphia: University of Pennsylvania Press, 2018.

Said, E., *Orientalism: Western Concepts of the Orient*. New York: Pantheon, 1978.

Sandoval, C., *Methodology of the Oppressed*. Minneapolis: University of Minnesota Press, 2000.

Sasson-Levy, O., "Research on Gender and the Military in Israel: From a Gendered Organization to Inequality Regimes." *Israel Studies Review* 26, no. 2 (2011): 73–98.

———, "Women's Memories of Soldiering: An Intersectionality Perspective." In A. Altınay and A. Pető, eds., *Gendered Wars, Gendered Memories: Feminist Conversations on War, Genocide and Political Violence*. New York: Routledge, 2016, 109–120.

Schaffer, G., ed. *Racializing the Soldier*. London: Routledge, 2013.

Shepherd, L., "Making War Safe for Women? National Action Plans and the Militarisation of the Women, Peace and Security Agenda." *International Political Science Review* 37, no. 3 (2016): 324–335.

———, *Gender, UN Peacebuilding, and the Politics of Space*. Oxford: Oxford University Press, 2017.

Shigematsu, S., "Intimacies of Imperialism and Japanese-Black Feminist Transgression: Militarised Occupations in Okinawa and Beyond." *Intersections: Gender and Sexuality in Asia and the Pacific* 37 (2015): http://intersections.anu.edu.au/issue37/shigematsu.

Sion, L., "'Too Sweet and Innocent for War'? Dutch Peacekeepers and the Use of Violence." *Armed Forces and Society* 32, no. 3 (2006): 454–474.

———, Can Women Make a Difference? Female Peacekeepers in Bosnia and Kosovo." *Commonwealth and Comparative Politics* 47, no. 4 (2009): 476–493.

Sjoberg, L., *Gender, War, and Conflict*. New York: John Wiley and Sons, 2014.

Skjelsbæk, I. and Tryggestad, T., "Women in the Norwegian Armed Forces: Gender Equality or Operational Imperative." *Minerva Journal of Women and War* 3, no. 2 (2010): 34–51.

Sloan, J., *The Militarisation of Peacekeeping in the Twenty-First Century*. London: Bloomsbury Publishing, 2011.

Smirl, L., *Spaces of Aid: How Cars, Compounds and Hotels Shape Humanitarianism*. London: Zed Books, 2015.

Smith, D., *The Everyday World as Problematic: A Feminist Sociology*. Toronto: University of Toronto Press, 1987.

Smith, S., *Gendering Peace: UN Peacebuilding in Timor-Leste*. London: Routledge, 2018.

Sotomayor, A., *The Myth of the Democratic Peacekeeper: Civil-Military Relations and the United Nations*. Baltimore: Johns Hopkins University Press, 2014.

Spivak, G., "Can the Subaltern Speak?" In P. Williams and L. Chrisman, eds., *Colonial Discourse and Post-colonial Theory: A Reader*. Hertfordshire: Harvester Wheatsheaf, 1994, 66–112.

Stavrianakis, A. and Stern, M., 'Militarism and Security: Dialogue, Possibilities and Limits. *Security Dialogue* 49, nos. 1–2 (2018): 3–18.

Stiehm, J., "Women, Peacekeeping and Peacemaking: Gender Balance and Mainstreaming." *International Peacekeeping* 8, no. 2 (2001): 39–48.

Streets, H., *Martial Races: The Military, Race and Masculinity in British Imperial Culture, 1857–1914*. Manchester: Manchester University Press, 2017.

Sylvester, C., "Empathetic Cooperation: A Feminist Method for IR." *Millennium: Journal of International Studies* 23, no. 2 (1994): 315–334.

Thakur, R., Aoi, C. and De Coning, C. E., eds., *The Unintended Consequences of Peacekeeping Operations*. Tokyo: United Nations University Press, 2007.

Tuana, N., *Feminism and Science*. Bloomington: Indiana University Press, 1989.

Tudor, A., "Decolonizing Trans/Gender Studies? Teaching Gender, Race, and Sexuality in Times of the Rise of the Global Right." *Transgender Studies Quarterly* 8, no. 2 (2021): 238–256.

Tudor, M., *Blue Helmet Bureaucrats*. Cambridge: Cambridge University Press, 2023.

UNHCR and Save the Children, *Sexual Violence and Exploitation: The Experience of Refugee Children in Guinea, Liberia and Sierra Leone*. London: Save the Children, 2002.

United Nations, *Report of the Panel on United Nations Peace Operations*. New York: United Nations, 2000.

Vahedi, L., Bartels, S. and Lee, S., "'Even Peacekeepers Expect Something in Return': A Qualitative Analysis of Sexual Interactions Between UN Peacekeepers and Female Haitians." *Global Public Health* 16, no. 5 (2021): 692–705.

Valenius, J., "A Few Kind Women: Gender Essentialism and Nordic Peacekeeping Operations." *International Peacekeeping* 14, no. 4 (2007): 510–523.

Väyrynen, T., "Gender and UN Peace Operations: The Confines of Modernity." *International Peacekeeping* 11, no. 1 (2004): 125–142.

———, *Corporeal Peacebuilding: Mundane Bodies and Temporal Transitions*. s.l.: Springer, 2018.

Wai, Z., *Epistemologies of African Conflicts: Violence, Evolutionism, and the War in Sierra Leone*. London: Palgrave Macmillan, 2012.
Walcott, R., "Nothing New Here to See: How COVID-19 and State Violence Converge on Black Life." *TOPIA: Canadian Journal of Cultural Studies* 41 (2020): 158–163.
Wegner, N., "Helpful Heroes and the Political Utility of Militarized Masculinities." *International Feminist Journal of Politics* 23, no. 1 (2021): 5–26.
———, *Martialling Peace: How the Peacekeeper Myth Legitimises Warfare*. Edinburgh: Edinburgh University Press, 2023.
Welland, J., "Compassionate Soldiering and Comfort." In L. Ahall and T. Gregory, eds., *Emotions, Politics and War*. New York: Routledge, 2015, 115–127.
———, "Violence and the Contemporary Soldiering Body." *Security Dialogue* 48, no. 6 (2017): 524–540.
Westendorf, J., *Violating Peace*. Ithaca: Cornell University Press, 2020.
Westendorf, J. and Searle, L., "Sexual Exploitation and Abuse in Peace Operations: Trends, Policy Responses and Future Directions." *International Affairs* 93, no. 2 (2017): 365–387.
Whitworth, S., *Men, Militarism, and UN Peacekeeping: A Gendered Analysis*. Boulder: Lynne Rienner Publishers, 2004.
Wilén, N., "Female Peacekeepers' Added Burden." *International Affairs* 96, no. 6 (2020): 1585–1602.
Williams, P., "The Security Council's Peacekeeping Trilemma." *International Affairs* 96, no. 2 (2020): 479–499.
Wood, E., "Variation in Sexual Violence During War." *Politics and Society* 34, no. 3 (2006): 307–342.
Young, I., "The Logic of Masculinist Protection: Reflections on the Current Security State." *Signs: Journal of Women in Culture and Society* 29, no. 1 (2003): 1–25.
Yuh, J., *Beyond the Shadow of Camptown: Korean Military Brides in America*. New York: New York University Press, 2002.
Zalewski, M., "'I Don't Even Know What Gender Is': A Discussion of the Connections Between Gender, Gender Mainstreaming and Feminist Theory." *Review of International Studies* 36, no. 1 (2010): 3–27.
Zanotti, L., *Governing Disorder: UN Peace Operations, International Security, and Democratization in the Post–Cold War Era*. University Park: Pennsylvania State University Press, 2011.
Žarkov, D., Foreword. In D. Žarkov, ed., *Gender, Violent Conflict, and Development*. Delhi: Zubaan Books, 2008, xi–xix.
Žbanić, J., dir., *Quo Vadis, Aida?* 2021.
Zisk Marten, K., *Enforcing the Peace: Learning from the Imperial Past*. New York: Columbia University Press, 2004.

INDEX

abolitionist perspectives, 145, 152, 158, 162–63
Africa: colonial rhetoric and, 37, 46, 48–49, 118, 120; disdain toward peacekept in, 137; global color line and, 27; public health epidemics and, 19; UN foundational thinking on, 52
Agathangelou, A., 27
All the Women Are White, All the Blacks Are Men, but Some of Us Are Brave (Combahee River Collective), 76
antimilitarism: feminist theories and, 8, 83, 158; limitations of military-centered life, 139–44; pacifist standpoint, 144, 158; peacekeeping practices and, 129; peacekeeping scholarship and, 5, 14, 20, 30, 70, 93, 109
Anzaldua, G., 75
Aoi, C., 15
Autesserre, S., 10, 14–15

Bacellar, U., 63
Bangladeshi peacekeepers, 55, 57, 65, 112–13, 117, 149
Beardsley, K., 14, 83–84
Belgian peacekeepers, 118
Belkin, A., 72, 92, 145
Ben-Ari, E, 110
Black feminist theory: abolitionist perspectives, 162–63; antimilitarism and, 144; intersectionality and, 27–28, 75, 144; peacekeeping scholarship and, 162–64; standpoint theory and, 24, 144; women peacekeepers and power relations, 73

Black Marxists, 75
Black women: coloniality and, 94, 137; community policing work and, 60; erasure from police violence accounts, 144, 162; multiple systems of oppression, 76; peacekeeper views on morality, 48–49; rhetoric of diseased bodies, 49; white feminism exclusion of, 76
Bosnia and Herzegovina, 23, 110, 118–20
Brahimi Report (UN), 52
Bring Me Men (Belkin), 145
British Colonial Office, 35

Canadian peacekeepers: as colonizers, 33; color line and, 27; gendered/racial peacekeeping, 8; national mythologies and, 7, 33–34, 44, 55; racist stereotyping and, 120; routine violence and, 118; violence in Somalia, 7, 9, 26, 33, 35, 38, 44
Carby, H., 75
Central Reserve Police Forces (CRPF), 84–85
civilian peacekeepers: altruism and, 38–40; colonial attitudes and, 39–40, 48; contestation of coloniality, 38–40, 54; martial politics and, 114–15; observer missions, 109; peacekeeping knowledge and, 25, 37–38; privileged positions of, 40–41, 54; on sexual exploitation and abuse, 48–49; UN-run recruitment process, 168n8

Clapham, C., 133, 167n3
close protection officers, 59, 90–91, 140
Cockburn, C., 6–7, 13, 16, 30, 73, 99, 106–7, 116, 119–21, 129, 132, 144, 155, 158, 164
Cohn, C., 105–7, 129, 151
Collins, P. H., 75
colonialism and coloniality: chaotic and uncivilized rhetoric, 27, 43–47; dirt and disorder rhetoric, 33, 43–46; financial rhetoric, 135–36; of gender, 73, 75, 93–95, 100, 145, 148; geopolitical inequalities and, 55, 58; Global North forces and, 64; Global South and, 14, 50–51; intersectionality and, 65; legacies in peacekeeping settings, 7, 9, 11, 19, 35–42, 132–33, 163; martial politics and, 108, 117–18, 162; peacekeeper rhetoric and, 47–50; peacekeeper violence and, 7, 33–34; peacekeeping scholarship and, 164–66; power relations and, 9, 45, 47, 50, 54–56, 58, 65, 72, 93–94, 134; racial hierarchies and, 132, 145; savior narratives, 69, 145–46; sexual relations and, 135; social organizing and, 58; social progress rhetoric, 45–46; stereotyping of Global South militaries, 37, 64–65; systems of dominance, 77, 112; work ethic rhetoric, 45, 136–38. *See also* decolonizing peacekeeping
color line. *See* global color line
Combahee River Collective, 75–76
Conrad, J., 15
Courtemanche, G., 41
Crenshaw, K., 27–28, 75–76, 144, 162
critical race theory: abolitionist perspectives, 145, 162–63; Global South and, 36; militarization of peacekeeping, 116; peacekeeping scholarship and, 9–10, 15, 66, 145
Cruz, C., 62
Cruz Report, 127–28

Dark Threats and White Knights (Razack), 9, 34, 37

Davis, A., 75, 162
decolonizing peacekeeping: critical approaches in, 132–39; Global North knowledge and, 157; humanitarian responses to conflict, 3–4; peacekeeping scholarship and, 71, 161–62; peacekept and, 31
De Coning, C., 15
de Leeuw, M., 119
demilitarization: humanitarian responses to conflict and, 3–4; of military peacekeeping, 139–45, 158, 161–62; of peacekeeping scholarship, 32, 165
Democratic Republic of Congo: colonial ideologies and, 15; peacekeeper relations with peacekept, 121; sexual exploitation and abuse (SEA) in, 26; UN mission in, 48, 63–64; violence against peacekeepers in, 61–62; women peacekeepers and, 59
development studies, 8–10, 38
Du Bois, W. E. B., 26–27, 75
Duffield, M., 10
Duncanson, C., 7, 13, 128
Dutch peacekeepers, 44, 120

East Timor, 38, 110
Elron, E., 110
embodiment: feminine-masculine continuum, 29; gender and, 82, 92, 151; geopolitical inequalities and, 73; Global North soldiering and, 73; militarized physical regimes, 79, 87, 89, 91–92, 140; patriarchal expectations and, 73; women peacekeepers and, 29, 90
Enloe, C., 56, 81, 99, 106–7, 113, 116, 121, 129, 132, 144, 146, 155, 158, 164
epistemic project of peacekeeping: as colonial practice, 36, 50, 66, 152, 154, 161; color line in, 26–29; conscious decision-making and, 21; critical approaches in, 17, 20, 31, 71, 165; Enlightenment values and, 152; everyday life and, 105, 161; feminist

standpoint theory and, 24–25; frontier metaphor and, 36; gendered/racialized, 35, 104; intersectionality and, 27, 73; knowledge production and, 3–5, 22, 32, 50, 104, 160; martial politics and, 30, 35, 152, 154; militarization and, 30, 32, 62, 104; national identity and, 28; patriarchal expectations and, 154; politics of location and, 24; positioning of peacekept in, 93, 131, 158; power relations and, 22–23, 25; repoliticizing narratives, 25, 160
Equal Opportunity Peacekeeping (Karim and Beardsley), 14

feminist theories: antimilitarism and, 8, 83, 158; Chicana, 75; colonialism and, 31; global sisterhood myth, 28, 77; intersectionality and, 24–25, 27–28, 75–76; intervention frameworks, 13; militarization of peacekeeping, 106, 116; on operational effectiveness, 81–82; peacekeeping scholarship and, 6–9, 12–16, 24–25, 161; peace studies, 4, 6–7, 30; politics of location and, 24; standpoint theory, 24–25. *See also* Black feminist theory
Fetherston, A., 116, 142
Filipino peacekeepers, 54, 79, 85, 124, 126

gender: binaristic views of, 29, 31, 69, 76, 84, 92, 94, 146, 151, 157, 161–62; coloniality of, 73, 75, 93–95, 100, 145, 148; division of labor and, 23, 57; empire building and, 61; expectations of, 61, 72, 80, 93; fixity of, 148, 151; as foil for embodied sex, 92, 101; identity and, 71–72; instrumentalization of, 72, 84; intersectionality and, 93–94; militarism and, 56–57, 83–84, 106–7; peacekeeper discourses and, 70–72; peacekeeping scholarship and, 11, 13–14, 71, 92–93, 151; power relations and, 23, 31, 72, 147–48; racial hierarchies and, 58; SEA and, 95–96, 134–35; standpoint theory and, 148; UN understanding of, 70; white women's oppression and, 76
Gender, Conflict, and Peacekeeping (Mazurana et al.), 8
Gender, UN Peacebuilding, and the Politics of Space (Shepherd), 71
gender awareness training, 8, 29, 99
gender relations: military masculinity and, 56–57; peacekeeping and, 2, 11, 29, 121; warfare ideology and practices, 106, 120–21, 123, 146; women peacekeepers and, 14, 29, 31, 57–58, 73, 84
geopolitical inequalities: forms of oppression, 96; Global South labor and, 36, 57–58, 160–61; intersectionality and, 28; legacies of colonialism and, 55–56; national militaries and, 149; peacekeeping scholarship and, 28, 71; peacekeeping spaces and, 21, 35, 41–42, 44, 62, 66, 77, 85, 102, 133; power relations and, 93; race and, 50–51; security institutions and, 58; UN complicity in, 4, 44, 70; wars and, 130
Ghana Armed Forces, 90
Ghanaian peacekeepers: community outreach, 60, 89–90, 114; division of labor and, 115–16; educational capital and, 89–90; national identity and, 89; superiority beliefs, 54, 89, 114; upward mobility through peacekeeping, 89; women peacekeepers, 60, 85, 88–90
global color line: colonial ideologies and, 65; division of labor and, 26–27, 31, 50–51; gendered burdens of security, 61; gender hierarchies and, 58; Global South peacekeepers and, 13, 157; intersectionality and, 29; racial hierarchies and, 50, 58, 65
global inequalities. *See* geopolitical inequalities

Global North peacekeepers: colonial ideologies and, 64; on embodied soldiering, 73; gendered-racial hierarchies, 58; gender expectations, 80; marginalization of Global South soldiers, 145; military masculinity and, 7–8, 73; peacebuilding operations, 6, 36; perspective on violence, 13; privileged positions of, 95; researcher privilege and, 20; romance narratives, 48; superiority beliefs, 47–50; women peacekeepers, 58, 148

Global South: burden of peacekeeping labor, 14, 30, 36–37, 50–52, 57–62, 66, 149, 160–61, 164, 166; colonial infantilizing of, 97, 102, 133, 136; gender-based violence in, 102; legacies of colonialism and, 14, 38, 40–42, 163; mercenary characterizations of, 46, 48, 136; as Other, 50, 152

Global South peacekeepers: ban on use of force, 64; colonial stereotyping of, 37, 64–65; gender expectations, 80; global color line and, 13, 157; global inequalities and, 95; Global North marginalization of, 145, 149; interactions with peacekept, 66, 135; intersectionality and, 28; militarism and, 51–53, 64–65, 75; oppression/privilege of, 66; risk and danger to, 62, 64, 66; socioeconomics and, 168n2; viewed as developmental forces, 37, 79, 149; warrior performances, 79, 87, 150

Global South women peacekeepers: advanced weapons training, 60, 70, 148–49; all-women contingents, 28, 67–68, 84–89, 148–49; colonial ideologies and, 58–59; driving qualifications and, 80, 112; exclusion of, 73; feminist expectations for, 77; gendered burden of security, 57–61, 66, 77; identity and, 68–70; intersectionality and, 28, 76; low status of, 58, 79, 149; male military spaces and, 73; martial labor and, 79, 87, 89, 101; as natural laborers, 59; patriarchal expectations and, 29, 78–80, 86–88; sex segregation norms, 86–89, 148; UN containment of, 61; viewed as docile and obedient, 58–59, 61, 79

Haiti: arming of peacekeepers in, 142–43; cholera outbreak in, 43–44; citizen insecurity in, 24, 152–53; gang-related violence in, 153; Global South peacekeepers and, 51, 65; hierarchies of peacekeepers in, 65; Lavalas supporters, 63, 168n9; non-French-speaking peacekeepers, 153–54; peace enforcement operations, 110; peacekeeper colonial ideologies and, 47; peacekeeper relations with peacekept, 121, 135; peacekeeper violence in, 26, 118; peacekeeping operations in, 23–24, 63, 108; women peacekeepers in, 29, 67
Hall, S., 75
Hammad, S., 103–4
Harrington, C., 13, 16
Heart of Darkness (Conrad), 15
Heinecken, L., 57, 84
Henry, M., 15, 26, 28
Holvikivi, A., 72, 151
hooks, b., 75
Howard, L., 15–16
Howell, A., 107, 116, 158
Hubic, M., 6, 73, 121
Hultman, L., 15, 128
humanitarian aid: colonial style relations, 35–36; crises and, 130; Eurocentric beliefs and, 35; geopolitical inequalities and, 35, 39, 41; militarism and, 122; peacekept and, 39; power relations and, 22; privileged positions of, 42

Improving Security of United Nations Peacekeepers (Cruz Report), 127

Indian peacekeepers: all-women contingents, 28, 67–68, 84–89, 148–49, 155; Central Reserve Police Forces (CRPF), 84–85; collective deployments, 85–87; force protection, 88; language learning, 155; male gaze and, 60–61; patriarchal expectations and, 78–79, 86–88; respectability norms, 87–88; sex segregation norms, 86–89; superiority beliefs, 28, 54; women's corporeal investments, 59, 87
Indigenous populations, 72, 108
Insecure Spaces (Higate and Henry), 2, 21, 118
internally displaced people's (IDP), 25
international development, 34–35
intersectionality: Black feminism and, 24, 27–28, 75, 144; Black Marxists and, 75; Chicana feminism and, 75; coloniality and, 65; color line and, 29; defining, 27, 75; feminist theory and, 24–25; forms of oppression, 76, 82, 92, 96, 139; gender and, 93–94; global inequalities and, 28; Global South peacekeepers and, 28–29, 81; marginalization and privilege in, 75–76; militarization and, 28, 74–75; peacekeeping scholarship and, 27–29, 74, 77; power relations and, 29, 66, 73–75; race and, 94; women peacekeepers and, 28–29, 73, 78–81, 95, 101
Italian peacekeepers, 47, 118

James, CLR., 75
Japanese peacekeepers, 126–27

Kaplan, D., 146
Karim, S., 14, 83–84
Karlsrud, J., 15
Kosovo: chemical contamination in, 43; Global North peacekeepers in, 48; peacekeeper colonial ideologies and, 47; peacekeeper violence in, 118; peacekeeping operations in, 23; services to Romani communities, 17–18, 43–44; UN martial branding in, 111
Kothari, U., 35
Kronsell, A., 13

Lemay-Hebért, N., 42
Liberia: civilian peacekeepers in, 155–56; colonial ideologies and, 47, 55; fieldwork in, 18–22; Indian peacekeepers in, 67–68, 155; martial politics and, 112–13; military peacekeeping in, 122; peacekeeper body work, 91–92; peacekeeper racism and, 55; peacekeeper relations with peacekept, 45–47; peacekeeper sexual violence and abuse, 26; public health epidemics and, 19; women peacekeepers in, 29, 68, 85–86
Ling, L. M., 27
Lorde, A., 75, 139
Lugones, M., 71, 75, 94–96, 145, 148

masculinity, 28, 98
male peacekeepers: domination of, 26; gendered violence and, 98; gender relations and, 2; machine masculinities and, 99; marginalization of women peacekeepers, 60–61; military ideology and, 5, 7–8, 26; sexual exploitation and abuse (SEA), 23–24; sexual relations and, 6, 48, 121; women's insecurity and, 24
Manchanda, N., 139
martial politics: civilian peacekeepers and, 114–15; colonial forms of, 108, 117–18, 162; defense intellectuals, 105–6; feminist approaches to, 106, 129; oppression of Indigenous, 108; peacekeeper ideals and, 117; peacekeeping and, 30, 32, 77, 104, 109, 139–40, 158; racialized, 126, 162; risk and danger in, 65; scientific/social practices and, 114; social/leisure spaces and, 112–13; state and, 107–8, 120; technostrategic discourses, 105–6, 127–28; UN symbols and, 110–12

martial violence: gendered/racialized tropes and, 119–21; male-dominated deployments and, 119; peacekeeper encounters with, 124–27; peacekeeping and, 117–19; power relations and, 119–20; routine acts and, 118; sexual violence and, 119; white supremacist/racist foundations of, 118
masculinity: body-centered, 141; gendered/racialized violence and, 99; gender hierarchies and, 74, 141; hegemonic, 123; homogenizing narratives of, 100; machine, 99; macho cultures of, 115, 117, 123, 129, 141; performances of, 122–24; predatory sexualities and, 98; sporting activities and, 53; technostrategic discourses, 105–6. *See also* military masculinity
Massey, D., 22–24
Mazurana, D., 8, 13, 30, 109, 129, 164
medal parade ceremonies, 59, 61, 87, 168n6
Men, Militarism, and UN Peacekeeping (Whitworth), 7
militarism: cultural products and, 106; epistemic project analysis of, 32; gender and, 83–84, 106–7; impacts on marginalized subjects, 83; inequalities and, 83; intersectionality and, 73, 107; organizing social principles and, 146; patriarchal, 57, 146; peacekeeping and, 30, 32, 96, 110, 158; peacekeeping scholarship and, 160–61, 163, 165; racial hierarchies and, 106; resistance to ideology, 104–5
militarization: burka and, 111; construction of, 116; feminist critiques, 108–9, 116, 126, 139; gender and, 1, 6, 56–57, 106–7; gendered power relations in, 61, 82, 90, 128; intersectionality and, 74–76, 107; macho cultures of, 115, 117, 123, 129, 141; martial symbols and, 104–5, 110–12; normalization of, 105, 113, 128–29; operational effectiveness discourse, 82; politics of, 106–7, 120; postcolonial studies, 139; postconflict settings and, 9, 12, 70, 126–28; violence and, 9; war systems and, 151
military masculinity: denigration of difference and, 146, 149; drinking cultures and, 115, 141; duty and sacrifice narratives, 26, 106, 142, 164; gender analysis and, 56–57, 149; gendered/racialized violence and, 99–100, 129, 159; intersectionality and, 28; machine masculinities, 99; martial symbols and values, 104–5; peacekeeping and, 5, 7–8, 23–24; performances of, 122–24, 149–51; repoliticizing narratives, 13; sexual predation and, 98; transgressive behavior and, 122–24; warrior practices, 99, 117, 123, 129
military peacekeeping: ambivalence in, 139–44; challenges of multinational forces, 63–65; colonial ideologies and, 46; defining, 168n4; defunding of, 31; demilitarizing, 139–45, 158, 161–62, 165; developmental arguments, 46; force for good narratives, 7, 44, 66, 118, 128–29; force protection, 88; fraternization and, 134; hierarchies of, 65, 113; martial habitus and, 139–42; martial politics and, 112–14; medal parade ceremonies, 59, 61, 87, 168n6; medical skills and, 90, 114; member states and, 1, 153–54; off-duty culture and, 121; patriarchal expectations and, 29, 146; peacekeeping practices and, 14; perceptions of, 52–53; physical regimes, 87, 89, 91–92; schedules and rituals, 115–16; sexual exploitation and abuse (SEA), 26; socioeconomic mobility and, 40, 78, 143–44; sporting activities and, 53, 115; stereotyping of Global South, 37, 64–65; superiority beliefs, 114;

women as, 77–78, 82–83, 85, 114. *See also* police peacekeepers
Mohanty, C., 50
Moraga, C., 75
multinational forces, 60, 63–65, 109–10, 122

Nepalese peacekeepers, 44, 54, 61, 85
Nigerian peacekeepers, 52, 65, 80–81, 97–98, 117
nongovernmental organizations (NGOs), 2, 17
Nordstrom, C., 116
Norway, 82, 85

observer missions, 64, 109
operational effectiveness: feminist pushback, 81–82; martial obsession with, 72, 82, 144; peacekeeping scholarship and, 160–62; women peacekeepers and, 14, 72, 77, 81–83, 162
Orientalism, 35, 65, 150
Otto, D., 13

Pakistani peacekeepers, 53–54
Paris, R., 10, 12, 36, 128
Parpart, J., 8, 13, 30, 109, 129
peacebuilding, 6, 36, 71–72, 96
peace enforcement operations, 109–10
peacekeepers: colonial ideologies and, 36, 45–47, 49–50, 54–56, 62, 64; color line and, 26–27; composition of, 41; construction of self and, 49–50; contradictory position of, 37, 40; enforcement operations, 109; gender awareness training and, 8, 29; Global South positioning, 62–63; inequalities and, 51–52, 69; neoliberal progress narratives, 40; patriarchal power relations and, 47; performance of humility, 54; privileged positions of, 28, 35, 40–41; racial hierarchies and, 49–50, 54–56, 62; SEA and, 6–7, 25–26, 44; second world, 168n4; sporting activities of, 53; violence against, 34, 61–64; white-identified, 45, 168n4. *See also* male peacekeepers; troop contributing countries (TCCs); women peacekeepers
peacekeeper violence: aggressive combat techniques, 24; by Canadians in Somalia, 9, 26, 33–34, 44; colonial ideologies and, 33, 35–36, 44–45, 65; military masculinity and, 129; national mythologies and, 33–34, 44; racial hierarchies and, 35–37, 65, 120; sexual violence and abuse, 25–26, 119; socio-legal insights into, 13; white supremacist/racist foundations of, 118
peacekeeping: androcentric, 7–8, 16, 127, 129, 145; as civilizing mission, 12, 145–46; as colonial practice, 7, 9–11, 14, 33–36, 38–41, 43, 69, 77, 96, 145–46, 163–64; degendering, 145–51; discourse of, 34–35; emergence of, 1, 108; gaze of, 151–56; geopolitical inequalities and, 35, 41, 62, 66; militarization of, 62, 96, 110, 126–29; observer missions, 64, 109; peace support operations, 109–10; politics and power of, 3–4, 30, 43; as surveillance, 16; viewed as neutral and objective, 3–4, 23, 54, 56, 159, 165. *See also* epistemic project of peacekeeping; martial politics
peacekeeping scholarship: abolitionist-inspired, 145, 152, 158, 162–63; antimilitarism and, 5, 14, 20, 30, 70, 93, 109; antiracist perspectives in, 12–13; Black feminist theory and, 162–64; colonial ideologies and, 39, 132–33, 164, 166; critical approaches in, 10–13, 17, 20–21, 24–25, 70–71, 152, 157–58, 167n4; critical race theories and, 9–10, 15, 20, 66, 145, 157; depoliticization in, 9, 12; effectiveness in, 15; feminist perspectives in, 6–9, 12–16, 20, 24–25, 157, 161; gender and, 11, 13–14, 71, 92–93, 151; global inequalities

peacekeeping scholarship (continued) and, 28, 62, 71; intersectionality and, 27–29, 74, 77; marginalization of peacekept in, 133, 144–45, 152; militarism and, 160–61, 163, 165; postcolonial studies, 9–11, 15, 24, 66, 145; qualitative methodologies and, 17–20; repoliticizing narratives, 5, 13, 20, 22, 24–25; researcher marginalization and, 18, 20; sexual exploitation and abuse (SEA) in, 16, 34, 101; theoretical interventions in, 5–16; women peacekeeping and, 82–83. See also epistemic project of peacekeeping

peacekeeping spaces: all-male military squads, 23–24; as chaotic and uncivilized, 27, 33, 43, 45; colonial ideologies and, 19, 36, 44–45, 55–56, 97; embodiment in, 73; functioning of, 18; global inequalities and, 42, 70, 102, 133; identities in, 68–69; patriarchal expectations and, 96; peacekeeper privilege in, 41–42; power relations and, 3–4, 10, 12, 16, 21–23, 43, 53–55, 70; racial hierarchies and, 36, 42, 55–56; SEA in, 1–2, 6–7, 13, 23, 25–26, 48–49; sexualized power relations in, 73, 95–97; social relations in, 17, 21–23; UN peacekeepers in, 41–43; UN symbols in, 110–12; violence in, 43, 63–65. See also postconflict settings

Peacekeeping Under Fire (Rubenstein), 11

peacekept: agency and, 29, 96–97, 100, 102, 121, 131, 165; children with peacekeepers, 121; colonial ideologies and, 36, 45–47, 102, 135–38, 165; containment of, 12; defining, 167n3; dehumanization of, 148; as inherent victims, 29; intersectionality and, 147–48; marginalization of, 31, 133, 144–45, 152, 154–56, 163; martial violence and, 64, 119–20; peacekeeping gaze and, 151–56; positive change and, 16;

power relations and, 43, 65, 133–35; social inequalities and, 28–29; standpoint theory and, 132; stigmatization of women, 95, 121, 147–48. See also sexual exploitation and abuse (SEA)

police peacekeepers: all-women contingents, 28, 67–68, 84–89, 91, 148–49; colonial ideologies and, 42–43, 47, 55; corruption and, 140–41; encounters with violence, 126–27; global inequalities and, 39; masculinist ethos and, 141; militarism and, 112, 122, 139–40; socioeconomic mobility and, 40, 78, 143–44; women as, 58, 60–61, 78. See also military peacekeeping

police violence, 144, 162–63

postcolonial studies: abolitionist perspectives, 145; militarization and, 139; peacekeeping scholarship and, 9–11, 15, 24, 66, 145; politics of location and, 24; SEA and, 101; UN foundational thinking, 52

postconflict settings: coloniality and, 35–36, 100; gender relations and, 6; geopolitical inequalities and, 70, 100; military peacekeepers and, 85, 109; peacebuilding in, 72; peacekeeper difficulties in, 63; peacekept in, 10; recovery in, 19–20; Romani community and, 17–18; SEA in, 1–2, 96. See also peacekeeping spaces

The Postwar Moment (Cockburn and Žarkov), 6

Pouligny, B., 10, 132

power relations: coloniality and, 9, 45, 47, 50, 54–56, 58, 65, 72, 93–94, 134; gender and, 23, 31, 147–48; geopolitical inequalities and, 93; imbalanced, 2, 10; intersectionality and, 29, 66, 73–75; martial violence and, 119–20; militarized, 12, 128; patriarchal expectations and, 47, 122; peacekeeping spaces and, 3–4, 10, 12, 16, 21–23, 70; peacekept and, 43, 65, 133–35; racial hierarchies and, 20, 23,

65; SEA and, 73, 93, 95–99, 134–35; sexual relations and, 96, 134–35; women peacekeepers and, 85
Pruitt, L., 13, 84

Quo Vadis, Aida? 159, 165

race and racialization: Black men's oppression and, 76; coloniality and, 65, 132, 145; gender and, 58, 94; geopolitical inequalities and, 50–52; global inequalities and, 49–50, 54–56; Global South peacekeepers and, 36–37; hierarchies of, 35–37, 50, 58–59, 62; peacekeeping and, 31, 36; peacekept women and, 94; power relations and, 20, 23, 65; war and, 120, 146; white superiority beliefs, 50
racial capitalism, 9, 94
racism, 9, 73, 118, 120
Raven-Roberts, A., 8, 13, 30, 109, 129
Razack, S., 9–10, 12–13, 15, 26–27, 34, 36–37, 40–41, 43–44, 47, 50, 54–56, 63, 65, 97, 116–17, 120, 128–29, 155, 162–64
Robinson, C., 75
Romani community, 17–18, 43–44
Rubenstein, R., 11, 110
Ruddick, S, 151

Sandoval, C., 75
SEA. *See* sexual exploitation and abuse (SEA)
sex: biological, 69–70, 84, 94–95, 151; embodied, 72, 92; essentialist ideas about, 77–78; gender and, 93–94, 101, 145–46, 148–49, 151, 157, 162; peacekeeper discourses and, 70; segregation norms, 86–90; UN definitions of, 70. *See also* gender
sex-gender binary, 92–94
sexual exploitation and abuse (SEA): all-male military squads and, 23–24; coloniality and, 72, 94; conflict-related, 16; European romance narratives, 48; gender training and, 29; intersectionality and, 95; military masculinity and, 99–100; peacekeepers and, 25–26; peacekeeping scholarship and, 16, 34, 101; in peacekeeping settings, 1–2, 6–7, 13, 23, 25–26, 44, 95–96, 120; postcolonial feminist perspectives and, 73; power relations and, 73, 93, 95–99, 134–35; predatory sexualities, 98; representations by peacekeepers, 72; as sexual imperialism, 16, 95, 97, 102; sexual violence and, 16, 96; women peacekeeper care and, 57, 121
sexual relations: coloniality and, 135; consensual, 97–99, 102; gender and, 97, 134–35; heteropatriarchal norms, 135; military policies and, 134; peacekeeping scholarship and, 71; peacekeeping spaces and, 73, 96; peacekept agency and, 96–97, 100, 102; power relations and, 96, 134–35; romance narratives, 48; sex worker-centered approach, 97, 100; UN policies on, 2
sex work, 97, 99–100, 134, 161, 164
Shepherd, L., 14, 71–72, 146
social relations, 17, 21–23
Somalia: colonial discourse and, 118; peacekeeper violence in, 7, 9, 26, 33, 35, 38, 44, 118, 162
Spivak, G., 69
Srebrenica, 44, 120
standpoint theory, 24–25, 132, 148
Subritzky, M., 104–5
A Sunday at the Pool in Kigali (Courtemanche), 41
surveillance, 16
Svedberg, E., 13

Tan, J., 168n1
troop contributing countries (TCCs): expectations of docile women laborers, 79; geopolitical inequalities and, 55; global governance discourses and, 37; peacekeeper ideals and, 117; UN funds and, 51–52; UN Security Council and, 57. *See also* peacekeepers

Ukrainian peacekeepers, 141
UN Gender Advisor, 67
UN Headquarters (UNMIK), 47
United Nations (UN): complicity in global inequalities, 4, 44, 70; Cruz Report and, 127; denial of responsibility for cholera outbreak, 43–44; dereliction in peacekeeping responsibilities, 44, 165; discursive knowledge and, 35; duty and sacrifice narratives, 26; expectations of docile women laborers, 79; force for good narratives, 44; gender equality failures, 57; gender training and, 29; geopolitical inequalities and, 61; idealization of military masculinities, 127–28, 149, 162; martial branding and, 110–11; martial politics and, 65; member states, 1, 167n1; peacekeeper employment by, 140; political neutrality claims, 4, 54, 56, 165; on sexualized power relations, 95–96
United Nations Security Council (SC), 1, 21, 57, 154, 167n1
UN Mission in Haiti (MINUSTAH), 63
UN Mission in Liberia (UNMIL), 53, 85
UN Mission in the Democratic Republic of Congo (MINUSCO), 63
UN peacekeepers, 36, 39–44
Uruguayan peacekeepers, 68, 115–16, 154–55

Violating Peace (Westendorf), 16
violence: Global North perspectives on, 13; martial politics and, 124–26; against peacekeepers, 34, 61–63; in peacekeeping settings, 43, 64; police brutality, 144, 162–63. *See also* martial violence; peacekeeper violence; sexual exploitation and abuse (SEA)

war: gender and, 106, 120–23, 146; global inequalities and, 130; heteropatriarchal relations and, 83; impacts on marginalized subjects, 83; normalization of, 105; peacekeeping operations and, 108–9; race and, 120, 146; resistance to, 104–5; sexual violence in, 98, 102, 119; system of, 151; vicarious experience of, 104
Westendorf, J., 16
Whitworth, S., 7–8, 13, 99, 128–29, 141, 146, 149, 155, 164
Wilén, N., 57, 83–84
women: colonial power relations and, 47–49, 58; European romance narratives and, 48; gendered-racial hierarchies, 58; militarism and, 82, 106–7; paid sex in peacekeeping, 6, 134; patriarchal power relations and, 47, 122; rhetoric of diseased Black bodies, 49; safety and security demands, 6. *See also* Global South women peacekeepers
women peacekeepers: added burdens of, 57, 83–84, 121; advanced weapons training, 60, 79, 148–49; body work, 87, 89, 91–92; challenges of multinational forces, 60; close protection officers, 90–91; collective deployments, 85–87; colonial ideologies and, 58–59; critical male gaze, 60–61; driving qualifications and, 80, 111–12; essentialist female ideas on, 77–78; feminine expectations for, 59–61, 84; as foil of empire, 72; gender relations and, 14, 29, 31, 57–58, 73, 84, 121; geopolitical inequalities and, 85; Global North militarism, 58, 73; informal labor and, 57–60; intersectionality and, 28–29, 73, 78–81, 95, 101; invisibility and, 88; lived experiences of, 13, 68–69, 72, 93, 157; local community work, 59–60; marginalization and privilege in, 76, 95; martial labor and, 79, 87, 89; military settings and, 72, 77–78, 82–83, 85–88, 101; operational effectiveness discourse, 14, 72, 77, 81–83, 162; patriarchal expectations and, 29, 31, 48, 78–79,

86, 88, 92; peacekeeping scholarship and, 13; politics of respectability and, 79, 87–88; power relations and, 85; racial hierarchies and, 58–59; reduction of SEA, 121; senior leaders, 90–91; sex segregation norms, 86–90, 93; situatedness in global relations, 72; viewed as docile and obedient, 79; violence against, 61–62; vulnerability and, 92.

See also Global South women peacekeepers

Wood, E., 98

Zalewski, M., 147
Zanotti, L., 12, 16
Žarkov, D, 6–7, 13, 16, 30, 99, 119–20, 129–30, 155, 158, 164
Žbanic, J., 159
Zisk Marten, K., 10, 132

ACKNOWLEDGMENTS

I have to confess to loving reading acknowledgments sections in the majority of books. Often before I've even begun to read a book, I peruse the acknowledgments. More than judging a book by its cover, it is about judging a book by the ways in which the author has paid its citational dues. I start my acknowledgments by mentioning the generosity of thought, time, and friendship from Cynthia Enloe, Sherene Razack, Carol Cohn, Cynthia Cockburn, and Lily H. Ling. Without these scholars and the way in which they so patiently listened and simultaneously pushed and challenged me, this work would not have been possible. I have had the fortune of being able to speak and share candid thoughts about so many issues surrounding gender, peace, and security with Cynthia and Carol; racial and colonial myths with Sherene; and sadly, I have lost this relation with the passing of Cynthia Cockburn and Lily Ling. Lily was the first scholar to invite me into conversations about peacekeeping. I can never forget Lily's big, bright smile, her whispers of insight during conferences and workshops, or her intellectual depth. I would have turned to Lily in the first instance with this book for advice and guidance, if it had not been for her untimely passing. Cynthia Cockburn has been an inspiration of feminist political activism—truly "living a feminist life" from the moment I met her and all of her contacts and friends in Cyprus, Bosnia, and beyond (Ahmed, 2016). I have been taken care of by so many of Cynthia's friends, who have welcomed me into their lives and facilitated fieldwork. Through these scholars I met and befriended a number of scholars who have provided the political foundations of this book—among them are Anna Agathangelou and Dubravka Žarkov.

Here I pause to acknowledge all those peacekeepers and individuals living and working in peacekeeping missions who gave up their time, took care of me when the Malarone gave me the worst side effects I have ever experienced, and consented to have their lives be the subject of research. The grace by which they afforded me space and time is unrivaled in academia. I want to preserve their privacy and do not name any of them here. Just know that I am grateful.

In Japan, while a visiting scholar at Hiroshima City University, I benefited from the intellectual rigor of a number of colleagues: in particular, Ulrike Wöhr, Masae Yuasa, Bo Jacobs, Yoshiaki Furuzawa, Michael Gorman, and Charles Worthen. I was welcomed into daily family life by Ayako Nozawa and her family and friends. In Kobe, I was reunited with Kaoru Aoyama; in Fukuyama, Yukifumi Makita provided emergency tea bags. While at Tokyo University, I debated peacekeeping, gender, and militarization with Ai Kihara-Hunt, Tomotaka Kawamura, and at other Tokyo-based universities with Masato Noda, Nora Beril, and Fumika Sato; I enjoyed engaging with international students learning about peace from a different vantage point. At LSE I have been supported by a number of colleagues throughout my time. In particular, Clare Hemmings has been a constant source of encouragement, inspiration, and laughter. Our shared common background in the humanities and in gender studies has meant that Clare has always understood the interdisciplinary pleasures and pains that come with situating oneself across different disciplines and fields of study. Ania Plomien has fed me, watched me weep, and been by my side as we walked on the peace march in Srebrenica—always rooting for me. Sumi Madhok has been an intellectual muse, a constant gardener, and a fellow lover of all forms of music. Leticia Sabsay, Sadie Wearing, Diane Perrons, Anne Phillips, Kalpana Wilson, Aisling Swaine, Anouk Patel-Campillo, Christine Chinkin, Louise Arimatsu, Punam Yadav, Nazanin Shahrokni, Samar Rodriguez, and Aiko Holvikivi have been mentors and stewards of teaching and a life of ideas. Kate Steward and Hazel Johnstone have on so many occasions reached out with love and affection—on one occasion, Hazel attended at the Ghanaian embassy in London so I could get my passport in time for a research trip. Hazel's unexpected passing in March 2023 has been a huge blow. Former and current doctoral students have altered my thinking with their brilliance and their gentleness at my so often frenzied schedules: Alexandra Hyde, Amanda Conroy, Nicole Shepherd, Harriet Gray, Aiko Holvikivi, Hannah Wright, and Niharika Pandit, Aynura Akbas, Lizzie Hobbs, Claire Wilmot, Florence Waller Carr, and Venera Cocaj. Colleagues in friendly departments at LSE have looked out for me on numerous occasions: Denisa Kostovicova became a friend, collaborator, and comrade. And former Master's students constantly sent me messages of support, amongst them Kasey Robinson and Saleh Sowad and so many more that are in my heart and mind so often.

I presented my work at various venues, in person and virtually—I have been presenting bits of the book for so long that I am sure I will leave out lovely audiences afar. However, Hannah Partis Jennings, Sergio Catignani, and Jonathan Agensky endured the PowerPoint presentations filled with book covers, and offered inputs. Close friends have buoyed me throughout the long *durée* of the book. Without Tom Slater, Carlo Tognato and Gurchathen Sanghera, I would have long ago given up on the completion of the book. The "Cool Kids" (Cristina Masters, Megan MacKenzie, and Amanda Chisholm), Toni Haastrup, and Swati Parashar provided emotional sustenance. Anna Stavrianakis, Maria Stern, Maria Ericsson Baaz, Kwesi Aning, Morten Bøås, Kathleen Jennings, Michelle Callanan, Jelke Boesten, Ali Howell, Melanie Richter-Montpetit, Paula Drumond, Peter Albrecht, Althea Maria Rivas, Frances Giampapa, Mandy Turner, and Alyosxa Tudor provided feedback, encouragement, and postcolonial rage when needed. Thanks to Jenny Tan from Penn Press; my editor Cecily Jones, a professional coach and editor after I finished working with Marianne Schofield, who guided me through the book process like a pro; and Joanne Kalogeras, Microsoft Word genius.

Friends patiently attended my mini-synopsis of the book and work. Irma Erlingsdóttir has provided the most restful and spectacular landscapes, cooked the tastiest dishes, and sustained me with stories of the life and times of growing up Icelandic. Neighborhood friends have lifted me up when I was feeling like I could not write a single drop more—Nikki and Jonathan Shaw pumped me up and Vicki Hook and Liz Edden fed me tea/coffee and took me out on dog walks. Friends and family back in Canada (or thereabouts) listened and waited patiently for me to finally finish the book: Niki Lederer, Heather Feeney, Susan Dowse, Mary Houle, Susanne Pereira, Jamila Hulme and Sandy Gunn. Fred Reinarz listened to me moan about the state of health care and world politics, Monique Reinarz sent me photos of my kids from the past, Eve Reinarz inspired me with lettuce, and the rest of the Reinarz clan around the world sent notes of love and care whenever possible. During the spring of 2011 and then autumn of 2018, when I lost my sister and then my mother, my brother, Maurice Henry, had done all of the caring work with barely a word of complaint and kept encouraging me to keep going forward, taking each day at a time. In the most recent years, if it were not for Amanda Chisholm, my muse, personal trainer, and best friend all in one, I would be sitting with one single line on the page (peacekeeping, it sucks). While writing her own book and putting down roots in London, she was there for me every single minute. Family and furry creatures also kept me real, especially when the abolitionist in me started to feel hopeless. Jonathan was a most excellent father during all those years, especially when I was away on many long fieldwork trips, enabling me to do the "deep thinking" I needed to. Theo, Audrey, and Conker tolerated the rushed meals and hurried walks. I guess it really does take a village to help someone write a book. What a whirlwind last couple of years, with challenges, new/old beginnings and yet, I found the space to write this. I hope it inspires a monumental change in the scholarship and practice of peacekeeping.